Human Ecology in the Vedas

Reconstructing Indian History & Culture

(ISSN 0971-3824)

1. Society in Ancient India; by Sures Chandra Banerji.
2. Political Thought in Ancient India; by G.P. Singh.
3. Early Indian Historical Tradition and, Archaeology; by G.P. Singh.
4. Vasantotsava: The Spring Festivals of India; by Leona M. Anderson.
5. Ecological Readings in the Veda; by M. Vannucci.
6. Vr̥ndāvana in Vaiṣṇava Literature; by Maura Corcoran.
7. Social History of the Tamils (1707-1947); by P. Subramanian.
8. Ancient Indian Coinage; by Rekha Jain.
9. Buddhism and Socio-Economic Life of Eastern India; by Bimal Chandra Mohapatra.
10. Chandragupta Maurya; by P.L. Bhargava.
11. Mr̥tyu: Concept of Death in Indian Traditions; by Gian Giuseppe Filippi.
12. Yama: The Glorious Lord of the Other World; by Kusum P. Merh.
13. Sacred Complex of Ujjain; by D.K. Samanta.
14. Vedic View of the Earth; by S.R.N. Murthy.
15. Society in the Atharvaveda; by B.S. Kharade.
16. Orissan History, Culture and Archaeology; by S. Pradhan.
17. Education in Ancient India; by Mitali Chatterjee.
18. Surà: The Liquor and the Vedic Sacrifice; by M.B. Kolhatkar.
19. Governance in Ancient India; by Anupa Chandra Pandey.
20. The Cultural Glory of Ancient India: A Literary Overview; by Sures Chandra Banerji.
21. Kautilya's Arthaśāstra in the light of Modern Science & Technology; by Sunil Sen Sarma.
22. History of Jainism - With Special Reference to Mathurā; by V.K. Sharma.
23. Cultural Tourism in India: Museums, Monuments & Arts - Theory and Practice; by S.P. Gupta; Krishna Lal; Mahua Bhattacharya.
24. Ancient Indian Historiography - Sources and Interpretations; by G.P. Singh.
25. Republics, Kingdoms, Towns and Cities in Ancient India; by G.P. Singh.
26. Facets of Ancient Indian History and Culture - New Perception; by G.P. Singh.
27. Kamakhya - A Socio-cultural Study; by Nihar Ranjan Mishra.
28. History and Culture of Tamil Nadu as Gleaned from the Sanskrit Inscriptions Vol. 1 (up to *c.* AD 1310); by Chithra Madhavan.
29. Lifestyle of the Vedic People; by Pranati Ghosal.
30. History and Culture of Tamil Nadu as Gleaned from the Sanskrit Inscriptions Vol. 2 (up to *c.* AD 1310 - *c.* 1885 AD); by Chithra Madhavan.
31. Matrimonial Alliances and Ancient Indian Polity (*c.* 600 BCE to *c.* 650); by Preeti Prabhat.
32. Artisans and Craftsmen of Northern India; by Kuldeep Singh Thind.
33. The Evolution of Historiographical Tradition in Ancient and Medieval India; by G.P. Singh.
34. Warfare in Ancient India, Theory and Practice by Soma Basu.
35. Sanskrit Education and Literature in Ancient and Medieval Tamil Nadu by Chithra Madhavan

Reconstructing Indian History & Culture, no. 19

Human Ecology in the Vedas

M. Vannucci

DK PRINTWORLD
Publishers of Indian Traditions

Cataloging in Publication Data – DK
[Courtesy: D.K. Agencies (P) Ltd. <docinfo@dkagencies.com>]

Vannucci, M. (Marta), 1921- **author.**

Human ecology in the Vedas / M. Vannucci. – Second impression.
pages cm. – (Reconstructing Indian history & culture ; no. 19)
"First published in 1999" – Title page verso.
Includes bibliographical references and index.
ISBN 9788124601150

1. Vedas. – Criticism, interpretation, etc. 2. Human ecology – Religious aspects – Hinduism. I. Title. II. Series: Reconstructing Indian history & culture ; no. 19.

LCC BL1112.47.V36 2018 | DDC 294.5921046 23

ISBN: 978-81-246-0115-0
First published in 1999
Second impression, 2018

Printed and published by:
D.K. Printworld (P) Ltd.
Regd. Office: "Vedaśrī", F-395, Sudarshan Park
(Metro Station: ESI Hospital), New Delhi - 110 015
Phones: (011) 2545 3975; 2546 6019
e-mail: indology@dkprintworld.com
Website: www.dkprintworld.com

To Erico and Dino
to whose incessant questioning
from the days of their first
'how' and 'why, 'yes' and 'no'
I owe much of my understanding

Errata

Page	Para	Line	*Printed*	*Correct*
xiii	—	20	*Śp Brā→Śatapatha Brāhmaṇa*	[omit]
48	2	3	of knowledge' Dandekar	of knowledge'. Dandekar
60	2	2	is present [omit]	
80	1	10	Trees forests,	Trees, forests,
85	1	10	*Ṛv*, X; 85, 37) provides	*Ṛv*, X; 85, 37 provides
106	1	12	too much anything	too much of anything
107	3	5	Mitra. Varuṇa's	Mitra-Varuṇa's
115	1	11	Angi	Agni
167	1	last	of the planetary system of Earth.	of planet Earth.
168	5	11	means	mean
172	top	4	*ṛṣi* Vasiṣṭha	*ṛṣi* Vasiṣṭha.
204	*at the end of para 1 add the sentence*: There were no watches, or time pieces at that time, *Mantras* properly recited are metres, a measure of time, a mean to measure time. Hence the number of *mantras* recited measures the length of slay and night.			
206	2	6	minor images	mirror images
206	3	2	mirror image	mirror images
209	1	5	sustainer *ṛta*,	sustainer of *ṛta*,
218	3	8	physiologist, said	physiologist said:
253	3	9	she he is an	she is an
287	3	1	Indra, riches of the	Indra, richest of the
312	*Atirātra*	2	of Soma sacrifice.	of the Soma sacrifice.
314	Capēre	1	Latin world from	Latin verb from
317	Fire	2	Agni is object and means and	Agni is object, means and
319	Intelligēre	3	Litterally: to find together	Litterally; to bind together
320	Kawa	4	plant, of the gemus Piper.	plant, of the genus Piper.
324	*Pariṇāma*	5	*Parjanya* [it is a new entry]	
332	*Upanayana*	1	rite of investitute	rite of investiture
333	Varuṇa	1	Āditya, unfound	Āditya, unbound
340	Volterra	3	*Lincel*	*Lincei*
341	Ahura		Mazada	Mazda
344	Ulyses		Ulyses, 87	Ulysses, 87

Preface

When I was writing the book *Ecological Readings in the Veda* I was very worried because I feared that I would be unworthy of the task. While I still feel that I am very far from the lofty heights, I am grateful to the Gods and to the many learned persons and scholars who encourage me to continue along the arduous path of learning from the Vedic lore. The passionate urge to understand that is peculiar to Man, as I wrote at that time, pushed me deeper and deeper along this path of studies, trying to absorb as much insight into Vedic wisdom as my personal limitations would allow.

Part I of the present book is vastly based on my earlier book '*Ecological Readings in the Veda*' and reflects my endeavour to express in simple terms what reason shows to be the understanding that the *ṛṣis* had of the universe. The eagerness to attain to the Absolute Truth caused the ancient sages to express in poetical metres the result of their observations of nature, of their studies of the relations of causes and effects, of the empirical and experimental science that they practised for survival, for better living and for war. In their search for the Absolute Truth, the Vedic and pre-Vedic sages uncovered particular truths, which are each and every one part of the Absolute Truth. The unveiling of *Ṛta* proceeded step by step; each step translated into norms and regulations for everyday healthy living; each one was then represented, reconstructed and lived over again through rituals. Clearly the Vedic sages had a notion of the fundamental pairs of opposites that keep the system going, such as Lord Agni and common fire. They perceived that matter and energy are the two interchangeable and interdependent extremes of a *continuum* and that Agni sublimates matter into energy, that solar energy and water create matter in mother Earth and in what grows from her. They realized that the life principle being undefinable, Hope, Bhaga, or the urge to go on living, is indelibly linked to Life and the sources of life were identified, hence the pair Savitṛ-Bhaga. The ancient sages also saw the *continuum* time/space, but that aspect of Vedic wisdom I have not dared approach.

The mental torment grew after the book was published and I felt more and more belittled by my audacity; I am fully aware that I was not entirely successful in expressing clearly enough my 'readings'. The wealth of knowledge expressed in concise and often cryptic form by the ancients is not tolerant of simple interpretation and explanation.

One of the serious omissions of that book is the absence of a discussion of what I consider to be one of the significant differences between Western and Eastern philosophies. In the West Nature, the environment, the universe were considered to be static in time. The word evolution did not exist and when it was first used in relation to evolving nature, it was anathemized. Nature was taken to be immutable since first created by God, the *Infinitum Ens* (the Infinite Being) and the idea is present already in the Aristotelic principles of classic Greek philosophy that bridled all creative thinking, from cosmogony to theatrical presentations. Judaic, Christian, Islamic philosophies willfully disregarded the obvious changes over time and the evolution of everything in the universe. One of the great merits I see in Vedic and Vedic-derived philosophies, and other oriental philosophies, is the recognition that nothing is ever static, everywhere in the universe. Hence the impermanence of everything, as the Epicurean philosophers of Democritus' school knew well.

Due to these reasons I revised the first text and selected a few hymns that support the above and that have remained living guides for mankind over the centuries. These show both the impermanence and continuous change of everything, the need for mutual adjustment of the components of the system and at the same time show that the basic laws of physics, chemistry, physico-chemistry, movements of the astral bodies, remain unchanged over infinite time and space, at least as man could detect them without powerful instruments. They further show that the interaction of the parts of the very complex time/space *continuum* inevitably causes changes and evolution of the constituent parts.

Part I of the present book contains much of the earlier text, revised and enlarged. The general conclusion is that the formulation of *dharma* is based on fundamental ethical laws of nature to which all living beings as well as man are subject. Further, because of his intrinsic nature and his position in the community, nobody can escape his *dharma*, though ecological constraints influence his behaviour and *karma*. Any deviation from one's *dharma* is an aberration that carries with it dire consequences for the offender.

Part II is the analysis of three hymns and discusses some aspect of two important personalities that offer much support to the concepts expressed above. The hymn to the 'Maṇḍūka' (the Frogs), *R̥V*, VII; 103, describes the seasonal cycles, the role of Viṣṇu as Preserver and the corresponding rituals to ensure man's participation in the cosmic drama in tune with R̥ta, the Law and Order of the Universe. The hymn for the wedding of Sūryā, the sun's daughter, *R̥V*, X; 85, focuses on the biological and social role of marriage and woman, valid even for present-day changing lifestyles. The third is one of the shortest of the whole *R̥gveda*, *R̥V*, X; 146. It is dedicated to Araṇyānī, the lady of the forest; it visualizes the forest as an ecosystem with a strong personality of its own, but not immutable. The first Appendix reflects the *r̥ṣi*s' perception of different aspects of reality, material and virtual reality, as personified in certain traits of the Great God Varuṇa and the King of the Gods, Indra. In the second Appendix I formulate the hypothesis that the inebriating drink: *soma*, was originally grapes' wine, though substitutes of the *soma* plant may have been and are still used at different times and places.

Finally, I would say as I presume, that the Great Truth discovered by the ancient sages is that the ethics of nature dictates the *dharma* of man and communities, and this in turn is subject to ecological imperatives which position the individual *karma*.

I acknowledge with deep gratitude the support given by the Bhandarkar Oriental Research Institute, Pune, and in particular Dr. Uma Chakravarty from whose constructive criticism I learned so much. Too many other generous persons have helped me and guided me in my search; it would be impossible to mention them all. To my publisher, Sri Susheel Mittal I am grateful for steadily and gently pushing me out of my innate shyness and laziness.

M. Vannucci

Preface

Kant's concept of Sublime: A Pathway to the Numinous, is the result of a project on which Professor Pabitrakumar Roy worked and lectured at Utkal Philosophy Department as a Visiting Professor under the DSA programme during March.2002. The Department of Philosophy, under the Special Assistance Programme sponsored by the UGC, has been bringing out the end products of serious research projects under the title *Utkal Studies in Philosophy.* The present volume is the tenth one in the series. Professor Pabitrakumar Roy, the retired Professor of Philosophy, North-Bengal University and at present the ICPR senior fellow, is an erudite scholar and a serious researcher of Philosophy. In this volume the readers will be exposed to his innovative interpretation of Kant's concept of the sublime.

Kant's trilogy of *Crtiques* has not yet received the uniform attention that it deserves. The first two *Crtiques,* namely the *Crtique of Pure Reason* and the *Critique of Practical Reason,* being highly imposing have inexplicably obfuscated the importance of the third *Critique,* viz. the *Critique of Judgement.* It is seldom realized that Kant's philosophical journey is a journey from the limited to the unlimited, from the phenomenon to the noumenon, from the sensible to the supersensible. In this work Professor Roy tries to trace the linking chains of this journey by highlighting on two vital concepts, viz. the concept of freedom and the concept of sublime.

It will not be a travesty of truth to claim that Kant's philosophy reflects his obsession with the concept of man. He was fully aware of the certain basic oppositions that may arise in the context of his perception of man. There may exist a form of confrontation between the concept of man as presented in his first Critique and his later works, like *Ground works of the Metaphysics of Morals* (Translated by H.J. Paton, London, 1941) wherein he conceives man as an end. To understand the nature of this conflict we have to first of all, focus on Kant's conception of "Man." In his first *Critique* Kant vindicates the role of human reason in determining the epistemological content of experience and the nature through what he calls the "Copernican revolution" in philosophy. At the same time this treatise projects human life as a part of the sterile content of empirical facts or else a part of the necessitated modes of scientific laws. But he intends to carve out a richer conception of man. By showing the limits of reason in its theoretical and intellectual application he opens the floodgates of human autonomy in the sphere of practical reason. His concern about the man as an end-in-itself finds a full-blooded expression in his treatises on moral philosophy. Here he introduces the postulate: "Man and every rational being exists as an end in itself, *not merely* as a means for arbitrary use by this will or that; but he must in all actions . . . *be regarded at the same time as an end*" (*Ibid.*, p. 125). This respect for man is gradually unfolded in his subsequent works. But can the projection of man as a part of the order of the scientific and necessary law coexist with the conception of man as an end? Here the concept of freedom may be seen as the connecting link.

To say that man exists as an end is to say that he has the ability to transcend the empirical order of nature and place himself in a higher order that motivates him to act and reach out to others so that the socio-moral dimension of his personality finds the full expression. This necessitates the human power of freedom. So, for Kant the term "freedom" does not signify the power to act as one wills, or the absence of obstacles. The recognition of our freedom means recognition of other's personality and freedom. The guiding principle of our freedom to act is "Act in such a way that you treat humanity, both in your person and in the person of all others, never a means only but always equally as an end" (*Groundwork of Metaphysics of Morals,* Preface). The idea of human freedom will lose its significance if there are isolated maxims for each person. Moral questions are not personal nor can man decide his actions without considering about others. So our rational law expresses itself as a universal law. If our rational law is not respected then it would render our social life impossible; and this would be tantamount to injuring the dignity of other persons and infringing upon the freedom of others. This universal law is not presented from outside, it is man's gift to himself. Thus Kant's use of the term "freedom" has a richer dimension. It is that sort of freedom which would allow a man to live in righteous harmony as a social being by evolving moral laws that are fit to be universal law for all persons.

The concept of freedom has a dominant role in Kant's second *Critique* as it helps Kant to focus on the social and moral dimensions of the human person. But the author feels that Kant's concept of freedom has still more rich significance, and points to a still higher form of harmony. Kant's third *Critique,* therefore, is an extension of Kant's concern about the creative power of freedom that could enable man to integrate the moral with the aesthetic dimensions of life.

Kant had always felt a need to explain the element of moral feeling, because the man, as an end-in-itself cannot act like an automaton without the moral motivation. The tension between the objectively conceived moral principle and the subjective motivation needs to be smoothened out. Here comes the role of the feeling of the sublime. Professor Roy very convincingly unravels its moral undertone of this aesthetic experience by interpreting this concept as the link that connects the gap between the objective moral principles and the subjective content of the moral motivation. So he calls it the doorway to the supersensible. One can decipher the exact implication of Kant's analysis of the term sublime by analyzing what he means by the word supersensible. In the third *Critique* Kant uses the term to refer to the unity that links theoretical and moral domains together. The concept of sublime, on the other hand, refers to a feeling that allows us to be conscious of "being superior to nature within and without." It is this highest feeling, with its accompanying sense of awe and respect, that a man is capable of. So this powerful feeling can serve as a ground human motivation to act. In this work, the author prefers to highlight on the moral dimension of the concept of sublime. He reasons out that the feeling of sublime can be "morally significant in that it helps to solve the problem of motivating the subject towards an objectively conceived goal." Thus the gap between the subjective moral feeling and objective order of the universal moral law can be bridged. Man must not act only on the basis of categorical imperative but also be motivated to act so that harmony can be achieved between the subjective and the objective, between the concept of "man" as a part of necessary natural order and as free autonomous person.

Professor Roy's presentation of Kantian philosophy is strikingly original. I am sure the readers would find it rewarding.

The Department of Philosophy at Utkal is deeply indebted to Professor Roy for kindly consenting to deliver a series of lectures on this interesting topic. I am thankful to Professor P.K. Mohapatra for sparing his valuable time to write the foreword for this book. I record my thanks to my fellow editors for the help in bringing out this volume. My sincere

Contents

Abbreviations

ABORI	*Annals of the Bhandarkar Oriental Research Institute*
AD	*anno Domini*, after Christ
AitBrā	*Aitareya Brāhmaṇa*
AV	*Atharvaveda*
BC	Before Christ
BP	Before Present
Brā	*Brāhmaṇas* texts of the Veda
BṛUp	*Bṛhadāraṇyaka Upaniṣad*
IE	Indo-European
KsBrā	*Kauṣītaki Brāhmaṇa*
MBh	*Mahābhārata*
MM	Max Müller
P	*Purāṇa*
Rm	*Rāmāyaṇa*
ṚV	*Ṛgveda*
Sam	*Saṁhitā*
Smṛ	*Smṛti*
ŚpBrā	*Śatapatha Brāhmaṇa*
Śr	*Śruti*

ŚtpBrā	*Śatapatha Brāhmaṇa*
SV	*Sāmaveda*
SS and SV	Swami Satya Prakash Saraswati and Satyakam Vidyalankar
YV	*Yajurveda*

Introduction

May Varuṇa distinguish wisdom and folly of man
Ṛ̥V, VII; 49, 3
AV, I; 33, 2

Ṛ̥ṢI Vasiṣṭa and other *ṛ̥ṣis* could distinguish wisdom from folly and *dharma* from *adharma*, truth from non-truth. However, when the relations between cause and effect were not apparent, they would use impossible or 'fantastic explanations' that we now call myths. The myth goes from the general to the particular and substitutes explanations, it substitutes logical deductions and jumps from the cause to the observed or desired effect. Myths are used as an 'explanation' *ad hoc* and never are generally valid. The myth gives no general explanation based on particular effects or consequences. There are no inferences in mythologies, this is why they are called myths, rather than legends, rules or laws. The short-cut from cause to effect is called a 'myth'. Myths are important for the development of the culture typical for each civilization, because they preserve a *quantum* of knowledge or wisdom of the collective mind of the people, generation after generation. Myths gradually fade away with time when the correct, logical, possible and factual, experimental and scientific explanations gradually substitute fantasy. For instance the myth of Rāhu devouring the sun and/or moon is a mythical and easily memorized way of 'explaining' eclipses, though the correct explanation, namely the projection of the shadow of the Earth on the sun or moon was well known already at the time of the *ṛ̥ṣis*. This could also be used as an example of how 'esoteric' knowledge which in all cultures is the science of the priesthood, was purposefully kept away from the masses, either because it is too difficult to explain to the non-initiated or because the knowledge could be misused.

In all cultures, myths and legends were also created to engrave into the collective memory of the people the tradition and history of their clan or race. An example from more recent times is the deification of Demetra into the goddess of agriculture in ancient Greece; she gave the knowledge and expertise which was purposefully transformed into a myth to ensure that the teachings be correctly applied. My studies show (Vannucci, under press in: Annals of the Bhandarkar Oriental Research Institute) that the 'Great Gift' that the Greek goddess Demetra gave to mankind was the practical knowledge of how to cultivate hexaploid wheat. History became legend and the legend was transformed into a myth and the religious practices called 'Mysteries' instituted by Demetra herself at Eleusis in Attika were performed for over 2000 years out of gratefulness because she gave the seeds of a special variety of wheat to a Greek called Triptolemus and taught how to cultivate it.

Legends are usually the poetical presentation of history or just wishful thinking. However the truths discussed in the Veda are mostly the result of the study of nature and of men's place in the universe, they are backed by carefully prepared rites and rituals, as were also the 'Mysteries' that took place at Eleusis.

The *ṛṣi* accumulated a great wealth of correct knowledge translated or not into myths. Much of this was used to acquire wisdom and is expressed in the sacred texts either in mythical or explicit language. Many hymns of the Vedas have maintained their validity over 50 or 60 centuries.

The fundamental difference between the science of the ancient *ṛṣis* and the science of the west, lies in the aims for which the learned persons of the priesthood sought truth: the 'unveiling of Ṛta'. Knowledge, in the West, was basically used to acquire power; technicalities had priority over pure knowledge. Even scholastic philosophy is in many ways the methodological and technical aspect of ancient philosophies, but discusses no new truths. In the East, as revealed clearly in the Vedas, knowledge was gained basically for the purpose of acquiring wisdom. Wisdom was the aim of the *ṛṣi* and wisdom was applied even for developing techniques to improve the quality of life, as for instance *Āyurveda* or *yoga*.

Vedic man had his views directed holistically towards the whole universe and was amazed at what he saw: the order and energy that reign throughout the world he lived in, these he called Ṛta and Agni and he consciously worshipped the orderly energy that is at the root of all movement, including all forms of life. The details of how the system functions, the dynamics of the universe and its parts were still beyond man's power of understanding. Though he often could see the effects he could not understand the causes. He instinctively had to obey and be in tune with the order that reigns supreme. Hence religion and the rites that accompany religions.

It was recently brought to my attention that speaking in biological terms, *dharma* and *karma* may to a certain extent be understood respectively as the **genotype** and the **phenotype** of man as a biological species. *Dharma* corresponds to the hereditary endowment, the genome, the DNA which is unique of each individual, while *karma* regulates the behaviour and action of each one of us. Behaviour and actions — the **phenotype** — as well as the physical aspect are the result of the forces of the world around us and within us: the outer and the inner worlds. All and every individual action and each person's individual behaviour bear consequences that act on each person's individual *karma*.

Part I of this book gives the general frame of mind, and the evolution of the thinking of Vedic man over several centuries, while man was migrating and living in a variety of different environments, prior to and much earlier than the written text. Part II gives some details of the wisdom acquired in relation to societal health of the community and of the individual. It further gives some details on the observation of the seasons, of the respect due to Nature and its preservation, and in general to some of the norms that should be followed for the well-being of the individual, the family, the community, to promote health of the body, of the mind and of the spirit.

Looking at the world we now live in, in spite of all the knowledge, the science, the previously unimaginable technological knowhow, the world looks very much like a mad-house and is much less wise than the world of the ancients. Personally I would like to express an utopic wish: that man would distinguish between wisdom and folly.

PART I

Yes, at thy birth, when thou hadst sat in glory
thou, Agni, wast the aim of invocations.
The Gods came near, obedient to thy summons
and thus obtained their ranks as chief Protectors.

R̥V, X; 6, 7 (transl. Griffith)

1

The Problem and the Hypotheses

We worship Agni, the Purohit, God, minister of sacrifice, who works through eternal laws, who feeds and sustains all that is divine and luminous.

R̥V, I; 1, 1 (SS & SV)

Be of easy access to us,
as a father to his son
Agni be with us for our sake.

R̥V, I; 1, 9

Two of the questions that have haunted me throughout life are: when and how did man, the anatomical Hominid called *Homo sapiens sapiens* learn to use reason to behave accordingly? What contributed to develop his power of reason and discrimination?

The man we are talking about here is the zoological species to which we belong and of which we are so proud. Maybe once again Linné selected the correct epithet when he gave us the specific name *sapiens*, but still this does not imply that man is generally wise. *Sapēre*, the verb from which the word *sapiens* is derived, in Latin means to try, to have the taste of, or to taste the essence of understanding that leads to or should lead to knowledge and wisdom. Knowledge of something that is different, new and previously unknown, something that is more than just *scīre* that also means to know, but somehow means crude knowledge without the taste of it, if I may say so; like a student who memorizes a subject to pass the examinations, he 'knows' the subject, but he does not really know it, he has not yet grabbed mentally the gist of it. Maybe it is the differences between erudition and knowledge. *Homo sapiens* is the zoological species that has the taste for, the firsthand experience of and the will to acquire and eventually use the understanding and wisdom derived from the observation of his inner and outer worlds. The urge to understand and thereby acquire knowledge is a basic trait of the human *forma mentis*. It is reflected in the common roots of such words as *scīre*, *sapientia*, *sacrum*, *sacrifacĕre*, *science*, *sacred*, *sachch*.

By whatever means one gains an understanding, one must be able to think and I do not subscribe to the school of thought (Piaget, 1952) according to which primitive man shares with infants and animals the inability to think. Based on scientific experimental observation I believe that thinking is not exclusive to man, hence it is not this particular ability that differentiates man from animals. Indeed experimental psychology teaches, and among the first W. Köhler showed with his experiments with chimpanzees carried out in Teneriffe during the First World War, that animals think. Recently Mandler (1990) has also disproved Piaget. Köhler's experiments culminated in his *Gestalt Theorie* (Köhler, 1947) that well demonstrates how qualitative observation, action and qualitative experimentation are inevitably linked together. Observation, action and experimentation are steps linked together in this order which requires logical thinking to carry out the reasoning, whatever number of intermediate steps have to be taken, to reach to a valid conclusion. A conclusion is the statement of a newly acquired bit of knowledge: a step in the process of unveiling *ṛta*. The opportune and accurate reaction follows the holistic perception of the 'surrounding' or 'outside' world. Behaviour by trial and error does not proceed along the same steps as the behaviour based on logical thinking.

We may visualize early man, or perhaps even the individuals of the species that preceded *Homo sapiens*, going beyond the consciously and perhaps subconsciously or even unconsciously rationalized perception of his inner and outer worlds by thinking and finally recognizing the relationships of cause and effect of the phenomena of the physical world. This I would call the *intelligĕre* phase; from *intelligĕre* the word intellect is derived. *Intelligĕre* literally means to tie, to unite, to relate one thing to others. It is the *scīre* and *sapēre* or the **testing** and **tasting**, as well as the *intelligĕre* phases that must necessarily come after the initial conscious endeavour to understand that which was observed; full understanding comes much later, if ever. To understand is *capīre* that comes from *capēre* that means to 'fill fully', 'to measure the fullness or capacity'.

It thus happened that towards the end of a lifetime of studies I realized that it was from the Veda that I acquired my present convictions.

When the intellect perceives the truth, the seer, the *ṛṣi* exclaims with joy: 'now thou art well my Lord and shall be really happy' (*ṚV*, VIII; 1, 34) and *Agni* (*l.c.*, 1, 33) is the great giver. The mortal, troubled by the need to understand, may then come to 'one of the seven pathways that the wise have fashioned' (*ṚV*, X; 5, 6), 'The seers with closed eyes understand through the intellect' (*ṚV*, VIII; 25, 9), 'even when they close their lids . . . they perceive'.

According to Sāyaṇa (SS and SV, p. 4380), in *ṚV*, X; 9, 1 'great happiness' means 'perfect knowledge' or the transcendental knowledge of *Brahman*; we could perhaps add: also *means* factual knowledge. The 'first seed of spirit' I take as the **desire to understand** and is 'what rose in the beginning' (*ṚV*, X; 129, 4); the *ṛṣis* could understand well what was not, or does not exist in the phenomenal world, but could not understand fully what they saw or sensed through the sense-organs and had to admit painfully: 'not this, not that' (*ṚV*, X; 9) is addressed to waters in general. Waters are invoked and eulogized because after Fire, Water is the next of the five basic ecological elements. Water is recognized as the cause of important developments, hence water in its liquid, solid as ice and water-vapour forms, helps to acquire 'perfect knowledge': for growing crops, for drinking, cleansing, preparing food and medicines, for health; water as seminal fluid is needed for procreation, so **Water** is the abode of **Agni** as energy. These are some of the correlations of cause and effect that were perceived by the *r̥ṣi*; they brought 'perfect knowledge' that caused 'great happiness'. Still, however, the *r̥ṣi* could not understand everything. The *r̥ṣi* realized that linking cause and effect is a step towards union with the *Brahman*, the Absolute Truth, Absolute Knowledge, the Self-Existent, but it does not yet indicate *how* or *why* the phenomenal world is as it is. It still does not explain the foundations of *r̥ta*. Then the *r̥si* painfully exclaims: 'not this, not that'. No full explanation or full understanding has yet been obtained.

Again eagerness to understand, to acquire knowledge is clear in *R̥V*, X; 88, 18: 'how many are the fires and suns in number? What is the number of the dawns and waters? Not jestingly I speak to you, O Fathers, Sages, I ask you this for information' (transl. Griffith). Incidentally, the verb 'to inform' and the noun 'information' that means 'to form internally' is the same as the mathematician Ernst Mach said: 'to understand something is to represent it mentally' or '**visualize**'. This type of quest of the ancients is sheer scientific enquiry and endeavour. **Agni**, the universal energy is the one who knows, Agni is the one who responds to the question and is 'he who will announce the sacrifice' (*R̥V*, X; 88, 17). 'All that existed then was void and formless, by the great power of warmth, Agni, was born that unit' (*R̥V*, 129, 3). 'The seven seers have given birth to Agni' (*AV*, XI; 1, 3), or 'Agni is born of the mouth of *Puruṣa*' (*AV*, XIX; 6,7). We may in other words say that the concept was 'seen' or 'formulated' that gave birth to the first God: Agni.

The eagerness and need to understand is eloquently expressed in *R̥V*, I; 71 and *R̥V*, I; 142, 6 where Agni signifies **Truth** and **Knowledge** and as such is the expression rather than the manifestation of God; he is the 'loved and loving one' who, together with the Aṅgirasas made the way to reach heaven and who burst the fortress of ignorance. Agni is the 'treasure-lord of treasures' (*R̥V*, I; 72, 1), forever granting all immortal bounties. In *R̥V*, I; 105, questions such as: 'may I know this?' are repeatedly addressed on different topics and the refrain says: 'why this, may I know, O Earth and Heaven? Which is the Truth?' Similar expressions of anxiety are formulated over and over again, as in *R̥V*, I; 75, 76, 105, where the refrain implores: 'let me know!' *AV*, XI; 5, goes a long way in eulogizing the *brahmacārī* and showing respect for him for his perseverance and learning. After listening to both concrete and incorporeal entities it is said that he is entitled to be respected because (*AV*, XI; 5, 20) 'the herbs, past and future, day and night, the forest trees, the year together with the seasons, are all born (this I read as 'born in the mind', or 'are understood and explained') of the Vedic student'. Questions frequently relate to natural cycles (*R̥V*, I; 113, 10), hence *r̥ta* or cosmic order. The ancient *r̥ṣis* were successful also in applying philosophical principles to satisfy the basic human needs of solidarity, generosity and transfer of material, intellectual and spiritual culture.

Rather than exclusive knowledge of god, the *r̥ṣis* sought all knowledge, or knowledge itself, because knowledge of the universe becomes knowledge of God. Thus as a consequence of the urge to understand, the concept or the idea of God must have taken shape in the mind of early man, long before the *r̥ṣis* elaborated on the concept. God is the entity that **is** everything and **is** therefore self-conscious and omniscient, while man realizes from experience, as can easily be demonstrated, that he is not and will never reach the state of omniscience. Thus man cannot be equated to God and in turn God cannot be fully understood by man. So man called 'God' all that he could not fully represent mentally. At a later stage, and this is the Vedic stage, man personified Gods, Ideas, Concepts to make them more readily intelligible; man can identify himself easily with personified ideas, concepts and gods and *thereby* binds himself to abstract ideas and concepts.

Agni is invoked: 'shine this blessing on us, may we attain to perfect understanding' (*R̥V*, VII; 3, 10) and 'Agni stay with us nor far away from the Gods' (*R̥V*, X; 11, 9). The antiquity of knowledge is proclaimed (*R̥V*, X; 17, 8) as personified by Sarasvatī 'who comes with the Fathers and rejoices with them'.

Observation of the phenomena of the world around us is essential to relate cause and effect and thereby acquire knowledge. In fact, we have all noticed how man, other mammals and birds, occasionally stop, look around, perhaps sniff the air and the ground or slightly change their posture, then trot or fly away in a chosen direction. We have all seen animals take detours to reach their objectives if there are impediments across the straight line, a fact that surely indicates that an analysis of the topographic situation was processed in the brain and was followed by instructions given to the locomotory organs. However, when and where the relationship between cause and effect breaks down or is not perceived by man, a sense of the supernatural, **God**, takes over.

Primitive man, hundreds of thousands of years ago, must have observed nature closely and drawn conclusions to guide his actions. Beyond satisfying the urge of hunger and reproduction, some individuals must have willed to act on their environment to improve what we now would call 'the quality of life'. It is the evolution of the genetic complex that gave to man the will to do, that in turn engineered *Homo sapiens*. The basic difference between man and the other primates and animals in general is that once the evolution of intelligence was set in motion, it could not be stopped because intelligence breeds constant self-improvement. Other Hominid species may have merged with ours or disappeared, while animals remain as they are or as far as they have intellectually developed for ever after.

MacKie (1988, p. 211) comments on what may have been the motives that moved the wise men of prehistoric times to build the megalithic structures of the British Isles, many of which are now proved to be some sort of solar calendars. MacKie 'presumes' that the structures were made 'for ceremonial reasons' and recognizes that 'more than one intellectual leap must be made' to use the structures as calendars. He argues that 'some reason would be behind the systematic attempt . . . to define the exact length of the year. . .'. I believe that the main reason, as mentioned earlier, is the human need to know and test one's knowledge or theory. The ancient Druids of the British Isles, or whoever the 'wise men' would have been, were scientists in their own right, moved by the same urge of scientific discovery as the genuine contemporary scientist. The main difference lies in the way they expressed themselves. The many megalithic structures of Brittany in France and of the British Islands were described by Thom, who studied in detail some 60 sites (Ferguson, 1988, p. 32); these studies indicate that great pain was taken to place and build the structures, transport and erect megaliths of up to 20 tonnes in weight. In the Kumaon hills, Bisht and I found some pre-historic megalithic structures that are aligned and oriented. We believe that they were used for ritualistic purposes probably associated to astronomical observations for the determination of calendar fixes.

It is not possible to prove whether the detailed study came first and the ritual associated to it followed, but it is hardly to be doubted that at first a rough observation of solar, star and lunar movements had to be made and that subsequently this would be verified and the observations refined by the use of instruments such as the megaliths themselves. Megaliths, menhirs, dolmens, stone slabs and rock alignments in Europe and those of Kumaon merely express the same urge to find out, to discover, to understand, to know, to unveil *ṛta* and to test the truth of one's discovery. In one word, 'to remove the veil of ignorance', as the *ṛṣi* said.

In conclusion, at one stage of the evolutionary process, man observing, thinking and then drawing reasoned deductions, must have formulated the idea of God **because** of the much that he understood and of the much more that he could not understand. He then learned to put to good use the expertise acquired and in fact Agni the God and *agni* the common fire have the same name. In the course of time, proud of their achievements, some men in all cultures equated themselves with God: 'if I, O Indra, were the Lord of riches!'... (*ṚV*, VII; 32, 18). Others identified themselves with Agni, as did *Vaiśvānara* and *Prometheus* or they deified other men and in doing so they again equated themselves with the Gods.

Man however realized very early that ignorance breeds fear and that truth or knowledge is freedom from fear (*ṚV*, I; 93); freedom from fear is reached through Agni-Soma: 'grant power to us and to our wealthy patrons, and cause our holy rites to be successful'. Such a powerful *ṛṣi* as Bharadvāja (*ṚV*, VI; 6, 1-3) reminds man of the multiple forms of Agni and that even the most humble form of fire must be kindled with 'newest worship' because that is only as far as man can go: kindling the manifestation of God, but not beyond. Agni God is 'the treasure Lord' (*ṚV*, I; 72) who 'forever grants all immortal bounties' and Agni bursts the fortress of ignorance (*ṚV*, I; 71, 2). In the recommendation for worship the importance of ritual is implied; it is spelt early (*ṚV*, I; 1, 9-10) and it continued to be recognized throughout the history of man as very important; but in modern times often religious rites and rituals are replaced by civil ceremonies. Antoine de Saint-Exupéry in the 'Little Prince' bitterly regrets that rites are being forgotten and people can no longer afford the time to 'dress their heart'. After being instituted, rites tend to grow in complexity and punctiliousness and when mistakes are made other complex expiatory rites must be performed to purify and redeem the offender. In the very last hymn of the last *maṇḍala* of the *R̥V* the desirability is expressed of establishing a religious organisation or a 'church'. *R̥V*, X; 191 is a hymn to Agni: 'assemble . . . let your minds be all of one accord. The place is common, common the assembly, common the mind, so be their thoughts united. A common purpose do I lay before you and worship with your general oblation. . . . One and the same be your resolve and be your minds of one accord. United be the thoughts of all that all may happily agree' (transl. Griffith).

The evolution of Man the Thinker is well represented by the very ancient God Savitr̥, the Great Vivifier, the Great Stimulator, the Enlivener, closely associated to *r̥ta* (Dandekar 1979a, p. 16). Savitr̥ is the expression of the idea and concept of life, to this matter I will return later.

Observation must have led the most intelligent among early men to make and use fire and at the same time they would have observed that fire is terrible, fearsome and dangerous, as well as very useful. In an earlier paper (Vannucci: Fire and marksmanship as transcultural values, in press), I made the point that the ability to make and control fire and the ability to take accurate aim are the basic properties that differentiate man from animals, but here I am only concerned with fire, the primordial God, the 'eye and guardian of *r̥ta*' (*R̥V*, X; 8, 5).

Fire as the most important element in the daily life of man and the one to which man owes the development of many of his techniques, had to be respected and venerated. Fire is multipurpose and multipotential, it is he 'who travels in various directions' (*R̥V*, I; 141, 7) and he is omnipresent as he pervades everything (*R̥V*, I; 31); 'Agni is the desire of what is and is to be' (*AV*, VI, 36, 3).

Man the Observer must have rationalized the many uses of fire while he was watching the outside world and the heat within himself. Not only the flames of fire must have entered into the realm of his thoughts, but a large number of other notions as well. Notions however are useless unless they are systematized, methodically and consciously. In trying to do this, man cannot have failed to observe the world's dynamics and as the mathematician Ernst Mach said that 'to understand something is to represent it mentally', man would have applied his knowledge methodically to develop his techniques. Much has been said and written on the perception by early man of the lunar and solar cycles, of the seasons and cyclic phenomena in general, but I would like to refer here to the more subtle observations of everyday life and death, those that shape the mind. One of them is the role of fire and heat in the normal functioning of life, another is that of order and cycles.

The rural, the mountain and the sea people and those of us who have had the good fortune to be exposed to and guided into observing nature, cannot help but see order everywhere; from the symmetry or orderly asymmetry of germinating and growing plants, of flowers and of the arrangements of leaves and buds, to the strict laws that regulate the structure and function of the human and animal bodies and the rhythmicity of all natural phenomena, except for episodic events, such as an earthquake. Early man perceived, sensed, got impressed and lived by and with the order in nature. When ploughing started to be practised, the convenience of ploughing through straight regular lines and seeding accordingly must have been as obvious as the regular alternation of even and odd numbers. Sītā, the furrow (*Ṛ̥V*, IV; 57, 6) is a basic aspect of Mother Earth, the good provider. The myth of the birth and death of Rāma's Sītā is a magnificent representation of the concept of cycles in nature further related to the *yoni*, as a symbol of femininity and thus of fecundity, generosity and compassion (Vannucci, 1992, p. 25).

Much later Lavoisier in eighteenth-century France, expressed the principle of Conservation of Matter: 'In nature nothing is created, nothing is destroyed but everything is transformed'.

Earlier the *ṛṣis*, for instance Bharadvāja had expressed the same in a figurative manner, as in *ṚV*, VI where Agni Vaiśvānara, as Jātavedas and Mātariśvan is said to pervade everything, that he needs air to live (combustion), returns regularly as observer of *ṛta* and as light he makes life possible on earth. The notion of order in nature is intuitively acquired through daily life, an experience most regrettably denied to the majority of today's modern life systems.

Dante Alighieri (Paradiso I, 103 *et seq*.) explains: . . . '*Le cose tutte quante — hann' ordine fra loro; e questo ĕ forma — che l'Universo a Dio fa simigliante*' (All things have order among themselves; and this is 'form' — that makes the Universe similar to God). Dante follows the philosophy discussed by Saint Thomas Aquinas in the '*Summa Theologica*' (pl. XV, art. 1) which is the corner-stone of dualistic scholastic philosophy according to which the world is distinct from God who created it alike, but not identical to himself: '*forma ad similitudinem cuius mundus est factus*'. Differently the monism that pervades the *śāstra* and culminated in Vedānta, identifies the whole universe with the *Brahman* or Self-Existent and therefore everything is sacred since it is **part of** and **not distinct from** the Godhead. Both philosophies, however, see **order** in all 'creation' **that** is what was '**created** by God' or in 'all the universe, that **is**' the Godhead or **Brahman** itself, as repeatedly stated in the Veda. While scholasticism sees order as a similitude, Vedism sees *ṛta* as **the** reality and therefore an expression or manifestation of the Godhead that man can apprehend and must accept, **though he cannot understand or explain it**.

Chaos is a word of classic Greek meaning confusion. In the history of the later intellectual development of mankind its meaning became the expression of a state of utter confusion beyond any sort of order, an unthinkable and impossible condition. However, mathematicians are now finding order even in 'chaotic states', though a very special type of order, a sort of deterministic randomness. Order is everywhere the rule and disorder the exception, as is inherent in the concepts expressed by these two words. Order comes before disorder in the mind of children and simple people as well as observers of nature. Before order set in there was nothing to be arranged in space and time. Chaos sets in when order and randomness break down; this presupposes that before the event, things were in order. Chaos is frightening because it causes and demonstrates the breakdown of the rule that makes everything possible, including life; the rule that gives a meaning to everything and its parts and therefore the concept of chaos cannot have existed in the mind of man **before** the concept of order was mentally formulated from the observation of nature. Chaos and disorder are universally confusing because they conceal order, the order that is necessary for logical thinking. Before anything existed there was void, emptiness (*R̥V*, X; 129), but: who knows? (*R̥V*, *l.c.* 6), 'the gods are later' (*l.c.* 7) 'he, the first origin . . . knows it, or perhaps he knows not'.

Order—*r̥ta*—is a basic concept derived, like the concept of the 'fireness in fire', from observation followed by logical thinking. Since man is not the artisan or maker of nature, he cannot be responsible for the origin of order. The concept of *r̥ta* arose as an inescapable necessity to represent mentally the realities of the physical world: it is based on the principle that order reigns supreme and is expressed by the statement of laws on which scientific theories were later based and further developed. *R̥ta* is therefore, like Agni Jātaveda (Agni omniscient), who is the essence of fire and who strengthens the concept of *r̥ta* as law (*R̥V*, I; 44, 14), a knowledge that must have been formed very early in the mind of man though neither *r̥ta* nor Agni are readily seen as a material entity. 'By *r̥ta*, *r̥ta* is restrained' (*R̥V*, IV; 3, 9). In other words, the universal laws of the cosmos are self-restraining or we could say: are automatic systems, where automatic means: self-starting and therefore, self-regulating.

As physical and mental evolution of the human species

progressed, at some very remote time man would have developed the ability to articulate stereotyped sounds to produce intelligible speech, a fact very important for the transfer of knowledge and for expressing abstract thoughts. The ability to pronounce conventional sounds that carry a specific meaning is evidenced, in the palaeontological record, by the development of the glottis and other anatomical structures, though unfortunately the glottis is not preserved well in the fossil record of the evolution of man. Though it is impossible to ascertain when and exactly how it happened, there is no doubt that the development of the organs of speech and of the corresponding parts of the brain went hand in hand. As speech and brain developed, so also did the ability to communicate with other men and to teach the younger generation, not only by example and demonstration, but also by explanation. The time when use and codification of sounds made into words was regulated to convey understanding, must have been a very exciting period in the history of mankind. It is not astonishing that later, Pāṇini who codified the means of expression in almost mathematical terms, is respectfully revered for setting the rules of classical Sanskrit. Classical Sanskrit is more precise and complex than modern simplifications, as is obvious with what has happened in its evolution into contemporary Sanskrit-derived languages.

It should be noted that the skript in which Sanskrit is written: *nagarī*, is the only ancient skript that gives perfect and detailed instructions on the pronunciation of the **word**: *Vāk*. *Nagarī* is comparable to classical XVII century italian music notation invented by Lulli and still in use worldwide. Those notations give the intonation and duration of the syllables besides indicating the tone. Classical and Vedic Sanskrit are read like music skript, which is an important tool for understanding the etymology of words. Classical Latin and to some extent classical Greek and a few contemporary languages of Indo-European extraction retain notations that indicate the sound of the written word.

Music is coding the laws that regulate the production of harmonious sounds, hence the importance given to 'vibrations', even if not consciously perceived.

Thus the concept of *vāk* must be as old, or almost as old as the concepts of Agni and *ṛta*. In the original order, I would guess that the succession was thus: first was formed the universal concept of Energy and Power, then the concept of Order and Law in Time and Space **as well as** of Cause and Effect and then, lastly the concept of precise and correct communication: Agni, *ṛta*, *vāk*: 'Bṛhaspati gave name to objects, sent *vāk* out first' (*ṚV*, X; 71, 1); **it should be noted that Bṛhaspati** was a man; words are sounds with a meaning and *vāk* is sent out to assist with the power of words.

These ideas, if I am correct, would have followed from pure philosophical attitudes and procedures derived from the need and urge that man, or at least most men have (*ṚV*, III; 31) to rationalize, to understand and communicate their findings; this would have satisfied part of the human eagerness to participate in the universal cosmic drama (*ṚV*, I; 10, 11) . . .' and (Indra) cause the seer to win a thousand gifts'. Contemporary science progresses essentially along the same conceptual pathways; it is a repetition of the basic and essential frame of mind of man, nowadays enriched by powerful instrumentation and cumulative experience; experimentation, knowledge and communication. Basically Leonardo da Vinci's aphorism: 'There is no truth that has not passed through our senses' is still valid if together with Leonardo we take truth as 'understanding' and if we agree with Indian philosophies that the mind is the seat of reason.

Indian philosophies recognize the existence of individual consciousness, *ahaṁkāra*. This is made up of eleven *indriya*s; *manas*, the mind, is the seat of reason that controls and coordinates the five senses, the; *jñānendriya*s by which the individual takes cognizance of the inner self and of the environment in which he lives, and the five faculties of action, the *karmendriyas*. Thus the mind stands supreme, it coordinates the stimuli received from the sense-organs with the organs of action, as for instance motion. It is clear that reason or mind, *manas*, is responsible for the behaviour of men at all times and circumstances. Thus the knowledge of Truth generates wisdom and appropriate behaviour through understanding.

Dandekar writes (1979a, p. 62): '. . . in the *R̥gveda* . . . we come across frequent reference to *r̥ta*, the cosmic-magic law which governs every happening in this world. . . The Vedic *r̥ta* . . . in a sense is the Vedic version of the Hindu doctrine of *karma*'. The laws of nature are unchangeable (*R̥V*, I; 73, 2), as 'the solar rays diligently bring daylight' (*R̥V*, I; 3, 8) and it is these that man endeavours to understand; man endeavours to acquire truth through the senses and finally represents the law, *r̥ta*, mentally.

A later epithet of *vāk* (speech) is *sasarparī* or 'swiftly moving' (*R̥V*, III; 53, 15); evidently the desire of fast and ever faster communication is not new to this century! According to Sāyaṇa, *vāk* being intelligence, dispelled the 'unintelligence of the Kuśikas'. The learned inherited the duty to teach other men and 'loosen the invoker's thought, Indu, as they clean thee' (*R̥V*, IX; 95, 5) while Varuṇa is 'held aloft above the ocean (of *avidyā*) by the ancient God Trita' (*l.c.* 95, 4) and the 'secret names are uttered' (*l.c.*; 95, 2). (*R̥V*, IX; 95), most probably refers to ancient rites of a propitiatory nature. Both Varuṇa and Trita are very ancient Gods, along with Savitr̥, who have their counterpart in the *Avesta*, under the names *Ahura Mazda* and *Tristha.* The magical power of *asura* Varuṇa is well known but Trita-Āptya is poorly known and is a rather mysterious personality. In the myth, while Varuṇa is supported by Trita very high above the sea of ignorance (*avidyā*) to avoid pollution, 'secret names are uttered'. This clearly refers to magical rites whereby knowledge and understanding were invoked for the benefit of man. The gods invoked are the most ancient and most endowed with magical power, a mysterious power beyond human knowledge and understanding. In *R̥V*, X; 71, *vāk* is actually almost identified with *jñānam*, or knowledge, a noun that appears only once and late in the *R̥V*. *Vāk* is invoked as the first, as the divinity who is concealed in the wealth of all subsequent auspicious knowledge; she represents oral tradition and symbolic speech; she represents sound and music and her power of discrimination is eulogized, including the hidden or esoteric meaning of all speech. The initiated understand the subtle meanings that are beyond the grasp of the non-initiated and only those who know the hidden meaning can follow the rituals profitably, with understanding, and they are those who come in triumph, having acquired knowledge. *Vāk* is also the means to convey prayers (*R̥V*, X; 114, 8) '*Vāk* spreads forth as far as prayer goes' . . . (*l.c.*, 9) . . . and conveys knowledge: 'what sage has learned the metres application? Who has gained *vāk*, the spirit's aim and object?' '*Vāk* bears Mitra and Varuṇa, Indra and Agni' . . .' by her own nature knew the supreme *Brāhman*' (*AV*, IV; 30).

Finally *Vāk* is feminine because she gives life and birth to ideas and thoughts (*R̥V*, X; 125) 'hear . . . all the truth as I (*Vāk*) declare it' (*R̥V*, X; 125, 4). Hence the importance of the word and of the name. It may be mentioned here that similarly, at the initiation rites of the Mysteries of Goddess Demetra at Eleusis (ancient Greece) only those who knew a very precise language, Greek, could be initiated to the highest level; the explanation given was that only those initiated would know the hidden meaning of the secret teaching. Each initiated received in great secret, whispered in the ear by the hyerophant, his or her own *mantra* or secret.

Inter-relation of all natural laws would have gradually been perceived. But since man could not then, as we cannot today, perceive or define all the relations of cause and effect, he had to resort to the concept of *asu* (Dandekar 1979a, p. 55) or magical power, to 'explain' the unexplainable. Thus to this day we still observe auspicious and inauspicious numbers, dates, hours and many other 'superstitions'.

The need to understand for the sake of having peace of mind is well expressed again and again, as in *AV*, X; 74 — *R̥V*, I; 76 — *R̥V*, I; 75 and it includes the urge to apply the knowledge gained to practical purposes. The need to communicate is implicit in the very nature and essence of the Veda, thus *Vāk* is frequently invoked though often indirectly so (*AV*, VIII; 3, 6) and is often referred to as 'the three syllables of the sacrifice'. Agni is also often referred to indirectly as for instance in *AV*, XIII; 2, 46 when he is 'coming as a milch-cow'. Furthermore the dual divinity Indrāgni that occurs not infrequently, indicates the concept of material and intellectual or spiritual understanding bound together.

In summary I believe that there is ample reason to conclude that philosophy as the search for knowledge came to man before religion. Philosophy is the science of primitive man who 'wishes to understand'. Philosophy and science are two words that express a host of ideas and concepts that were differentiated only much later in the process of systematization of man's knowledge. An Eskimo man told Rasmussen (Radin 1941, p. 50) that 'our fathers were instructed by their fathers, they preserved ancient habits and rules that are the product of the experience and science of countless generations'. This is absolutely correct because to a large extent science and tradition are the cumulative experience of many generations selected for what is good, positive and useful and expurgated of what is bad or ineffective. Tradition also forms an important part of the *corpus* of all religions.

I use the words 'philosophy' and 'religion' in their original sense of 'wish to understand' or 'friend of knowledge' and 'uniting or binding man to God' respectively, because the concept of God or the idea of a Supreme Being and Ruler of all the world could have been conceived and could have originated only **after** the order prevailing in the world, or *r̥ta* was perceived, recognized and unconditionally accepted. Only then could conceptual ideas be deified with consequent personification. Once the order of the universe was recognized and accepted, then man would implicitly know that he is part of the system subject to its laws and forces, subject to *ṛta*. This knowledge would necessarily bring with it the strong desire to be a participant rather than a mere spectator of the grand drama unfolding in — and outside — himself. Most of the Vedic sacrifices, in addition to being propitiatory rites, are also and foremost participatory rituals.

Radin (*l.c.*, p. 8) refers to religion as a 'sentiment and an ensemble of acts, customs, beliefs and concepts associated to the sentiment . . . a mechanism invented by man'. Here Radin contradicts himself, because if religion is a **sentiment** it cannot, implicitly and by exclusion, be a **mechanism invented** by man. Other modern 'definitions' of the term 'religion' fall into comparable contradictions.

Of the three basic concepts, Agni, Ṛta and Vāk, Agni Jātavedas, the all knower, is obviously the natural *Ur-Gott* of man. Recognized as the original energy and power, he is adorable and frightening, protector of good and bad (*ṚV*, I; 31, 6); he is four-eyed and sees in all directions. He enlightens and gives knowledge and above all he gives the power of discrimination because he is the Great Purifier, purifier of matter — concrete and abstract.

Agni, the Purifier *par excellence* (*AV*, XII; 5) extracts the essence and turns matter into spirit: 'O Agni who separatest what was mixed' (*ṚV*, V; 8, 3). One is tempted to paraphrase this into: 'Lord Agni, who turns the material into ideas, concepts and knowledge of the abstract'. *ṚV*, I; 72, 2 is a very important hymn that goes a long way to show the dual personality of Agni as God and *agni* as common fire. He is here recognized as the highest God by the other Gods who had not 'found him' until they understood his philosophical meaning and knowledge. Agni is the giver of spiritual and material food and Agni is also the preserver of mysteries and rites; Agni is therefore also the Hotṛ *par excellence* and is the one with awful power (*ṚV*, I; 127, 11 —

R̥V, V 10 — *R̥V*, X; 71). He is the sagest of the sages (*R̥V*, V; 42, 3), the all-pervading energy though not specifically mentioned by name in some of the hymns to the Viśvedevāḥ (*R̥V*, V; 41, 42). Agni (*R̥V*, VI; 1, 1) is the worker of marvels and the bestower of strength and wisdom.

Thus the study of Lord Agni became the corner-stone problem to be tackled before any other.

Finally I would like to say that I regard religions as the simplification of philosophy and science for the use of the common man since it is not possible or desirable to make philosophers of every human being. Religion presupposes the acceptance of dogmas as undisputed **truths** by which individuals should abide without hesitation or discussion, but with **Faith**. Religions demand unwavering faith on the part of the believer, hence the need of a scholarly, inspired, learned class of people to assist man in his quest for God.

To enforce or make attractive the dogmas, teachings and practices of all religions, rites and rituals are developed and mythologies are created to illustrate what is obvious and to produce a story behind what is **not obvious**. Mythologies enable the masses to identify themselves with and thereby feel closer to the God they worship. Mythologies also bring easily accessible religious principles to the doorstep of every mind, whether simple or evolved. Finally mythologies go hand in hand with faith and tend to explain the truths of factual reality as recognized by the 'intellectuals' or 'scientists' but for which a logical or experimentally reproducible result or immediate explanation has not always been found. There is much magic and there are many myths also in twentieth-century science and much blind faith in the acceptance of its infallibility.

In conclusion, after intensive reading and re-reading of the sacred texts, my hypotheses in formulating this work are:

1. The will to know and to understand natural phenomena

are the first movement of the human mind;

2. The observed relations and correlations of cause and effect, or science, that cannot be fully understood are deified and/or explained as 'magic';
3. Religion is born to unite man to the entity beyond his power of understanding; religion begins at the ultimate boundary of philosophy, where and when logical explanations of natural phenomena cannot readily be found;
4. Rites and rituals are developed to approach, propitiate and worship the ideas/concepts/Gods;
5. Religions, with time, develop their own philosophies that are no longer empirical or experimental science.

The study of the Veda helped me to formulate these working hypotheses and guided me towards an understanding of the evolution of the intellect, science and knowledge of man.

> *To me who understands hath Varuṇa spoken, the names borne by the Cow (Vāk) are three times seven;*
> *The wise God, knowing the place's secret, shall speak to teach the race that cometh.*
> R̥V, VII; 87, 4 (from Wilson and SS & SV transl.)

2

The Quest for Sources

Agni the undeceivable, who spread out all the worlds,
keeper is he and guard of immortality'
ṚV, VI; 7, 7

THE fossil record bears witness to the evolution of man's body; the artifacts found in association with human fossil remains bear testimony to man's increasing technical performance; paintings and sculptures of animals, human figurines and 'hominoids' as well as ornaments suggest the development and evolution of growing mental faculties. Much of what we know or presume we know at present about the evolution of man's mind is to a great extent the outcome of circumstantial rather than direct evidence. The ancient roots of man's way of thinking must be sought in the oral tradition; the folklore, the myths, the legends and the shamanistic practices and chants of the people of the world, while the ancient-most are lost in past aeons. The Vedic lore is unique in that it has come down to us through an uninterrupted line of teachers with its roots and links in the most remote past. It is however, a difficult task to find out what were the early thoughts and reasonings of man since the oral and written records begin at a very late stage of the evolution of man's mind; inevitably research in this field cannot be but speculative to some extent.

The Veda state the **Truth** — or **Knowledge** — but do not explain how this was acquired. For instance a hymn to Dadhikrās (*R̥V*, VII; 44) appears to indicate the annual cycle of the sun and how to forecast the calendar, but no details are given on how the science was developed. The oral and practical instructions would be sufficient to transmit the expertise; the hymns of the Veda are often mainly mnemonic aids that express concepts and functions as represented by the Gods involved in that particular branch of science.

The evolutionary process of man's mind and the increasing development of manual ability took something like a million years or perhaps more to concretize, as indicated by palaeontological remains of man-made fire. The oldest known remains of fire used by man for roasting purposes and/or sharpening tools comes from the Swartkrans cave in South Africa, and are dated approximately one to one and a half million years BP.

Evolution was slow and our knowledge of the prehistory of man is fractional and to some extent conjectural. Early history is also insufficiently documented. Though the records of historical Egypt go back some millennia, much of the history of the development of thought and science of ancient comparative Egyptians is lost. Chinese records also go back a few millennia; they have been rendered in English language and were studied in detail by the lifetime monumental work of Sir Joseph Needham, a distinguished biologist whose first book, published at a very early age, is a landmark treatise on comparative Experimental Embryology and Development. Unfortunately the intellectual and philosophical aspects of man's story were often kept as well guarded secrets or esoteric knowledge of a restricted number of initiated members of the priesthood; in the course of time most of the oral and written records perished, victims of changing times and persecutions or destructive warfare. Thus the teachings of Hermes Trismegistus of ancient Egypt that could have given us an insight into the evolution of Man's intellectual processes, were only partly revived by the Greek 'mysteries', mainly at Delphos, and they have come down to us only as a few scattered references that do not permit a reliable fully representative reconstruction of the body of knowledge of that school of thought. The Veda are the only body of ancient knowledge that has come down to us as an extensive and cohesive whole, through an unbroken chain of teaching, both oral and written. This immense body of knowledge can, even at this late stage, help us to form an idea of how the human intellect and religion evolved, at least among the Āryans and perhaps in a comparable manner among most of the Indo-European people, and perhaps others as well.

It is therefore in the Veda that I have tried to trace the origin of Man's beliefs. The remarkable feat achieved by the Āryans who migrated to India of memorising the whole of the Vedic lore, generation after generation, brings forth almost intact the thoughts of ancient man. The oral tradition and later the written transmission of the Veda covers such a long period of time that it allowed for enrichment of the primordial thoughts with later findings. The personalities of the Gods themselves evolve as knowledge develops and as everything else in the universe evolves, throughout the *R̥V* itself, as Dandekar has shown (1979a, p. 142). The evolution of the personality of Indra, for instance, was well illustrated by Chakravarti (Xth World Sanskrit Conference, 1997, and 1997). Knowledge was gradually made accessible to more initiates and it percolated in part to the common man by the addition and interpolation of mythological tracts as well as by adding empirically acquired knowledge of the phenomenal world. It therefore appears to me that the Veda, as we have them, mostly have:

1. a literal meaning;
2. a figurative or esoteric meaning;
3. a magico-divine-spiritual-religious purpose for propitiation of the divine and of each divinity in particular

through chanting and incantations to be used mainly or exclusively by the initiated brāhmaṇas.

Throughout the Veda, specially the *R̥V*, there is a constant questioning and unremitting search for answers made by men who try to understand what goes on around them (ex: *R̥V*, I; 161). Consequently my question was, would traces of the basic conceptual ideas be identifiable in the *R̥gveda Saṁhitā*? Since my basic hypothesis is that original ideas can only be derived from the observation of the working of biological and ecological principles of general validity and since the Vedic and Hindu traditions are remarkable in their ecological visions, in them indeed is to be found the original *forma mentis* of Diogenes' 'naked biped'.

It should be pointed out that this approach is radically different from the often quoted, though now outdated, school of thought that regarded the Gods of the Veda as personifications of natural phenomena. What was indeed divinized by the ancient *r̥ṣis* were the identified and rationalized relations of cause and effect and the scientific principles that the *r̥ṣis* gradually discerned. The II, VI and especially the VII *Maṇḍala* of the *R̥V*, the Vasiṣṭha hymns, can be read and are to a great extent, scientific books. Much however, still remained unexplained and could not be represented mentally; all that was then relegated to the realm of magic, as amply documented in the *AV* that, unlike the *R̥V*, is practical rather than speculative. Some of the Gods, and most important among them Indra, the **King** or **Chief** of the Gods, were historical figures deified, a practice common to all people who at some point or other of their cultural evolution have gone through a stage of 'hero-worship'. Even nowadays, in at least one developed country, Japan, the divinity of the Emperor, on which the ancestral Shinto religion is based, is seriously discussed. Dandekar analysed in detail the evolution and deification process of the personality of Indra (Dandekar 1979a). Incidentally it could be pointed out that the principal

God of the Kafirs of Kafiristhan (later Nuristhan) who are descendants of Indo-Europeans, probably Āryan stock, and similarly the Kalash of the Gilgit-Hunsa area, still have as their main God **Imra** (or **Indra**) for the Kafirs and **Balumain** for the Kalash, who arrives at festivals on horseback, or who are represented by carved wooden horse-heads, though the people themselves do not have horses any more. The horse is one of, the important and representative domestic animals of the Indo-European people if not the most important of them. The god and his horse arrive at the winter solstice celebrations, but they are seen only by the shaman, or oracle, in trance.

Chakravarti (1997, p. 106) points out that 'the general mode of life the Āryans lived, was a life full of conflicts and clashes against their enemies, non-Āryan and Āryan, with Indra as their chief'. Again (*l.c.*, p. 113) she writes: '. . . the R̥gvedic poems are a series of songs of their victory. Life in a general way was not that divine, but quite a common place existence with its quota of love, jealousy or hatred against each other'. While I would agree on the whole with Chakravarti, I would like to add that most if not all the hymns to the Great Leader Indra, are a self-eulogy of the great feats of the Āryans arrived after earlier waves of Āryans to the land of the Seven Rivers, *Saptasindhu*. The earlier tribes had already settled down and made alliance with local people, as is obvious of what is well known of the *Dāśarājña war*. In reading the Veda, specially the *R̥V*, we must be aware that it is not an unbiased representation of the feats of a conquering warrior people, the Āryans. Many hymns, therefore, have as their primary scope to put in evidence the battle prowess of their people, personified and symbolized by king Indra. By eulogizing Indra, the Āryans eulogized themselves, hence the large number of hymns to Indra that have come down to us. But apart from these political songs, there is an even greater number of philosophical songs. Many of the hymns to Indra are in fact for the purpose of kindling bravery in their own people or inspiring terror in the enemy and traitors. In a parallel manner, the history books of the West, until recently, were essentially a history of wars and battles, related in a biased manner by each and every nation. Furthermore, it should be remembered that the *Saṁhitās* as we have them now, are an anthology of songs composed over many centuries.

The process of direct acquisition of knowledge, is in fact described in many hymns, specially in *R̥V*, *Maṇḍala* IX, all of them dedicated to Soma Pavamāna. Many of these can be read as perceptions acquired during wake-up observations (*R̥V*, IX; 95-96), others could be read as descriptions of supra-sensory perception perhaps induced by the use of different plant-extracts; *soma* is, at places, mentioned in the plural. Supra-sensory perception could also be reached by self-induced hypnosis and deep meditation. All of these are well-known techniques to acquire enhanced perception, to control body functions and to bring the unconscious and the sub-conscious to the fore at conscious level; 'born out of time as finder of treasures' (of science)... 'king of all existence... as Soma Pavamāna you have been flowing to the earliest man'... who sought knowledge.

Once the relationships of cause and effect were conceptually grasped, the understanding acquired had to be mentally crystallized, so to speak, into *an* entity above suspicion: a God. But since nothing in the phenomenal world is ever fully understood, nor can any event be ever forecast exactly or even anticipated accurately in all details, except for astronomical cycles, the **Entity** is much above man; **It** obviously knows and understands *r̥ta* and all that man is unable to fully grasp mentally. God is implicitly omniscient and of course present everywhere and at all times; **it** is omnipresent, because phenomena **are living entities**, they are in the process of being and becoming, everywhere, always. Man accepts that he is not nor will ever be capable of being omnipresent and omniscient. This scientific attitude and logical frame of mind is the golden thread that runs through the Veda. The ancient seers kept their mind open to recognize and admit new knowledge as understanding progressed. They then incorporated the new knowledge making use of their power of reasoning and discrimination. Evolution of everything, including of the personalities of the Gods was thus implicit. In fact, ideas and concepts and science itself evolves as knowledge progresses.

I believe that the first God, primordial idea of God was **Agni** (fire, light, heat, energy) who underlines all phenomena of the living and non-living. *R̥ta* could not be divinised, because it is the recognition of a *status quo* and not a concept. *R̥ta* **Is** and has to be submitted to, obeyed, preserved, analysed and known as far as possible; it is better to abide by it because it is how things are and because first of all *r̥ta* determines one's place in the universe, one's duties and one's functions and therefore one's *dharma* as well as one's own rights. *Vāk* also could not become a God because *vāk* is a means to an end: the transmission of an understanding. *Vāk* is the means by which mankind and all domesticated animals and plants benefit from the studies carried out by the *r̥ṣis*. The contemporary counterparts of *vāk* are scientific and educational journals, books, teaching aids such as photos, posters, maps, films, videos, TV and so on.

R̥ta and *vāk* are not original Gods, in my thinking, not the same as Agni is god, though they are respectfully deified, they are seldom personified or even represented iconographically, they are often called **ancient ones** and they call for the utmost obedience; they are present, though often indirectly, throughout the Veda.

R̥ta is the result of the cosmic sacrifice of creation (*sacrifacĕre*: in Latin means to make sacred) *R̥V*, III; 6, 6-10 at which Lord Agni is present to provide all Gods with 'noble worship'. Agni is unconcealable and kindled by all the Gods (*R̥V*, X; 64) with whom he is permanently associated. Gods are clearly differentiated from natural elements that are listed later in the same hymn (*l.c.*) as rivers, floods, trees, mountains to **conquer** which Agni is again invoked. But Agni is not invoked only figuratively; he is also invoked physically and practically to vanquish enemies, animals, men, demons or wicked spirits. The destructive power of the jaws of agni, (*R̥V*, X; 87), the flames, are repeatedly called to aid; Agni is also called to be destroyer (*l.c.*, 12) of the 'fool who ruins truth with falsehood'.

While studying the Veda, I made three assumptions:

1. The *śruti* are stated to be revealed truths, consequently it would be impossible to find in the texts the explanations of how the knowledge stated therein was acquired. We either accept them as a revelation or we assume that the knowledge-acquisition process was kept secret purposefully. In either case it will be impossible to find out from the text **how** the knowledge was obtained; we can only put on record **how far** the understanding had progressed at the time when the Veda, especially the *R̥V*, were formulated; the *r̥ṣi* sought **Truth** that 'is the basis that bears the Earth' (*R̥V*, X; 85, 1). There are, however 'two truths, the apparent and the one that is concealed . . . known only to those who are skilled in highest truths', who, in my reading, are the initiated few (*R̥V*, X; 85, 16). Furthermore, the ancient *r̥ṣi* were primarily concerned with physical and spiritual or divine truth that are the matter-of-fact of nature, rather than ethical or sentimental truth that are human expressions.

2. The *śruti*, as we have them, are a **transcription** of the ancient oral tradition. This necessarily had to be concise in its expression. When the oral tradition was written down, similar with what happens with the transcription of all ancient scholarly texts, the language used had to be a sort of code, because:

   (a) pen, pencil and paper were not available and writing came much later and material was scarce, cumbersome and limited; records had to be brief and easily memorized;

(b) aphorisms, metrical poetry and music are obvious means for correct and easy transmission of ideas impeccably repeated; they serve as captions and allusions to best recall the oral teachings of the *ācārya* and of the *guru*;

(c) secret knowledge can be imparted to only a few carefully selected or initiated, tested and trusted *śiṣyas*. Esoteric language is often purposefully enigmatic and has to be interpreted and explained by the *guru* or the *ācārya*.

3. The *śruti* contain the **basic scientific speculations** and conclusions obtained by observation, logical deduction, empiricism and experimentation, and they are rendered by figurative and symbolic imagery.

In conclusion, I realized that most Gods represent ideas, concepts and laws that altogether make up a body of knowledge that relates to different aspects of the inner and outer world of man.

Science, Art and the Veda are fundamentally similar in that they describe and communicate the meaning and function of the many aspects of our inner and outer world, but they differ in the means and ways by which they communicate their insights. Typical scientific-bio-ecological aspects are those with which I am conversant and an **example** of how they are expressed is clear in *R̥V*, VII; 76: 'dawn illumines the path to be trodden by the sages and all men long for dawn', where dawn is what precedes sunrise: it is the beginning of 'seeing' or 'understanding' for which men are longing; dawn is what comes before knowledge and 'light unveils the darkness of ignorance' and puts in motion life and the food web (*R̥V*, VII; 75). Dawn, Usha, is (*R̥V*, VII; 80, 2) beautiful, youthful and unquestioned. 'She has turned thoughts to the sun and fire' of life. 'Thus the fathers could find the light that lay in darkness' (*R̥V*, VII; 76, 4) and 'the ancient sages true to law eternal were the God's companions at the banquet'. Sage Vasiṣṭha (*Ṛ̥V*, VII; 87, 4) also reminds man that there is still much yet to be known. More specific examples I will give in the chapter on the bio-ecological aspects.

I shall discuss Lord Agni in more detail later. Agni who, as God, is not the same as common fire that appears in multiple forms. The antiquity of Agni as concept of energy and as God is further attested by the fact that it is seldom personified and represented as such. Visual and personified representations of Gods came late, they were preceded by a long period of symbolic representation in graphic, sound and totemic form. Stylized and symbolic representations of fire are ubiquitous throughout the world to this day, in all cultures.

After Agni, the original God, perhaps the first concept grasped and deified by man was Savitṛ̥, the great Vivifier, Life and Hope, who is represented as a struggle; to win the struggle one needs the determination provided by Agni to acquire wisdom and power (*Ṛ̥V*, I; 66). The concept of life and motion, and perhaps also of Time that is inseparable from life and motion is deified in the Great God Savitṛ̥.

The antiquity of Savitṛ̥ is mentioned over and over again and is further confirmed by the fact that there are few representations of Savitṛ̥, which means that by the time iconography was developed, he was already so ancient that he was implicitly accepted as ever-present, as embodied in the Sun that is the giver of life on Earth; at that time new divine personalities had probably developed and were represented iconographically. We could, however, speculate that the *svastika* and *cakra* which represents the wheel of life, and is derived as a symbol from the *svastika*, are symbols that occur throughout the world in many different cultures. The *svastika* is already found in old ceramics from about 5000 BC at Samarra in Mesopotamia. Amongst other meanings the *svastika* indicates rotation around a centre, therefore marks movement, cycles, regeneration, action, life and rhythms. In the *cakra*, including the *dharmacakra* of Buddhism, the centre is often represented as occupied by Agni. The *svastika* represents infinity, like Aditi, and sacredness or transcendental reality. The *svastika* and *cakra* are universal symbols of the Sun and Life. Incidentally it could be mentioned that most *svastika*s are represented forward moving, from left to right, indicating progression for right-handed persons and for those writings like Sanskrit that proceed from left to right. The nazi *svastika* was turned the other way round, to the left; was it an unwilling and unwitting recognition of regression and degeneration, a significant Freudian slip? Or was the Nazi *cakra* an attempt to place infinity and sacredness into the temporal and profane?

Man learned to make and use the fire that was first brought by Mātariśvān, but as the apprentice sorcerer he is, he feared his own invention. Man therefore needs to propitiate Agni, the messenger of cosmic sacrifice, by treading the path of **Truth**, with worship, reverence and offerings (*R̥V*, I; 128, 2 *et seq.*). Man learned to control man-made fire, but there are limits to man's power: runaway forest or grassland fires are difficult to control, as repeatedly mentioned. Therefore the protection of Lord Agni is always to be invoked. But Indra's thunderbolt will never be controlled by man (*R̥V*, I; 129, 10).

In conclusion, the Veda read with a biological-ecological decoding key show a profound knowledge of the relations of cause and effect of natural phenomena, specially those that are related to life processes. The Veda are a treasure-mine of information about the science of ancient man and, even more important, of the way man thought, **understood or not**, and transmitted his knowledge to others.

May the most glorious Pitr̥s aid us ...
R̥V, I; 106, 3

3

The Concept of God

Agni, thou encompassest the Gods as the felly encompasses the spokes of a wheel

R̥V, V; 13, 6

Two elements appear to be indispensable to visualize and then formulate mentally the concept of God; first, the existence of a powerful mind incessantly intent on understanding natural phenomena and second, the mental capacity to formulate or give a body or formula to abstract ideas and concepts. This non-material body is what was later called the **forma** or form. The second step is an immense leap forward in the evolution and development of the human mind.

All of us are imbued with the concept of God. To us God is no longer just an idea but is a mental reality whether modern human beings believe in **IT** or take great trouble to dispose of **IT**. Implicitly it appears natural to us that the idea of God existed throughout the ages of man's mind. This, however, cannot be so and at some stage, either by revelation, by inspiration, by a 'stroke of genius', by a sudden thought or idea, or whatever we want to call it, or by step by step thinking and logical deduction, as for instance expressed in *Īśa Upaniṣad*, man must have conceived of the idea of an Entity, invisible yet present, intangible but that can be felt, omniscient, omnipresent and omnipotent, with no beginning or end in space and time, better known from the effects of its existence than known in itself. Indeed it is stated that the Supreme Being is so formidable that man cannot apprehend the concept in its entirety. The concept of infinite and infinity is significant in this context: Aditi, the mother of infinity existed since ever; a concept that covers space, time and existence. Hence the abstract idea of infinite as a mathematical reality akin to the Supreme Being, the Absolute Truth.

What man could understand of it was expressed as knowledge of the world he lives in; the whole world that is sacred because it is part of the Ultimate Reality. And what man could not understand, that too was inherent in the concept of Ultimate Reality or God; thus man, to appease his eager mind, had to create **approximate** understandings and representations; they appear in legends, myths, magic and visual representations. Sound itself is made a revelation or *śruti*, as the syllable *AUṀ*, ॐ that sets in motion all vibrations. Nature and magic are inseparable and magic is as old as mankind, and of course it includes prayers, incantations, exorcisms and shamanistic practices that are all part of the acts or rites that man developed to satisfy his urge for active participation in the Cosmic Drama and Cosmic Order. These acts are included in the power of *asu* Varuṇa, so well analysed by Dandekar (1979a, pp. 28-67; 312-31) and are incorporated in the rites and ritualistic performances of ceremonies, religious and laic (*R̥V*, I; 110). The concept of God and Agni as God is expressed in *R̥V*, VIII; 11, 6: 'Sages, we call the sage to help; mortals we call God to aid, we call Agni with our songs' (transl. Griffith).

Once it was recognized that there is something unexplained and therefore mysterious in this world and in the universe at large, something that is beyond the grasp and control of man, faith, religion and dependency on this entity were born. Man had to develop rituals to bring himself in closer relation to his God; rites and rituals were probably first created to propitiate the invisible Omnipresent. At the same time it must have been recognized that the role of empirical and experimental science, though not specifically described as such, was of fundamental importance for the survival of man who is not particularly gifted physically. The *ṛṣis* were good scientists in their own right; not scientists as we visualize them today, going around in white laboratory coats and dealing with sophisticated equipment, but scientists in the full acceptance of the term, meaning 'those who understand and know; those who endeavour and work to acquire understanding and knowledge' of the inner self, of the outer self, of the visible and the invisible, of the tangible and intangible, of the past and future. The VIIth *Maṇḍala* of the *ṚV*, can most of it be read as a book of science culminating in intense devotion to *asura* Varuṇa. In other terms, Varuṇa of infinite magic power, takes over when and where man can no longer understand and explain nature with his own limited intellect. Dandekar (1981, pp. 113-21) discusses vividly the *bhakti* aspects of the devotion of Vasiṣṭha to his God, Varuṇa.

Prof. Dandekar (pers. com.) objected to my reading **science** in the *ṚV* saying that no scientific theories were developed by the *ṛṣis*. This is correct in the contemporary acceptance of the expression **scientific theory**. Theory is defined here as a body of doctrines used for the explanation and prediction of a phenomenon or a series of phenomena. Though the ancient *ṛṣis* probably did not see the need to knit together the knowledge acquired into a well defined and formulated whole or **theory** having general validity, they did recognize the importance of factual knowledge and of the establishment of cause and effect relationships for the understanding of the phenomenological world. They based their understanding on observation, logical deduction and experimentation. Maybe they did not formulate theories because they did not see the need for generalization since the particular explanation was sufficient to the purpose; or perhaps they did not have sufficient correct information to generalize their understanding. Most probably the concept of **theory** did not arise in the mind of *ṛṣis*; the intense devotion that Dandekar rightly recognized in *ṛṣi* Vasiṣṭha is indicative that *asura* Varuṇa is the embodiment of all understanding and that he himself and He alone is the explanation of the Universe, since He is the *asu* of the universe, the infinite magical power that permeates everything; originally Varuṇa is himself **the** theory.

The establishment of a theory requires taking a big step from the particular to the general. While this is relatively a direct procedure in the exact or mathematical sciences, it is a very complex one in physical and chemical sciences and is extraordinarily more so in the biological sciences where the number of factors and variables is practically infinite. The world of the Vedic man is essentially a biological and ecological world, therefore one whose mysteries are difficult to unveil. Incidentally, the word theory can be derived from the same root as God in Greek; *Theo*, and would therefore mean: 'what pertains to God'. Consequently all knowledge is the science pertaining to the *deva*, same root as *deus* in Latin and *Theo* in Greek. I believe that the *ṛṣis* progressed in a genuine scientific manner as far as they could go, but where they could not give a clear answer they had to explain the world as 'God's magic'.

The great achievements of the ancients as they have come down to us through teachings of the Veda, are:

1. a critical attitude that stresses the power of discrimination of man as different from animals; the power of discrimination enables man to identify what he knows and what he does not know;
2. the recognition that everything in the cosmos is subject to perpetual evolution, that there is a continuous change over time of the whole and of its parts, so much so that even the personalities of the Gods evolve;
3. the recognition of the cyclic aspect of natural phenomena as perceived by man living in an Euclydean world and that these cycles can be broken down by cataclysmic events.

Coming back to the very early man that had just emerged as *Homo sapiens* and who had learned to **use**, then also to **make** and **control** fire, we can easily imagine him to be quite bewildered as the apprentice sorcerer he really had become. Fire indeed has all the attributes to become the precursor God and by a process of identification and assimilation, God himself; witness to this is the sublimation and disappearance of matter caused by fire. Fire, **the** '*ur-gott*' of thinking man is lovable and fearful, gentle and terrible, destructive and generous, it takes and gives, it is good and bad, above all it is powerful and omnipresent, great, imposing, giver of light and warmth, giver of life and food, and never fully understood since it is ever somewhat mysterious. We have all experienced at sometime or other the hypnotizing power of fire. Man learned to kindle fire, but he could not similarly kindle the attributes of Agni, the 'fireness' in fire: 'Agni bring hither Agni's self' (*R̥V*, I; 44, 7-8), such as for instance the fire of life: Agni Tanūnapāt, is Agni son of himself. Primitive thinking man must have had the idea and must have then developed the concept that the entity, God, that he could not really define or understand, **expresses** itself through fire, more than just **manifests** itself. It expresses itself by what it can do and by the uses it can be put to. That which fire consumes disappears into nothing and this power of sublimation makes Lord Agni the Purifier *par excellence* and, later on, the ideal intangible, spiritual messenger between man and all Gods that were born later in man's mind and that exist everywhere, in space, air, earth, water and within man himself as thought and as the fire of life. 'He alone of all these Gods . . . hadst been born living from the dry wood; then all were pleased with thy wisdom' (*R̥V*, I; 68, 2) . . . 'within the laws of *r̥ta*' (*R̥V*, I; 70, 2). Agni grants spiritual vigour and gives immortality to the Gods (*R̥V*, I; 3, 4), 'the Gods gained immortality from Agni, at first only Agni was immortal'.

I concluded that partly because not everything about fire could be understood by man, fire was developed into a god, Lord Agni who is the essence of fire, who appears as flames, heat, warmth, energy, light, sun and who hides away in waters and wood in his **potential energy** form, but not revealed aspects. In all the manifestations of Agni there is a common principle; he is omnipresent as energy (*R̥V*, I; 27, 2), unexplained, undisclosed, mysterious and adorable. These aspects of fire are aspects of God, because by definition God is never totally comprehended or mentally visualized. The kindling of the innermost fire of one's enlightenment is well described in *R̥V*, V; 2. The original and supreme God cannot be fully represented mentally because of human intellectual limitations; unlike God, man cannot unravel all mysteries. This is nowhere expressed better than in the simple common prayer:

> O Lord, forgive three sins that are due to my human limitations.
> Thou art everywhere, but I worship Thee here;
> Thou art without form, but I worship Thee in these forms;
> Thou needest no praise, yet I offer Thee these prayers and salutations;
> Lord forgive three sins that are due to my human limitations.

As God, Agni 'by whom the sages gained their wisdon' (*R̥V*, IX; 108, 4) and through whom the wish is expressed: 'may we accomplish all that we are capable of' (*R̥V*, X; 2, 3), came to be mentally realized, the need arose to invoke, propitiate, beg and adore the mysterious entity that was forced on man's mind by his own reason (*R̥V*, I; 19) and was expressed through Agni; rites and religions were born, hence also the appellation 'divine fire' that becomes more and more frequent. Fire divine as knowledge and wisdom; knowledge as Truth. Truth is the obsession of the Āryans (*R̥V*, I; 71—*R̥V*, I; 72—*R̥V*, VII; 66, 13) as is also evident throughout the history, legends and myths of most Indo-European people, as for instance the Celts, to mention only one group. The inner fire of consciousness later became the fire of *tapas*, as in *R̥V*, I; 73, 4. Fire is also the source of life, physical and spiritual but according to the eternal duality of everything when one takes a coin, one accepts the other face as well. Fire creates life and also destroys it.

The sublimation of Agni into God is a good example of how abstract ideas rather than physical phenomena were made Gods and, in my opinion, it is the best example of the fact that the Vedic Gods are not just the deification and personalization of natural phenomena, but are instead the representation of **philosophical principles** and concepts. In other words I believe that ancient man crystallized his knowledge into Gods, though he also deified successful leaders, chiefs and teachers, as for instance Indra, King Indra, king of the Gods, great conqueror and representative of the valour of the Āryans in battle and glorified over and over again. Figurative myths and legends are useful instruments to instruct other men and perpetuate historical facts. Gradually the scientific, historical, mythological and existential experience of the early Āryans who migrated towards *Saptasindhu*, the land of the seven rivers, were condensed into that formidable body of knowledge that are the *śruti*.

In historical times, the details of the evolution of the Buddhist sects, for instance the *Jātaka* stories, show clearly how mythology develops **after** and not before the philosophical religious aspects of the doctrine have been established and how they adapt to the conditions of the pre-existent cultural and ecological environments.

Radin (1941, p. 203) says that 'the Australian Aborigines, the Andaman tribals, Negritos of the Philippines, the Lalkman of Tierra del Fuego have no myths of creation, the Supreme Being is not considered a creator . . . no prayers are addressed to him, and there are no rituals associated to his cult'; further Radin adds: 'there is no religious belief properly, though only **he** is always good and just'; 'there is only a philosophical notion'. By saying this Radin indirectly expresses the same views as given here that 'philosophy' comes to the mind of man before religion.

Humility is the characteristic of the early stages of religions (*Ṛ̥V*, VII; 89); arrogance in man likening himself to God and considering that it is God's duty to satisfy his wishes, desires and prayers, as well as representing God in the image of man, come at a later stage.

One is tempted to read the origin of the concept of God directly at many places in the Veda, for instance in *Ṛ̥V*, I; 65, Lord Agni is said to be born in the womb of *ṛta*; in other words, the idea of god is born from observing nature's and all laws of the universe by which man must live (*Ṛ̥V*, IX; 63, 14-24). In *AV*, X; 2, man the observer examines himself and the outside world; he finds out how wonderful is the anatomy, the structure and function of the organs and systems of the human body and he exclaims in awe: 'the Gods did it', 'the voice, the brain, the thoughts, the pleasure', 'the Gods did it'. All structures and functions are analysed; then the final great question comes naturally; it expresses the idea of God: 'By whom was the mind put in him? Wherever does he dwell upon the Gods?' and the concept of fire as energy is at the root of all thoughts. Agni as thought, body heat and energy is the expression of the invisible and intangible God.

Traditionally the significance of fire-worship is to imbue wisdom in man: 'Agni impart to me wisdom, *brāhman* impart to me *brahman*' (*AV*, XIX; 11, 4). Agni as the fireness in fire is knowledge, wisdom and mental power, but fire also burns dirt and confusion (*Ṛ̥V*, I; 79, 12) physically, spiritually, intellectually through the power of discrimination that is his gift to man. Fire burns evil thoughts and provides energy for keeping and acquiring more knowledge. There is a clear distinction (*Ṛ̥V*, I; 79) between Agni the spiritual and intellectual entity and 'agni of the pointed flames' (*l.c.*, 10). However both Agni and common fire are, like everything else in ecology, closely related to other Gods as is evident from the frequent recurrence of the duals Agni-Indra;

Agni-Mitra; Agni-Soma; Agni-Varuṇa and Agni the lofty *asura* (R̥V, V; 12), all-pervading and present everywhere at all times. (R̥V, I; 149, 151). The individual as well as the collective society need to have their internal world attuned to the external world of which they are a part to achieve ecological inner (psychological) and outer (physical well-being) balance. Accordingly there is a need for 'seasonal offer of the inner sacrifice' (R̥V, I; 170, 5), which is a renewal of the self in tune with the seasonal changes of the environment over which man has no power. These are phenomena that can only be influenced through magic or religious practices performed preferably at the solstices or equinoxes. Usually the winter solstice marks the beginning of the year and the spring equinox is specially significant as marking the re-awakening of nature after the winter stasis. In this context, in addressing the sun, the horizon is called 'the lap of your mother Earth', which is more than just a poetical expression, but indicates astronomical fixed points. Natural cycles are a recurrent theme of great importance (ex: R̥V, 29; R̥V, I; 105, 9).

In the Veda the concept of Dhātr̥ as Creator must have evolved naturally from the fundamental triad Agni, R̥ta, and Vāk. If Dhātr̥ is indeed the idea of a Creator or Maker, rather than a fully developed divinity, I would place him at a very early stage of the development of the Āryan man's mind when the gradual acquisition of knowledge imposed the logical assumption that 'what **is** had to be **made**'. Dhātr̥ as an idea, rather than a God, belongs to philosophy rather than religion; in fact, in the evolution of the Vedic thought, from philosophical to religious, Dhātr̥ gradually fades off and becomes a secondary divinity. On this point I would not follow the conclusion (Dandekar 1979a, p. 16) that 'abstraction . . . divinities belong to a later phase of the Vedic religious thought'. I would repeat here that I believe that pure abstract concepts are the root and precede religions; elaborate thoughts evolve into religions, rather than the other way round.

I mentioned above the Āryan obsession with Truth that is strong to this day in all forms of Hinduism. It could have originated from the fact that originally the two concepts of **Truth** and **Knowledge** were interchangeable and were used as synonyms. **Knowledge** is power, hence the need to acquire it and in so doing, **Truth** becomes sacrosanct.

Once early man developed the concept of God, the knowledge of God would have been the ultimate goal, because man recognized the 'magical potence of knowledge' Dandekar (1979b, pp. 149-61) stresses the point of how this fundamental trait was retained throughout the history of Hinduism as 'respect for knowledge, and trust in the practical religio-philosophical efficiency of knowledge'. 'Do not forget, O Agni, who art a Sage possessed of knowledge' (*R̥V*, I; 71, 10).

Finally I would also mention that it is made clear at a few places (ex: *R̥V*, I; 164, 10) that some aspects of knowledge must be kept secret, therefore knowledge of the mysteries should be given only to a few selected initiates. Knowledge can only be reached by unrelenting mental and spiritual exercises, training and strong willpower. Complex rituals, sometimes performed secretly and elaborate permanent structures such as temples, churches, places of worship are constructed. They are useful to explain the doctrine to the masses that must also be impressed and filled with awe, respect and admiration. Rituals and impressive permanent structures may also be an unconscious attempt to capture and retain God as an honoured guest.

When did I worship the deities of falsehood
or when did I think adversely of the Gods, O Agni?
Why art thou angry with us, O Jātavedas?
May destruction fall upon those who lie against thee.

R̥V, VII; 104, 14
(from Wilson and SS and SV transl.)

4

Ecological Aspects

He (Agni) who gives food, like patrimonial riches
and guides aright like some wise man's
instruction,
Loved like a guest who is received with respect,
may he as Hotṛ, bring prosperity to the house
of his worshippers Ṛ*V*, I; 73, 1

Weal to thee be Agni, together with the waters,
Weal be Soma, together with the herbs
AV, II; 10, 2

THE ecological validity of the Veda is not exclusive to them. St. Francis of Assisi expresses much ecological wisdom in his *Cantico delle Creature* (Canticle of all Creatures); Chief Seattle in his letter to Franklin Pierce, then president of the United States of America, is detailed and explicit in his defence of the environment and he bases his arguments on valid ecological principles; he declares beautifully how he and his people are an integral part of their environment: 'how is it possible to buy or sell the sky or the heat of the land? . . . as we do not own the air or the lustre of the waters how could they be bought? . . . each small piece of soil is sacred to my people!'.

Books have been written and more could be added about the mystics, Rumi and the Sufi tradition, the Christian, Jain, Buddhist, Tibetan as well as some of the Chinese and Japanese poets and even the great mathematician Omar Khayyam and other Iranians whose views on the permanence or impermanence and cycling of all matter and energy are ecologically sound in modern scientific terms. Giordano Bruno could be revived from the stake for his 'heretical' views, but I will strictly adhere to my first purpose. The Veda, as we have them, constitute a considerable body of knowledge, codified in rigid metrical form and collected in the *Saṁhitā*. In fact, I started with the aim of studying the ecological aspects of the *śāstra* at large; by gradually trimming down my ambition, I am at present concerned only with the Veda. The wealth of information I see in these would be enough to fill a lifetime with assiduous study, while my own lifetime is quickly approaching its end.

The *Saṁhitā* are the product of a highly evolved and evolving culture; a culture that to this day has kept alive and creative the memory of its roots and beginnings. The critical ideas, thoughts, concepts, conclusions and technicalities of the ancients are present in every verse, crystallized as myths, pronounced as teachings, rendered in poetic form, memorized as sound and metre, spiritualized as invocations and laudations, dictated as techniques. All these aspects are grafted on the ancient roots of a system that preserves as sacred all knowledge acquired and keeps its doors open to any useful addition 'from the four quarters'.

Indian tradition admits three distinct ways in which the Vedic hymns may be interpreted. The inner subjective way (*ādhyātmika*), the objective literal or material way (*ādhibhautika*) and the godly or spiritual way (*ādhidaivika*). What precedes is mostly my personal subjective way of reading the hymns as a biologist. What follows is an objective interpretation from an ecological point of view. Saraswati and Vidyalankar (1977, SS and SV) have done a beautiful work in rendering the *ṚV* in an integrated manner, with emphasis on the *ādhidaivika* aspect as well as the *ādhibhautika*; their monumental work has been the beginning and basis of my studies. Of course, I would not add anything to the learned expositions of the commentators, specially on the *ādhidaivika* aspects. For instance, under *R̥V*, III; 35, 8 they write '. . . extraction of medicinal elixir from herbs . . . needs an expert . . . pressing stones . . . and water, and is sweetened with milk . . . on the metaphysical plane, the worshipful sentiments are sweetened with intellect, austerity (stones) and pure thoughts'.

Traditional Way of Life

When reading the Veda from a biological and ecological point of view, one should alienate oneself from the contemporary world and environment. The best way to visualize how the Vedic *r̥ṣis* saw themselves, their fellow men and nature, is to figure out how man lived three or four thousand or more years ago in the areas inhabited by the ancient Āryan tribes and before them by the local populations whom they collectively called Anārya and with whom they came in amicable or not-so-amicable contact. It is indispensable to try to identify oneself mentally with the world as it was at that time to avoid such elementary mistakes as for instance taking tree-worship as worship of the sacrificial post (*yūpa*). One must imagine how impressive must have been the giant trees of the extensive forests of those distant times and read Vanaspate literally: 'O Lord of the forest'; 'O tree'. When in the text of the Veda the sacrificial post is meant, it is stated so. The 'interpreted' erroneous translation of tree or lord of the forest into '*yūpa*' (see Griffith, 1889, p. 8, note) is just one of the many examples that indicates how distant the learned scholars who worked in their libraries in far away places were from the environment and realities of everyday life of the Vedic people: 'Vanaspate, O Lord of the forest, give forth thyself and call the Gods for sacrifice'. . . . 'May Agni, God intelligent, speed our oblations to the Gods' (*R̥V*, I; 142, 11) where the tree is invoked as the wood that will sustain the fire through which Lord Agni expresses himself. Tree-worship is a very ancient practice still alive in one form or another in most cultures; it is particularly significant in present-day Hinduism and Buddhism which have carried it over respectively from the ancient forms of Vedism and Brāhmaṇism. It is recurrent in Palm Sunday's waving of palm fronds and olive branches, as the 'tree of life' of Christian texts, as the Christmas tree and other trees in the Christian tradition that still maintains some products from trees as important elements in the liturgy and mythology, such as incense and the symbolism of the olive branch of peace brought by a pigeon. Incidentally the pigeon has no gall bladder; this could be one reason why it was taken to be a non-bilious animal and was chosen as a symbol of peace.

The South-Siberian Turks consider the *axis mundi* to be a tree and the shaman's drum is made from that tree (Marazzi, 1984, p. 11); they also pay homage to the 'rich tree of the Altaï top' [invocation to the *Altay Azi Akalar* Spirit (*apud* Marazzi, *l.c.*, p. 110]. Tree-worship is still a daily practice for devout Hindus.

The migrating Āryan tribes were originally given mainly to pastoral activities in highlands, hence the importance given to cattle; only secondarily they became agriculturists for the sake of daily mainstay food. This they found in barley that grows better in highlands and was domesticated before wheat, already around 8,000 BC among proto-Sanskrit-speaking people. To this day many devout Hindus offer barley grains in preference to wheat to the family deity; it is common to find a few plants of barley in the vegetable garden, sowed specially for this purpose. Migrations took many centuries as they stopped at convenient places for shorter or longer periods of some years or some generations. The best pasture or agricultural lands would be disputed away from earlier colonizers if any were present and the prize of land was the cause of disputes and wars between the Āryan families and clans themselves, but eventually a strong desire to settle down grew among the people on the move (*ṚV*, VI; 49, 15): 'give us a lasting home' and 'one rich with nature's God-given bounties'.

It may have taken something like three thousand years before the tribes coming from Central Asia east of the Caspian sea settled down in their respective territories, but as far as one can estimate from the present-day life in some remote areas, life-styles would not have changed in any fundamental manner since then. Loude and Lièvre (1984; 1987) lived for two years among the Kalash of Chitral and Gilgit and before them Robertson (1887) lived for one year and visited several times the Kafirs of Kafiristhan or Bashgal. Their observations and those of others are invaluable aids to help us visualize how the Vedic man lived. Several anthropologists studied the habits and customs of Dards, Kafirs, Kalash people, who are all descendants of ancient Indo-European, perhaps Āryan migrant tribes that became isolated and separated from the major stream.

Vedic people were one with nature (*R̥V*, VIII; 58, 2-3; *apud* SS and SV, a *Vālakhilya* hymn): 'One is that which manifests in all', which in contemporary ecological terms is expressed as 'everything is related to everything else'; it could also be interpreted as the energy resting in everything, alive or dead, organic or inorganic, which exists either as dynamic or potential energy, or both. It was essential for the survival of ancient people to learn how they could interfere with the world around them to improve quantity and quality of food, shelter, health, hunting and fighting potential; this is how agriculture and animal husbandry were engendered. Man had to recognize what powers of nature he would be unable to control and he was thus compelled to resort to magic and religion to win the cooperation of winds, rains, regularity of the monsoon and astronomical recurrences, for the control of earthquakes, landslides or dam-bursts, forest or savannah fires, river flow and all major elements of nature. All these are described, invoked and prayed to in the Veda, with fear and respect. Interference of the Gods was sought for the repetition of favourable phenomena such as regular rains to ensure rich pastures and good crops, healthy cattle, horses, goats and sheep, as well as fecundity of the land and of women.

Rites would be performed also to forestall destructive natural events. Man learned that there were also natural phenomena with which he could interfere and with which he could collaborate after having understood how the **system** worked. Thus rational agriculture and the use of natural products such as provided by plants, or the smelting of metal ores and improvement of the wheel, the plough and irrigation devices as well as harnessing of horses and bullocks were already well developed in **R̥gvedic times**.

The seeker of nature's laws is rewarded: 'the fathers found the light (knowledge) that lay in darkness (ignorance) and with effectual words begat the morning' (teaching of knowledge, or acquired science) (*R̥V*, VII; 76, 4). In fact, we would not be here if our forefathers **had not been wise** and ingenious.

The intimacy of man with nature is expressed with great joy (*R̥V*, VIII; 31, 10) 'we solicit the happiness afforded by the hills, the rivers, the sun . . .'. 'Agni the first God . . . who makes our fields prosperous' (*l.c.*, 14). It is clear from *R̥V*, X; 85, 1-19 and the interpretation given by SS and SV mainly based on the *Nirukta*, that many rites and rituals **derive directly** from the observation of natural phenomena and cycles, and not the other way round: the phenomena are not **explained** by the rituals, as was often repeated by commentators. Rituals are not an attempt at explaining the natural phenomena.

Communication of Knowledge

The *r̥ṣis* who retreated to their *āśramas* to study and apply the fruits of their studies to practicalities, had ample time also for meditation and for religious practices and thus became the famous *ācāryas* who imparted theoretical, spiritual and practical knowledge to such youngsters as were eager to learn. Apprenticeship lasted for many years of unremitting, arduous work under trying conditions aimed at strengthening the body, the mind and the will, thereby elevating the spirit. Evidently, the concise texts of the Veda reflect only the essence, or the conclusions of the vast amount of empirical and experimental scientific knowledge that was accumulated generation after generation of *ācāryas*. Physical, intellectual and spiritual abilities were transmitted practically and were impeccably memorized thanks to strict discipline, to *yoga* practices and to metrical (rhythm and sound) laws without written transcription; memory was also aided by an extremely rich mythological lore that is still growing through addition of new myths or the addition of details to old myths. There are, for instance, several traditions on how the right (or left) tusk of Gaṇeśa was broken. I believe that the oral tradition, which is mathematically musical, guarantees exact transmission of knowledge, better than the written tradition. The reason is that there can be no errors in the rendering of metrical poetry, and if a mistake was committed, it would be immediately spotted. In the written tradition, however, the copyist can unwillingly enter errors in his script, specially considering that in those remote days there was no refined equipment as we have now and a थ can easily look like a य and a ध like a घ, and so many others. In other words, the oral tradition guarantees a more faithful transmission of knowledge than the ancient written tradition. For instance, the Mysteries of Eleusis in Greece, were celebrated for a period of about 2000 years, well into the Christian Era about the middle of the second millennium AD; they left no written record, unlike other Greek and Roman 'mysteries', but the rites were impeccably calebrated at Eleusis until the end.

Material Culture

In their migrations from the steppes of Central Asia and the South Caspian and south-eastern Caspian Sea, through Balkh in Khorassan (Dandekar, 1979a, 1981) the ancient Āryans came in contact with many new environments and different materials. The wealth of the rich valleys of *Saptasindhu* inevitably favoured the development of many new abilities 'with the mind of a seer and the acts of a sage' (*ṛṣimana ya ṛṣikṛt*; *ṚV*, IX; 96, 18). During earlier times the most important objects of daily use would have been those of pastoral people; in fact in a hymn addressed to Pūṣaṇ (*ṚV*, VI: 53, 9), the guide, the pathfinder (Dandekar, 1979a), the 'goad with a horny point' is mentioned. Though it is not certain that the word *gūpaśā* means horny material, there is no doubt that leather straps, objects and containers made of hooves, horns and hides were of common use; such were trumpets from horns, chords, from sinews for bow strings and reins, thongs and latchets for footwear, straps and cover for the drum, whole hides to make drinking water-bags, covers for shelters and inflated hides as floats to ford rivers. Fat and bones of domestic and hunted animals were used by all shepherds and hunters of all cultures as raw materials, as well as cow or camel dung dried and mixed with straw as fuel. The ancient *Ṛgvedic* man was no exception. In my childhood farmers in Tuscany used cowdung cakes as fuel and we liked the milk boiled on those fires better than any other 'because it smelled of our friend the cow'. Cattle or camel dung cakes are used to make fire throughout Asia. Over the centuries techniques were improved, for instance by curing (tanning) leather with the bark of certain trees rich in tannins, a very ancient practice that wandering people would have learned from one another. Raw leather however, is still in use in remote arid areas where fuel is scarce and there are no tannin producing trees, such as the Tibetan plateau or among the Dard nomads of Ladakh. The importance given to the tree and consequently to the forest is obvious (*ṚV*, VI; 47, 26 *et al.*) since a large variety of useful products are obtained from them. Species diversity, or presence of a large number of different plants and animals, must have been a most astonishing and wonderful experience for people coming from steppes, savannahs and grasslands to forested areas, specially the rich land of the seven rivers, *Saptasindhu*. Conservation practices and judicious use were still practised until recently; among the Kalash, live trees were never felled because they belong to the fairies (Lièvre and Loude, 1990), branches were chopped out of live trees and only dead trees are fully utilized, a practice that was observed throughout the Karakorum-Himalayan ranges and most of India to date. It is only in the nineteeth and twentieth centuries that local people have succumbed to the greed of vested powers and mountain forests have been mercilessly plundered with disastrous consequences such as changes in climate, decrease in rainfall, drying out of water springs, dryness of the land, landslides, loss of pasture land, increase in summer temperature and decrease in winter temperature, loss of species variety of flora and fauna and impoverishment of human health. Not only organic materials were used, metal ores were smelted for the extraction of metals; it is possible, but not certain that *aya* means iron, though it could mean metals in general. Smelting of iron ore and the making of steel are very ancient practices in India (Vannucci 1989, p. 131). Fire may have been used for fragmenting rocks and boulders by heating: 'by the *ṛta* the Aṅgirasa have broken the rock and cleft it asunder' (*ṚV*, IV; 3, 11).

Materials are otherwise taken for granted in the *ṚV* and the *SV*, and are seldom mentioned specifically, not so in the *AV* which is more pragmatic. As such the *AV* illustrates the everyday life of the Vedic people, their fears, their difficulties, their aspirations as well as their material culture and the source of raw materials, better than the *ṚV*, or the *SV*. The *AV* also illustrates upon the materials used in the rites to invoke help from the divinity and those which could have been used to enhance the powers of the mind to seek help by prayers and invocations. The most immediate worries of the Vedic man appear to be, as is natural, about food, its availability and quality, then health, birth, death, the number and health of domestic animals, progeny and marriage, but throughout there was a constant communion with nature.

It is not clear when the conch, the shell of the marine mollusc whose zoological name is *Xanchus pyraeum,* came into regular use in war and rituals; it was probably late. At the beginning it must have been rare and would have been used for jewellery only by kings, princes and perhaps their *purohitas*. It is indicative of trade with coastal dwellers since early days as it was probably already in use as the conch at the time of the war of the ten kings and of king Sudās. In *R̥V*, VI; 47, 29 *et seq.* the *dundūbhi* is mentioned and was correctly interpreted as the war drum, but the conch is not mentioned; it was probably unknown in very early R̥gvedic times. According to *AV*, V; 20, 21 the drum is made of wood of the forest tree and headed with cowhide and belongs to all *gotras*! The making and use of the shaman's drum, used in the rituals of the South Siberian Turks who are Indo-European language speaking, are described in detail in many contemporary shamanistic chants; the practice begins with invocation to the tree chosen by the spirits and from which the hide-headed drum is fashioned and proceedes all the way up to the animation of the drum itself (Marazzi 1984, pp. 174-224 *et al.*), which has a personality of its own.

Domesticated species of plants and animals play a key role in the life of people conscious of being one with nature. Among the animals, horses, cattle, camels, goats and sheep and among the plants barley first, then wheat, grapes and some medicinal plants and other species of grasses were important; apart of course, of the *soma* plant that is still an enigma as to its botanical identity. My conviction is that the *soma* plant was one of the various species of wild grapes native to India; probably it is *vinifera* which is the common table and wine making grapes. This is a point on which I will elaborate in a future paper. Trees and forests would have been worshipped as they are by all people, specially those coming from steppes, savannahs and arid or high places devoid of trees or having only a few scattered ones. The use of natural products would have followed along with the technicalities developed to make better use of these materials. The settlement of migrants would also favour the habit of tree planting for shadow, for fruits, for beauty and for worship.

There is an extensive literature on the ethnological, scientific and archaeological aspects of the long process of domestication of plants and animals; it is not my purpose to review the large amount of information obtained in this domain by traditional and modern science. Rather I try to visualize how the ancient *ṛṣis* saw the process of living, the phenomenon of life and how life-giving elements of nature were used.

Non-material Culture

Apart from satisfying the basic physical needs of food, shelter and reproduction, thinking man must have developed in early stages both the desire for immortality and the desire to learn the art and acquire the power of divination, since either would enable him to have a greater participation in the cosmic drama that unfurled under his very eyes. Both of these desires are still unfulfilled but they are not dead and they still stimulate most individuals in one direction or other. Throughout the *ṚV*, the *SV*, the *YV* and the *AV* we may read these desires openly or hiddenly declared. It was finally granted that immortality can be achieved through good deeds that will be rewarded in future lives according to the theory of *karma*, the germs of which Dandekar (1979a, p. 341) reads as early as *ṚV*, VII, the Vasiṣṭha hymns. Immortality is likewise achieved through the oral tradition and by the deification of excellent personalities like Indra.

It is interesting to note that though the *ṛṣi* prayed for material benefits and gifts, such as victory over the enemy and rich spoils in war, cattle and other riches in general, they did not pray for miracles. In other terms, the reward should not come as a free-gifted miracle; the reward should be a well deserved recognition of bravery in battle and should proceed from true understanding and knowledge imparted by the *ācārya* and based on the *ācārya*'s own knowledge. This is a totally different attitude from that of the Sumerian-Babylonian myth of the 2/3

God and 1/3 man *Gilgamesh*, king of *Uruk* who was defeated in his quest because he wanted immortality of the body, not only of the soul, of his name, his fame and his deeds.

The desire to acquire the power of divination is present in people of all cultures is present in latent form in all invocation to Agni who, as messenger of man to the Gods, is also requested to bring the Gods and their spouses to man to fulfil man's prayers and thereby tell him what the future keeps in store for him (R̥V, VIII; 38, 39): 'Lord Agni (*l.c.*, 5) knows all that comes from Gods, he knows the mystery of men', while also the Viśvedevas become omniscient and seers of past, present and future. The desire of immortality is alive and 'He (Agni) gives us kinship with the gods' (R̥V, IV; 10, 8 *et al.*). Immortality can be reached by acquiring fame and is later rationalized as the fruits to which man legitimally aspires: *dharma, artha, kāma* and *mokṣa*. Intimacy with the Gods whose life ends at the end of each *kalpa*, also enables man, who equally has a finite life span, to ask for protection and gifts.

Vedic man was technically bound to nature. There is an interesting parallel of the Greek 'Gordian Knot' in R̥V, VIII; 40, 6, where Indra-Agni are invoked: '. . . may you cut the evils . . . like tangles of the creeping plant', the string to be cut is made of natural vines! The Vedic man shows his intimacy with nature as he sees health as the law and disease as the breakdown of order or law, which in this case is the breakdown of the equilibrium among internal factors of the body, of the mind, of their physiology as well as the breakdown of the balance between body and mind on one side and the environment on the other.

Man perceived that life is constant changes at different levels and knew that life is maintained as long as there is movement; everything evolves and develops and stillness spells death. Similarly in human society. '. . . the one to whom you give so that he may give again (to others)' (R̥V, VIII; 52, 6, a *vālakhilya* hymn); to this day the custom is observed of distributing sweets and of feeding guests and visitors at all occasions, a custom that also seals deeds and ensures observance of agreements; it is recognized as valid by law. Movement such as recycling of matter and energy are observed in everyday life; everything is recycled in India, down to the minutest objects, even new materials developed by twentieth century technology are recycled.

A guest or visitor is God himself and is to be honoured and fed, his requests are to be granted and from him blessings are expected in return; a sort of recycling of intellectual and spiritual power.

An incidental remark may be made here: *R̥V*, VIII; 51, 1 is addressed to Indra who drinks *soma* with others, including Nipātithau; the meaning of the name is: one who carries oblations to Gods and protects the *yajamāna* who is named Nipa. A mangrove species of stemless palm-tree bears the scientific name of *Nypa* which was taken from the popular name of the plant given locally in some islands of Indonesia. All parts of the *Nypa* palm are useful and utilized, but most important is the sap tapped from the inflorescence that produces abundant liquid that is fermented into an alcoholic drink and that can be further processed into sugar, alcohol or vinegar. The *Nypa* palm occurs in India and was formerly present along the whole coastline. Could ancient Indian travellers to the Indonesian island have carried the name with them? Personal names in Indonesia are often of Sanskrit or Pali origin.

Participation of Man in Nature

The Veda probably took shape in Balkh (Dandekar, 1981, p. 25) at the time when the Āryans lived there before migrating further towards *Saptasindhu*; the *Saṁhitā* form that we have now took shape at a later stage. The subject-matter of the Veda originated from a continuous process of intellectual creation and revelation that spans a long time, probably many centuries of oral tradition.

Innumerable studies and scholarly texts have been published on this subject, but whatever the historical details or texts may be, the Veda as we have them, specially the *ṚV*, the *SV* and the *AV*, are the expression of very ancient seers who, to my mind, were also good scientists: observers of nature, technicians, engineers and medical doctors. We have the names and know much about many of these seers and the lineage of most of them is traced and known down to the present. The *ṛṣis* of the Veda were historical men and at least one woman, Lopamudrā, even if modern critical historical analysis considers 'proofs' to be insufficient. The seers/poets/scientists who formulated the hymns lived with nature that they studied and used. A strong feeling of man's participation in the universal order pervades the Veda; man is inseparable from his cosmic environment, he is not distinct from it but imbued in it. Man becomes immortal through his descendants and through his spirit that merges with the universal spirit on the death of the body. Fire as energy is present in **movable** and **immovable** natural things; Agni, the original power or God is present everywhere at all times, even in stones (*AV*, III; 21, 1) and Agni expresses and manifests itself in many forms. Energy and matter as well as the essence of God and man are one, the same and interchangeable and when bodily life ends, man like other movable or immovable things, merges with infinity or, in modern ecological terms, matter is recycled and energy is one under many interchangeable forms. In fact, even human mind is part of the cosmic soul, or energy.

At whatever place or time the songs of the *ṛṣis* were formulated, they invariably express a deep sense of communion of man with God. Nature is to be understood as friend, revered as mother, obeyed as father and nurtured as a beloved child. Nature is sacred because man depends entirely on it and because of this everything is sanctified, including man and the terrifying aspects of nature itself, such as glaciers, landslides, earthquakes, storms (*AV*, XVII) that have to be taken as they are, even if difficult to bear. Even bad people such as thieves are part of nature and have to be accepted with tolerance for their bad habits and have to be redressed with wisdom and according to *dharma*. Clearly the ancient saw that there is a relation of cause and effect in everything, even if man and the seers themselves could not always perceive all the hidden meanings, purposes and relations among the multiplicity of natural phenomena that they observed. Natural phenomena are manifestations or expressions of the Gods, not the Gods themselves; they are manifestations of and express the principles that govern the world and cosmic order, **Ṛta**

The Vedic Āryans saw Truth in *ṛta*: 'True to *ṛta*, born in *ṛta*, strengtheners of *ṛta*, terrible, haters of falsehood (Mitra, Varuna, Aryaman)'. 'In their felicity for best defence may we and the seekers dwell' (*ṚV*, VII; 66, 13). To this day to tell a lie is an even greater sin than to commit a theft, but **Vedic Truth** is to be understood also as knowledge, 'which is a gift of God to all men', hence it cannot be betrayed by human lies. **Knowledge** in the Vedic sense has much in common with what we now call **science**, hence **Truth** in the Vedic meaning of the word is science as was practised and expounded at the time when the basic instruments of study were the sense-organs, which are controlled and coordinated by the mind which, in Vedic terms, is the 'seat of reason'. All intellectual thinking was considered to be spiritual.

Fire and Heat

Fire and heat were perceived as the central force of life and of most natural phenomena, while in scholastic philosophy the *primum mobile* is God as Love, expressed by Dante Alighieri in the '*Divina Commedia*' as 'Love that moves the Sun and the other Stars' (*Amor che muove il sole e l'altre stelle*). Fire as light is necessary for the growth of plants and as warmth in birds and mammals, it is linked to life and movement; cold-blooded animals are inert in cold weather and a lizard basks in the sun to warm up and move. At high altitudes, in glaciers, mountain lakes and mountain peaks 'only Gods, spirits or fairies (*parī*) live'. Life, even if warmth is not detectable, implies that energy is moving about, for the process of living, for growth and reproduction.

Other forces also govern the world: the most difficult to perceive was gravity that was guessed, so to speak, indirectly and only from its effects, but could not be understood through the weight and fall of objects; however the effects of the pull of gravity or weight of missiles and weapons in general was considered in practice for marksmanship (Vannucci), for building chariots and habitations and for all matters of daily life. Astronomical phenomena also were observed, measured and predicted through their effects and by markings, rather than explained. Prediction was necessary for seasonal migrations and pastoral activities, such as taking the herds to the mountain high pastures or sowing at the right time of the lunar and solar cycles for best results. The relationship between lunar cycles, day and night (circadian rhythms) and the physiological cycles of women and domestic animals were known and taken into account, even if not explained. Ancient man lived in an Euclidean world as we still do in practice; in our everyday life there is no relativity or fourth dimension. In an Euclidean world, which is the simple geometrical reality readily perceived by man, natural phenomena are cyclic, except perhaps for ageing of biological systems, including ourselves, though at present scientific methods of rejuvenation of tissue cultures break even that aspect of the **arrow of time**. The Veda must be read as a function of an Euclidean system of natural philosophy since all the speculative hymns are within the constraints imposed by the perceptions of the sense-organs.

Fire and heat in nature were and are still used to improve the taste and nutrition qualities of food by boiling and roasting. According to Vesci (1985) the art of cooking the sacrificial offerings endows them with a divine status; Vesci goes as far as stating that cooking is the most important part of the preliminaries of any sacrifice in the Vedic tradition, a statement, however, that could be questioned. To a certain extent cooking is a magical art, therefore an art divinely inspired. In fact, some of the most common foods, like for instance beans (many of which the Vedic man did not have), are mildly poisonous if consumed raw; the heat of fire degrades and therefore destroys the poisonous molecules.

Food and Medicines

About fermentation and the role of fermented food, much could be said. Fermentation is a process that both requires and generates a certain amount of heat. Man has always availed himself of the **purifying** or we could say, **disinfecting** effects of the fermentation processes. Fermentation in essence is the creation of a culture medium specifically 'chosen' by specific micro-organisms, such as only that species will survive and reproduce while competing micro-organisms are eliminated because they cannot live and multiply in the new conditions created in the medium by the dominant species of micro-organism. In preparing fermented foods, including wine, man aids the selected species of micro-organism to eliminate all competitors, by boiling and then adding some substances, in order to have a **pure culture** as desired. Different varieties of curds, yoghurts, cheese, wines, vinegar, broth and other foods owe their different tastes and properties to the original culture medium, milk, broth, casein, fruit juices, and others, and then to the action of the specific micro-organism introduced by man as *inoculum* that induces fermentation and develops a monospecific culture. Fermentation increases the nutritious value of foods by increasing their protein and vitamin content and also increases the lifetime of foods because it avoids 'spoiling'. **Spoiling** is due to contamination by other micro-organisms which was avoided by the fermentation process itself. Contamination gradually changes the properties of the culture; spoiled cultures are correctly called **impure**. People living close to nature are great experts at handling fermentation processes to produce drinks, foods and manure and to loosen vegetal fibers from their matrix to produce textiles. *Soma* is a fine example of an excellent fermented drink.

In addition to working in the field as draft animals, cattle give dung which is used as fertilizer and to make fire and they give food as milk, meat and milk products; ancient Vedic man was not vegetarian. Milk is thickened and sterilized or purified by boiling and is further made into *panīr* and curds by fermentation and butter is clarified as *ghī*. All these items last longer and are concentrated food more easily transported by man as he follows his cattle that moves about from pasture to pasture and during the seasonal migrations uphill and back. The bull is powerful, hence Indra and Agni are often likened to the bull; the cow who is generous is called mother and the giver of the five gifts, pañcagavya, or milk, *ghī*, curds, urine and dung. The high content of ammonia in fermented dung is an efficient disinfectant of the house floor. To this day the life of many Indians is a real symbiosis with their cattle; these practices are ecologically wise in that they provide full recycling of organic matter and avoid waste. Nature must be treated parsimoniously.

Milk and milk products along with barley and wheat were the staple food of ancient Āryans, though a certain percentage of them, like any other group of human beings, does not produce *lactase* in their stomach after ten or fifteen months of age. Lack of *lactase* makes it impossible to digest raw milk. Among Indo-Europeans there may be as many as 15 per cent or up to 20 per cent or more people who do not produce *lactase* in their stomachs; these are the persons who say that they do not like milk or that they cannot digest it, which is true. Fermented milk derivates in their various forms have been pre-digested by the micro-organisms that cause the fermentation, hence humans have no difficulty in digesting the milk-derivates. Shepherds of every culture know this well and feed their cheese or yoghurt, which are pre-digested in the process of making them, to children and elders, ailing persons and puerperal women. 'By kine may we pass over ill conditioned misery; by barley . . . over hunger. . . .' (*AV*, VII; 50 (52), 7).

The use of barley and wheat as staple food is indicative of the geographic origin of the Vedic Āryans who must have been to a certain extent seasonal nomads even before embarking on the long distance displacements which they later undertook. Bread wheat, *Triticum aestivum* (hexaploid wheat) has its origin in the south Caspian Sea area: and may have been introduced in India earlier than 2,000 BC. Barley was cultivated in India already by 6,000 BC. Archaeological remains indicate that *durum* wheat (tetraploid wheat) was cultivated much earlier. Rice was not a staple food and was introduced much later in the diet; it is extolled at many places, specially in *AV*, XI; 2. Rice is even now not the staple food, rather a luxury for mountain people, though dietary habits change with time, as imposed upon people by ecological constraints of new environments.

Agni and the Aśvins are requested to send abundant food **from the east**. This could be interpreted as follows: in their eastern migrations the Āryans entered some or many Hindukush-Karakorum-Himālayan valleys that run roughly N-S or NW-SE where their descendants still live. These beautiful valleys must have been heavily forested; the people that they met must have had a more varied diet than they had. The plains of *Saptasindhu* must have been rich in edible vegetals, hence the request: bring us 'good food', meaning 'varied food', rather than the monotonous diet they must have been used to, and teach us how to plant it, raise it, collect it and hunt it or fish it. The same applies to medicinal plants, hence the invocation to the Aśvins. It was recognized that much could be learned from the local people: 'the little girl of the Kirata, she digs a remedy . . . with golden shovel, upon the ridge of the mountain' is said in a paragraph against snakes and their poison; it illustrates well the process of syncretism of cultures in the making (*AV*, X; 4, 14).

Fuel

In trying to follow the Vedic people in their migrations towards the Indian sub-continent, we do not only perceive changes in attitudes towards a changed environment, but also a change in habits. Different foods would have to be prepared in different manners, then the use of fire would have changed accordingly; mud ovens and *cūlās* of the types still in use, must have been invented early, they are cheap and can easily be abandoned without any loss before the next season or displacement; easily they are made anew and quickly when necessary; they cost next to nothing, though they are not very efficient; but thermodynamics had not yet been invented by man, though of course it existed and deforestation began and grew with growing populations who depended on firewood to cook their food. There would also have been increased use of fuelwood and correspondingly more cattle dung would be used as fertilizer when agricultural practices were intensified and less dung would be used as fuel. The extensive forests provided all the fuel needed but at the same time the newcomers would have learned and accepted from the local people the concept of **sacred forests** (Gadgill, 1992; Ramakrishnan, 1992, Vannucci, 1991) and would have seen the value of good management practices.

The smelting of iron ore and making alloys with other metals required the production of high temperatures and efficient forges had to be invented or copied from pre-existing expertise; the *lohārs* are nomadic to this day; the simple forges that they use at present may have already been in use thousands of years ago. Agni is mentioned in association with iron (*AV*, V; 27-28) since no extraction from the ore and no steel can be made without fire, needed also to fashion tools. Fire was used to reduce rocks to fragments, cold water may or may not have been poured on the heated rock to burst it open (*R̥V*, IV; 3, 11); and the help of fire for this purpose is also mentioned elsewhere (*R̥V*, II; 15); 'may we flaming break the rock that contains the prize of the contest'.

What is meant here probably is the breaking up of copper or iron ore bearing rocks, before smelting: '. . . our ancients . . . clearing the earth they disclosed the red . . .'; copper is red, but copper ore is shining yellow, as chalcopyrite or is dark green as malachite or others; limonite which is a poor grade iron ore is rusty red and good grade iron ore is shining red or dark steel colour as hematite and magnetite or shining yellow as pyrite.

Three main environmental novelties would have faced the migrant Vedic people as they came to *Saptasindhu*. The first would be the encounter with major perennial rivers; the second would be the high-rise dense forests and a much greater variety of plants and animals; the third, seasonality of rains: the monsoon. Adapting to these changes required innovative capacity and the will to settle in the newly found haven as well as the will to learn from the local people.

Rivers

The first major geographic-ecological novelty encountered was the perennial great rivers with abundant supply of running water available for as long as they would settle along the river banks and fields. This would have been a marvellous situation for people coming from dry climates and steppes, no wonder that the rivers are repeatedly eulogized and invoked. Water was hailed as the great cleanser; extensive and intensive agriculture became possible. The dialogue between *ṛṣi* Viśvāmitra and the rivers (*ṚV*, III; 33) now called Beas, formerly Vipāśā, and Sutlej, formerly Śutudrī, does not only illustrate the sentiment of marvel that the Āryans felt in the presence of the great rivers, but it also shows the urge to gain knowledge through understanding of what goes on in nature; in fact the water cycle is accurately described: evaporation, cloud formation, precipitation, percolation, formation of rivulets and rivers, then the ocean and evaporation again. The hymn also describes how a dam caused by a landslide that blocked the river flow was destroyed by Indra's thunderbolt. Again here the life-giving role of water and its importance for agriculture is made visible. Interestingly the names of trees, rivers and places have not changed much since Vedic times and they are mostly readily identified at present. The reason why it may be difficult to know for sure what the *soma* plant was, could be due to the fact that probably many species of plants were clustered under the single name *soma*; in fact at some places of the Veda the word is in the plural form. Some of these plants had a **milky sap**, in other words they were latex producing which indicates that they probably are members of the families Euphorbiaceae or Asclepiadaceae which are native of the sub-continent or the sap of which contains poisonous alkaloids, some of them with curative powers or psychotropic effects. Some commentators interpret this by translating 'milk was added to the juice of the *soma* plant'. Both interpretations are puzzling.

Forest

Changes related to new vegetation cover in the new habitat may already have been partly met by the Vedic man during the migrations southward and eastwards. The major novelty would have been the tall forests and dense vegetation of the pre-Himālayas. Food habits would have been influenced by the changed conditions and the daily menu enriched. The importance of goats and sheep would grow and that of the horse and cattle would acquire a different connotation. To the use of the *soma* plant, whatever it was, was added the use of a great variety of local species. Timber would be available to build larger and stronger chariots and carts; horses and bullocks would have to be bred stronger. Houses could be built with the help of timber and rafters, windows and doors; walls and roofs could be made of stones and slabs of slate. The change from the nomadic to a settled life brought with it changes and enrichments to the material culture that can be clearly read in the Veda, specially the *AV*. Still man had to learn the peculiarities of the new environment and how to use it best.

Thus the Aśvins are more and more often invoked and historical studies show that the pre-Āryan people had to be befriended to learn from them. Additional uses of fire were introduced in the culture of the new-comers, specially important being the use of plants and natural products new to them; hence the ritualistic preparations, including rice, that required special treatment and the help of fire to be processed.

Climate

The seasonality of rains, the regular swelling and rising and even flooding of the rivers, the vigorous monsoon, the alternation of dry and wet seasons required many types of adaptations. These may have implied the adoption of pre-existing techniques of water storage and irrigation and many others, as for instance the adoption of local expertise including for the determination of calendar fixes such as solstices and equinoxes. Appreciation of the culture of local people implied the acceptance and incorporation into the Vedic pantheon of the Gods and relative myths peculiar to the new environment. For instance, the Kailāsa-dwelling Lord Śiva is identified with the Vedic Rudra by a process of assimilation and syncretism caused by and required by an expanded culture. Tolerance of the newly-met culture was an imperative necessity for survival and development. All of the above implies careful observation and study of the new world facing the incoming migrant tribes; it also implies adapting physically and culturally to the new conditions, a process that would have taken many generations of continuous efforts and many wars that are mentioned with pride and that are reflected in the frequent prayers for victory over the Dāsa and others. Lord Agni is throughout the Hotṛ, messenger of the Gods and benevolent leader. Fire as one of the physical manifestations of Lord Agni would also be used in an increasing number of new rites; most important cultural enrichment may have been the improvement of the smelting processes and of the manufacture of iron and steel objects, as well as the improvement of medical practices: fire purifies instruments used by the medical practitioner and purifies decoctions, medicines and food by boiling. Purify here means also 'disinfects'. It could be noted here that food, including meats, was and still are more often cooked and boiled for a long time rather than roasted, in the mountains.

As routines were established and methods perfected, Agni became almost a **matter of fact God**; in rites and rituals and in homes, his place was assured and insured, thus Lord Agni ever-present to this day, always invoked and respected, becomes less and less mentioned directly; physical fire, however, with the development of new techniques and the refinement of old ones, becomes relatively more and more important, more frequently mentioned and used.

Time Measurement

The *śruti* as revelation received by the ancient seers was transmitted orally generation after generation until when they were put into writing by later generations, the major credit for this immense work being given to Veda-Vyāsa. Besides traditional spiritual knowledge, mythology and practical teachings were incorporated, including music. Religious and other ceremonial rituals and rites in general were regulated, but ancient learned men had their own way of expressing themselves before the art of writing was invented. One way of expressing themselves was by building structures with a meaning, besides using a variety of signs and symbols. In Part I, I briefly mentioned a large amount of such structures in Europe that are now considered to have been created and probably used for rituals and astronomical observations. Some of them, where organic remains were found, were dated to be as old as 5,000 BP with confirmed dates of around 2,000 BC for many of them. The megalithic cultures that flourished in India were studied from the point of view of burial rites, hero and ancestor worship and are of much later period. In April 1987, H.S. Bisht and I found in a distant place in the Kumaon, two megaliths with hemispherical cup-like excavations that could be used for grinding seeds or other matter. The megaliths are lying on two hill-tops of the Kumaon. They are aligned and oriented and they could have given astronomical fixes much more accurately than would have been necessary for common agricultural or pastoral practices. I believe that rituals and ceremonies were also performed at the site, since there are numerous indications in the Veda that hill-tops were used for ceremonial and religious purposes even in pre-historic times. In the present context what matters is that such pre-historic structures are evidence of the scientific pursuits of the ancient seers for the unveiling of *ṛta* and thereby understand the non-living and living environment in which we live. We regard these megaliths as instruments in a scientific sense, of which ancient man availed himself; but their use and meaning are lost in time. The present-day myths associated with these megaliths suggest their pre-historic antiquity and are supposedly related to the exploits of Bhīma, the strong one among the Pāṇḍava brothers.

Most authors consider the numerous megalithic structures studied by palaeo-archaeology in Britain and Brittany, France (Ruggles, 1988), including the famous Stonehenge, to have been associated with religious ceremonies. While this is probably true, my question is whether scientific discovery, the study of natural phenomena and the building of instruments to better understand the phenomena is not a ceremony in itself that entails a series of ceremonial methodical acts, related to religion **because** they are a means to acquire knowledge. The pursuits of modern science are a rite that similarly entails a long preparatory phase of study and the ritualistic performance of certain acts in a pre-established sequence regularly planned, as the scientific method requires and as every laboratory or field manual teaches. Many authors go a long way to enquire why pre-historic man would have gone through so much trouble as building the structures. My tentative answer is very simple: pre-historic man shared with modern scientists the inquisitive frame of mind that is typical of man and that has made man, **Man**. Man cannot have changed so much in the relatively small number of generations of the past 10,000 years or less. Having found out something **significant**, man would then succumb to the challenge of knowing more and more, and for the purpose of understanding more, he would accept and face the great task of building impressive structures to enable him to learn more and better from mother nature. The word **Mother** is here extremely significant. Man the scientist and engineer is basically the same all over the world, then and now. The reason why it took so long for man to emerge from the early thinking stages to some 10,000 or 12,000 years ago when he took a big leap forward, may be the small number of human beings on Earth to begin with, hence the rarity of the advent of a genius. Furthermore there was an enormous difficulty in the transfer of knowledge that could be done only practically and through example, being therefore restricted in space and time. Finally language was not yet fully evolved and codified and abstract thoughts and ideas would not have been easily expressed or understood.

In India, the amount of effort and time that would have been necessary to transport uphill stones weighing several tons and the amount of precise knowledge needed to align and orient them accurately would have been matched only by the determination of somebody and the importance given to the study of natural cycles. The knowledge obtained would also have been used for practical purposes, such as the ritual preparation of medicines and the performance of religious practices that are powerful psychological tools that give hope to man and strengthen his will and self-reliance. The areas on levelled hill-tops where the megaliths of Kumaon are placed most probably were sacred areas for the performance of Vedic rituals.

Astronomical observations are important for nomadic people living in open spaces without landmarks, load stone or compass and at times when there were no roads or road signs. Megalithic structures, however, would only be constructed when migrants decided to settle down for good. Hence they were built respectively by Celts or pre-Celtic people and Vedic or pre-Vedic people, though they have come down to us as having no apparent purpose. *AV*, IX and X indicate markings of the year and seasons and the course of the sun is given as 360 days (*R̥V*, I; 155, 6 *et al.*). *R̥V*, I; 136, 137 gives hints of calendar determinations, mainly for fixing solstices and equinoxes. All religious practices are influenced by local environmental factors and in turn they play a role in the ecological perception of the relationship between man and God. Religions that consider that all nature was created for the benefit of man and that man is the master of nature, are permissive of ruthless exploitation of natural resources; on the other hand 'primitive' and nature sensitive cultures always have some tenet in their religion about the sanctity of natural wealth, for instance of water and on the merit of conserving water. All religions mark key festivals and anniversaries to coincide with natural phenomena of the lunar and solar cycles. For the Vedic people the winter solstice or the spring equinox marked the beginning of the year; the Kalash to this day commemorate the winter solstice and the spring equinox with prolonged and meaningful ceremonies related to rebirth, the awakening of nature after the winter depression, with fecundity and purification rites after the old year is disposed of.

Following the observation of sun, moon, cardinal points and their movements, man observed the stars, the eclipses and other astronomical phenomena, all well documented and paraphrased into the myths of the Veda, of the Chinese ancient texts, of the Mediterranean, American and Mesopotamian and other people of the world. There are no humans, however primitive, that have no myths and legends, which is one aspect of Vāk. As a matter of fact, one of the important aspects of Vāk is that one clarifies one's ideas by putting them into words.

In the Veda usually the observations are correct, though the interpretation and explanation given is not always of the type that nowadays we would consider to be scientifically correct and valid. Man resorts to myths as a substitute explanation of the direct cause-effect relationship that he has not yet understood fully. For instance, solar and lunar eclipses were correctly observed to be caused by the shadow of the earth or moon cast on the other celestial body, but the explanation given of the phenomenon, was mythological. Conclusions, however, are usually sufficiently correct to be used for practical purposes.

One of the greatest merits of the Veda is to have put on record in the oral and later in the written tradition, the understanding and knowledge to be transmitted to the next generations for the benefit of all. The *ṛṣis* and the ancestors are duly remembered with infinite gratitude.

Ecology and Biological Cycles

Ecology is the study of each individual's and each species' or association of species' requirements and of their limits of tolerance in relation to environmental factors. Ecology is the study of the exchange of energy and matter between living beings and between living beings and the non-living elements of the environment. Individuals live, grow, multiply and die and the species continues to exist and evolve. The inter-relations among individuals of one and the same species and of different species among themselves and with their environment are the core of ecological studies; hence the best definition of ecology is 'the study of the distribution and abundance of species and individuals'. The environment, including other species present, is evidently a decisive factor in determining the presence or absence and abundance of individuals and species.

The distribution of individuals of one species in space and time indicates the maximum limits of tolerance for individuals of that species in relation to environmental factors such as temperature, humidity, salinity, other species present and so on. The abundance of individuals of one species indicates where, everything considered, the optimum environmental conditions for that particular species are to be found. This includes both active and reproductive living stages of plants and animals, as well as dormant stages like seeds, propagules, embryos in the womb of hibernating mothers, resistance to diseases and so on.

In conclusion, the study of natural cycles of living and non-living things, the analysis and measurements of the multiple aspects of *ṛta* in space and time, is the true meaning of the word Ecology: the 'science of the house'. House here means the living and non-living environment of which man is a part, whether he wants it or not.

Of all natural cycles the diurnal or circadian rhythm is the most readily perceived. It is the first one to which new-born babies coming from the uniformly dark and warm environment of the mother's womb must adapt. The baby's chemical circadian rhythms are primarily regulated before birth by the chemical rhythms of the mother's organism, but the final adaptation to the alternation of day and night of new-borns may take days or even months to be completed. Children learn quickly that nights are not all alike, some are shorter and some longer, but they also learn that the second most spectacular heavenly body, the moon, waxes and wanes according to its own laws. The day-night cycle brought about by the most important heavenly body, the sun, is something which children get attuned to automatically, they learn to welcome the short nights of summer and dread the long cold winter nights. Cycles of summer and winter, rain and drought, cycles of the flowering and fruiting of plants, of shedding of leaves, and of animal reproduction, nesting of birds and emergence of butterflies, migration and hibernation and aestivation of all kinds of animals from insects to mammals, are concrete manifestation of *ṛta* into which children grow often without a **conscious** perception of their knowledge. If we look back at our own past or observe the development of infants and children, it becomes obvious that after birth we are at first assimilated into a world, or I would call it a mathematical hypervolume of knowledge and only gradually, and almost painfully, we begin to acquire personal, internal, **conscious knowledge**. While understanding is a marvellous experience, the conscious acquisition and storage of knowledge is a heavy burden. It is a burden because it increases the personal responsibility towards oneself and others.

Children who live in rural areas or away from big cities learn the events of nature without being taught, except by example, so did early man; some of them, gifted with specially inquisitive minds must have started to observe closely, to make correlations among natural phenomena by taking measures in time and space, seeking precision and accuracy.

Most studies of the ecological aspects of nature did not leave a record in stone but rather in the language of the Veda and most of all in the oral tradition. They refer to the five traditional elements of eastern and western Indo-European cultures, earth, water, air, fire and void or *ākāśa*. These are represented by the five-headed *nāga*, common in Hindu and Buddhist arts. It is significant, for instance, that the bronze image believed to be a replica of a very ancient and very large, estimated to be 3 m tall, stone image of Aghoreśvara in the temple dedicated to this deity at Ikkeri in Shimoga district of Kerala and built about AD 1566-70, stands with the right hand in *abhaya-mudrā* and the left in the *varada-mudrā*, under the protective canopy of the five-headed *nāga*. Innumerable five-headed *nāga* are represented, but with time, more heads were added, as sculpture, painting and carving became more elaborate as art forms.

Mother Earth, Pr̥thvī often identified with Aditi, the infinite, the 'free from bonds', as well as with water, air, fire and *ākāśa* proceeds from the down-to-earth beginning of everyday reality, to the imponderable, present but intangible concept of space or void, the existence of which is inferred by reason rather than observation.

Most of the ecological traits of the *Ṛ̥V* and the *AV*, as would be expected, refer to the wide Earth, its features and produce, while the central figure is, of course, man. For man's survival there is a constant preoccupation with food and medicinal plants. Vegetarian habits came late and only in the wake of Buddhism. Hunting must have been a common practice in ancient times, yet there is little mention to this type of activity in the *Ṛ̥V* though cooking of meat and other parts specially of the body of goats, is referred to. The main source of meat must have come from domesticated animals, probably mainly goats and sheep. People must have relied heavily on the winter crops of barley and later of wheat for their staple food. Winter wheat or *durum* tetraploid wheat is still the most commonly cultivated in the mountains.

Rice came into cultivation, first in Asia, about 2,500 years BC, much later than wheat or barley that was cultivated even before wheat. There is still much daily ado among the people of the Hindukush, Karakorum and Himālaya ranges with plants, specially grasses, trees, medicinal plants and grapes. Where the word *soma* is in the plural, SS and SV have translated the word as '**medicinal plants**' or '**medicinal herbs**', which gives a better interpretation of the hidden meaning. The *Soma-yājña* was one of the most important rituals preferably conducted on hill-tops, about which there are frequent references in the Vedas. Detailed instructions for the performance of the Soma sacrifice are mainly to be found in the Ṛ̥gvedic *Brāhmaṇas*. There are remains of stone alignments or slabs on many hill-tops in the Kumaon, on which I have climbed; they are markings of some sort. Sacredness of mountains and hill-tops is frequently mentioned (ex: *Ṛ̥V*, V; 41, 42) and still observed at present. The rites probably evolved into the preparation of several different plant decoctions with different effects on the human body, inclusive curative of human diseases and those of his animals. Preparations were always made with the help of fire and invocations to Agni, the Aśvins, Agni-Aśvins and other Gods.

The migrant tribes did not only find an abundance of animals to be hunted and plants to be used for different purposes, but they would also have a different type of soil under their feet and on which to build their habitations; the air and water, the whole climate would be different and have different forces. Powerful natural forces would have to be appeased (*R̥V*, I; 151 — IV; 20) hence the supplication to understand what is going on: 'give mental power to him who sings the sacred song' (*R̥V*, I; 151, 2) while the same hymn can also be read as a good description of an earthquake. Trees forests, rivers, winds would be the good providers but also a constant menace when unleashed in their fury. A whole hymn is dedicated to the lady or Goddess of the forest: Araṇyānī (*R̥V*, X; 146), 'the mother of all forest beings who tills not but has stores of food'. The hymn also shows that flora and fauna were studied carefully. To this day the deity of sacred groves are Goddesses; I know of only few exceptions, one is the very ancient masculine *Puttu* in Tamil Nadu, who is the presiding deity of a mangrove sacred forest. The Goddess of the Sunderbans in Bengal is called *Banodebi* or *Banobibi* and is prayed to equally by Hindus and Muslims who would never venture into the forest without invoking her protection against encounters with tigers and other mishaps; they also need her permission for hunting, fishing and collecting other bounties as honey, wax, fuel-wood, timber, medicinal herbs, tan-bark from her domain, the mangrove swamp.

The association of man with forests was an expansion of the field of studies of the immigrant Vedic people. As pastoral migrants and nomads, the Vedic people were exposed, until when they reached the Balkh area, to a restricted environmental variety, physical and biological; steppes and savannahs are monotonous and extensive and people's best friends were their domesticated animals, intimate partners in good and bad times, companions in joy and adversity. Domesticated animals participate in family affairs and in the festivals of the community during which they are decorated with genuine pleasure equally for the decorator as the decorated: they are the pride of all. The sacredness of the cow was an ecological imposition since in good times the cow was the giver of all, the female of the bull, mother of the bullock and she was the symbol of femininity and the generator of new lives. The cow was the symbol of the mother Goddess, almost as much mother as Earth, Pṛthvī herself; the cow naturally became the embodiment of all that is good in the female world and the giver of the basic needs for the life of the body, including warmth; indeed mother cow is generous in life and after life. Even in times of adversity the cow would not be sacrificed since she was the only hope for the future and the production of new bounties. The greatest praise to Aditi, the universal mother of deities, unbounded, unfettered mother of infinity, is: 'Aditi, the cow, the sinless, injure it not' (*ṚV*, VIII; 101, 15). The bull on the other hand was respected as the embodiment of strength and power.

The wonders of the new environment are frequently referred to: 'the big rivers of Saptasindhu can be forded' (*ṚV*, X; 113, 10) but it is important to know the right time and places where and when they can be managed. Indra, the deified leader of the Āryan people, king of Gods, is extolled in ecological terms, among others in *ṚV*, X; 134. The gentle gesture common to all shepherds whose wards depend more on trees than grass for fodder is described: 'as for a goat... O Maghavan, draw down the branch' thus allowing the animal to browse on the lowered branches of *Prosopis, Mimosa, Acacia* that grow in semi-arid regions where pastures are scarce and most of the food comes from trees. 'Head of the world is Agni at night' was interpreted by scholars as Agni being the moon though what is meant here obviously are the home fire and the camp fire that are kept burning all night. New environments, specially in the mountains, are inhabited by ghosts, demons, fairies and wild animals that must be kept away by fire and light, while man and his domesticated animals sleep. As centuries roll by, carnivorous animals once very abundant, become rare, but ghosts, demons and fairies become more pressing as the human population density grows and more people invade their dominions. Man continues to apply more and more pressure on the environment at higher and higher altitudes, provided as he is with the powerful means of modern technologies. Mountain slopes are deforested, fairies and *yakṣa*s lose their abodes and cry loudly in the unchecked winds, demons let loose avalanches and landslides come down on their own, with no vegetation cover to keep loose boulders and soil in place. Downhill floods become more frequent, widespread and devastating . . . but that is a sad story of the present, when the conservation practices expressed in poetic injunctions by the *r̥ṣi*s are no longer heeded.

For the Vedic man the mountain valleys are perennially great: 'untouched by time, never lacking green trees and vegetation, with their voices they have caused heaven and earth to hear' (*R̥V*, X; 94, 123); 'from the mountain came the pressing stones' and probably other tools as well. Stones are respected as an important and useful element of earth and mountains are the maximum expression of immortality: the hardness and permanence of rocks. The high peaks looming in the distance inspire elevation towards God. Stones are spared even by Agni who 'eats **everything** else' and 'who in his wrath shaves a hill as a barber shaves a head' (*R̥V*, X; 142, 4). Agni's fury can be terrible (*AV*, VII; 70 (73), 4,5), the 'Rudra that is in fire' . . . 'to that Rudra, to Agni, be homage' (*AV*, VII; 87 (92), 1). Fire and smoke are also used to frighten away enemies (*AV*, VIII; 8, 2). Agni is present even in water as dynamic energy in waterflow, rivers, mountain streams, ice and snow, avalanches, torrential rains that could be harnessed for different purposes; Agni becomes the associate of water to create plant and animal life (*R̥V*, X; 142, 3, 4); 'Agni descending with water impregnates in the plants' (*RV*. X; 21, 8).

And the Vedic people decided to settle in the wonderfully promising land. They came in more than one wave and knowledge had to be sought and was obtained from the earlier inhabitants, the local people collectively called Anārya and the resources of their territories are designated as the 'treasure of the Panis' (*Ṛ̥V*, IX; 111, 2). Their knowledge is represented figuratively by the myth of the stolen cows hidden in the cave, kept in the darkness of ignorance and liberated by the light of knowledge who is Agni as Soma Pavamāna or alternatively liberated by the war power of Indra, the great chief. Significantly all of *Maṇḍala* IX is dedicated to Soma Pavamāna though the hymns come from different *ṛ̥ṣis*. The name Soma Pavamāna can be understood in many ways, Agni-Soma, spirit and body, theoretical and practical knowledge. Pavamāna means 'self-purifying', since knowledge is always correcting itself and only Agni is repeatedly called 'self-purifying'. Soma-Pavamāna is therefore the self-purifying Agni: the fire and source of knowledge.

Plants

Plants of the new environment gradually acquired meaning and value as knowledge of their use was worked out or otherwise received from the local people; thus began the fusion of cultures. A corpus of knowledge was formed on the use of natural resources for building, for making roofs and containers for grapes juice to make wine, for water, milk and grains; irrigation ditches and tanks hewed out of the rock and soil, appropriate agricultural processes and the use of harder woods for the plough and the hoe, for rafters, windows, doors and chariots were developed or improved. Instructions are given on all these matters and more; specially interesting here are the instructions given for making the *araṇis*, with the softer wood of the *aśvattha* tree or *pīpal* (*Ficus religiosa*) that is energetically rotated to create heat by friction and sparks on the lower, harder wood of the *śami* (*Acacia suma*). The appropriate type of grass to collect the sparks is also mentioned. Plants are 'those that grew in old times' . . . 'much earlier even than the Gods' (*Ṛ̥V*, X; 97, 1) and are 'different from many different places'. Incidentally, this expression 'earlier than the Gods' fully recognizes and admits the fact that the idea or concept of God was born in man's mind at some stage **after** man had gained the power of discrimination that made him man and enabled him to study nature.

There are also plants that have 'departed far away'. This probably refers to those that were typical of the places where man dwelt earlier and from where he had migrated to new places having a different flora. There are also 'plants with flowers and without, with fruits and without', 'plants that (*soma* is here in the plural form) give us different things' which, in this context, means different natural products, including what probably are intoxicating or psychedelic drugs; 'be glad and joyful in the plants' (*ṚV*, X; 97, 3) and 'bring back the very self, O man,' (*l.c.*, 4). It also indicates that mixtures of medicinal plants extracts were prepared (*l.c.*, 14) because they 'help and lend assistance to each other'. In Āyurvedic medicine, mixtures are used rather than purified extracts of single plants. The *ṚV* and the *AV* on the whole contain a good summary of scientific knowledge of plants and animals, the latter being divided in biped and quadruped.

Finally it is Agni who says 'in plants and herbs, in all existing beings I have deposited the germ of increase. All progeny on earth have I engendered and sons in women who will be hereafter' (*ṚV*, X; 183, 3). Agni is the energy materialized at the inception of a new life when the fecundation of the plant or animal ovule by the sperm cell takes place; it is at that time that energy becomes operative in the embryo of every existence (*AV*, V; 25, 7), plant or animal.

Indra, the powerful is addressed as *sahasramuṣka*, the one having one thousand testicles, to express his valour and strength (*ṚV*, VI; 46, 3); the reading of the corresponding verse in the *Sāmaveda* is biologically a watered down expression: Indra is said to be Sahasramanyo, or having a thousand powers; this expression, according to Ludwig, is more aesthetic, but biologically speaking it is evidently and undoubtedly less powerful and less meaningful, even less correct. Sahasracakṣu is an expression that would come naturally to the mind of pastoral people given to animal husbandry and living in daily contact with their animals. It is sad to note that the Western translators failed to see the powerful vitality of the expression and shyed away from the naturalistically beautiful and scientifically correct expression to adopt a less faithful but more prudish word as 'power' or 'ardour' that only poorly corresponds to the joyful, healthy and full of vitality expression used in the *R̥V*. Incidentally, ardour comes from the Latin verb *ardĕre*, which means to burn. *R̥V*, X; 85, 37) provides another example of a prudish translation that is in reality an impoverishment from the healthy vigour of the original text. Where Griffith sees 'pleasure' the Vedic poet sees a normal biological function charged with biological, psychological and ecological importance. Two renderings of the line:

> 'loving whom we embrace' or 'in whom originated by desire we may beget progeny' or: 'men sow seed' (where *sepah* is a synonym of penis, acc. SS and SV).
>
> or: 'and welcome all my love and mine embrace...' (acc. to Griffith).

The Indra-Agni dual is interesting in that wherever the dual divinity is invoked, Agni is addressed with intellectual and spiritual epithets while Indra is eulogized in concrete biological and human terms. It is logical to eulogize the great chief and leader, fearful in battle, winner of wars, the king of the Gods, himself deified because of his greatness as a conqueror with the epithet *sahasramuṣka*, or more often, the bull. If Max Müller and H. Oldenberg (repr. 1990, p. 305) are correct in their reading, there are other biologically interesting examples. Fire is compared to the erect male genital organ or *prajānana* (*R̥V*, III; 29) and the *pramantha* used in the generation of fire has the shape of the male organ. The *pramantha* is the upper fire stick and the two *araṇis* are addressed as *mahī viśpatnī*. Agni as energy that drives life is said to 'stir the wearied man to pleasure and great joy what time the longing gifts approach him as he comes'.... In other words Agni is also physiological potence and his power can revive old age and impotency.

Maṇḍala IX is entirely composed of hymns addressed to Pavamāna Soma, or self-purifying *soma*. It is not clear how and why plant juices could be self-purifying. However, on the basis of several references in these hymns and because Agni is self-purifying, self-generating and is the life-energy in all living beings, the hymns make good sense if they are read as the close association of *soma* with Lord Agni. Soma, extracted with the help of 'mountain given pressing stones' becomes divine though not a God after being purified by fire. Soma is made pure by Agni (*ṚV*, VI; 8, 1), most probably by boiling, and perhaps boiling and distillation. Nature reveals its secrets to the seeker of knowledge (*ṚV*, VII; 5) and Lord Agni is the formless deification of the concept of understanding. But a form must be given to the concept and Soma often appears to be the mediator or the one who facilitates* the acquisition of the process of understanding and the acquisition of knowledge. 'Soma Pavamāna teaches the secret name of the Lord' (*ṚV*, IX; 95, 2). Soma appears to function almost as a wise elder: 'preeminent for wisdom, leader along the straight path... by thy guidance our forefathers dealt out among the Gods their share of treasure'... 'praise loving lord of plants' (*ṚV*, IX) and ... 'the mortal man in thy friendship has delight... the mighty sage befriends' (*ṚV*, IX). Agnisoma 'in cooperation have revealed the light of heaven' (*ṚV*, I; 93, 5), and are 'makers of the path' (*AV*, XVIII; 2, 53).

---

* Facilitation is a physiological process by which the transmission of the nerve impulse from nerve ending to the effectors, for instance a muscle fiber, is facilitated or quickened and made possible by pre-conditioning the receptor to accept the stimulus and to react to it.

Whatever substance or plant *soma* would have been originally, it was obviously a substance that exhilarated, inebriated, intoxicated and gave **enhanced powers** mentally, physically and perceptively, perhaps by extrasensory perception. Maybe the *soma* plant was just grapes out of which fermented wine was and still is ritually made and consumed during the winter solstice celebrations of the New Year of the Kalash and Kafirs to this day. One is reminded of the few-days-old wine made by Ulysses to inebriate Polyphemus and thus make possible his escape and that of his companions from the cave where they were held.

There is an unending literature on *soma* that is not to be discussed here; it appears certain, however, that with time other plants were added to the original one, some of which could have been producers of psychotropic drugs that give altered or enhanced sense perception. The word *soma* appears to have become almost a synonym of medicinal plants in general, and thus the original bio-socio-ecological meaning of the word **soma** would have been greatly amplified. Maybe the revelation that is the object and subject of the *śruti* was in part obtained during periods of exalted awareness. Hence the **visions** of the seers, often mentioned. There are hints that states of supersensory perception were induced by 'herbs' (*R̥V*, IX; 25). The human brain also normally produces opiates and other psychotropic drugs like endorphins, the production of which may increase during periods of deep meditation, thus increasing perception.

Medicinal plants extracts would be included in the collective term *soma* since they are something that interferes with the normal functioning of the body and mind: 'flow on to Indra, Soma Pavamāna carefully effused, let sickness stay afar together with her friends' (*R̥V*, IX; 85). However, already in the first *Maṇḍala* the realm of *soma* appears to be made of many elements and the word *soma* appears to be a collective term not restricted to a single species of plant. 'The herbs that thou has generated' (*R̥V*,

I; 91) and **Agnisoma** 'have freed man from the fetters' (*R̥V*, I; 93, 5). Fetters of fear, in other words, the knowledge acquired through **revelation** disperses fear, as much as faith also liberates man from fear of death and worldly evils. Fear is the most powerful agent of destruction of mental balance, fortunately Agnisoma 'found the single light for many' (*R̥V*, I; 93, 4).

Soma 'bestows heroic powers' (*R̥V*, IX; 43, 6-*RV*. IX; 53, 3) and also has healing power (*R̥V*, IX; 79, 2—*R̥V*, IX; 91) but many other plants are also recognized as having medicinal or intoxicating properties: 'the juices (plural) with a thousand powers' (*R̥V*, IX; 42). The Vasiṣṭha hymns of the seventh *Maṇḍala* make frequent reference to medicinal plants and to their preparation, important elements being the pressing stones, water, the woollen filter, fire as fire and fire as Lord Agni who is joy of living and is knower of the correct rites and technicalities needed for the preparation of medicines. 'Aid the pious through heat to life with your (Aśvins) assistance' (*R̥V*, VII; 69, 4); 'delight yourself . . . in plants and waters when the *r̥ṣi* give them and ye find they suit you' (*R̥V*, XVII; 70, 4) which is a hymn to the Aśvins, the medical experts with whom Agni collaborates. 'The juices (*soma* is not mentioned, but liquids or water) that exhilarate are mingled, injure us not, but come with happy fortune' (*R̥V*, VII; 73, 4). And to the Aśvins . . . 'man's dear priest (Agni) is seated who brings sacrifice and offers worship' (*R̥V*, VII; 73, 2) and in another hymn also to the Aśvins (*R̥V*, VII; 71) Vasiṣṭha alludes to the preparation of medicines through fire, where Agni is present as fire technically and as God for the invocations; as God he performs the rituals of the sacrifice. **Sacrifice** retains in all the translations of the Veda into Indo-European languages the original meaning of 'making sacred' or 'sanctify', or 'sanctifying' or 'sanctified'. **Sacrifice** literally means 'to render' or 'to make sacred'. In the Roman Catholic liturgy, the Holy Mass is called the 'sacrifice of the mass' and the Christian act of the Eucharisty is partaking of the sacredness of nature through the oblations made to God of wheat and wine, which are vegetal food made sacred. Thus the scholastic theory of the transubstantiation of bread and wine into flesh and blood or of flesh and blood into bread and wine, is biologically and ecologically correct.

Agni is intimately related to all other elements that he sanctifies by his own sacrality. Drinking of *soma* excites and 'gives direct access to the Gods' (*R̥V*, IX; 44) and Soma as the moon, Indu, has something to do also with mental disturbances, as is also expressed by the word 'lunatics'.

Āyurvedic medicines are often mixed with food, milk or honey to make them palatable or more efficient or both. Soma Pavamānaḥ is described as of 'many colours' and as coming from different places, including mountains. In fact, also different parts of a plant have different colours and produce or store in their cells different chemical compounds that have different pharmacological properties and medicinal uses. 'Coming from different places' could also mean different species of plants; 'Soma Pavamāna, a doer of many acts, is dwelling in wood as Varuṇa in rivers' (*R̥V*, IX; 90, 2) and is also giver of enlightenment (*R̥V*, IX; 61, 16). Soma Pavamāna is gifted with a very important attribute: he 'stirs the waves of sound, is by song a poet and a sage by wisdom' and 'teaches the secret name' (*R̥V*, IX; 96, 17; 18). It is proper to ask here: what is in a name? In Vedic terms, a name is not only a word, it is also the essence, the meaning, the intention. He gives the best gift, intelligence and wisdom. 'Let Indra . . . drink of the juice of wisdom' (*R̥V*, IX; 109, 2). An ancient Latin proverb brings to us a similar notion from the Romans: '*In vino veritas*' (truth in wine); it is recalled to this day at the holy communion of the Christian rites as it was at the last supper of Jesus Christ.

Great importance is given to the tree, the 'Lord of the forest' . . . 'whose praises never fail' (*R̥V*, IX; 12, 7); the tree is a symbol of life that always regenerates itself and is immortal, like the *aśvattha* on whom the Maruts rested, that germinates and grows in the air (above ground, on other trees or structures), which regenerates itself and from which the upper *araṇi* is made. The concept of sacred forest is very ancient and sacred trees or sacred forests are specially significant in the Hindu and Buddhist cultures. 'Sacred forest' is undoubtedly a pre-Āryan concept and it was probably adopted by the immigrants because of its far-reaching significance and importance. Forest use and management would have been learned by the new-comers from the local inhabitants.

The perception of nature's cycles includes not only astronomical bodies, but plants and animals as well; 'the soul of the plants, the fatness of the waters and let there be long life — ye Gods — to Agni' (*R̥V*, X; 51, 8) who is the energy that recycles everything; ecologically speaking it is the creation of life, its death and decomposition and re-creation of living matter through the all-pervading energy of Lord Agni. Clouds are thus called the 'son of fire' (*R̥V*, X; 31, 10-11) because of the heat that causes the evaporation of water, that after condensation into clouds pours down as rain.

Water, Fire and Life

Water is the great cleanser, second only to Agni, the Great Purifier; in contemporary terminology we would say that water cleanses and fire disinfects or sterilizes. 'Waters have healing powers, they drive disease away; they have a balm for all, let them make medicines' (*R̥V*, X; 137; 6, 7); this reminds us of the fact that water is the substance that has the greatest dissolving power. A very large amount of substances are water soluble.

An important role of all religions is their action on man's psyche; 'the tongue that leads the voice precedes — then with our tenfold branching hands — with these two chasers of disease — we stroke thee with gentle touch' (*R̥V*, X; 137, 7). Invocations, rituals, exhortations and magic power of chanted *mantra*s sooth and strengthen a vacillating mind, spirit and heart, before or during the process of treatment of the body. They strengthen the will to endure painful interventions to dress wounds or set broken bones or other affected parts of the body. This verse may also indicate the use of massage, as is common for many ailments, and bone or muscular strain; massage is a common practice and a real science in *Āyurveda*.

Fire as life energy (*R̥V*, III; 22), as the energy responsible for the dynamics of nature or, in ecological terms, the agent of the continuous exchange of energy and matter and constant evolution and development of everything uninterruptedly, fire as Agni is the ecological factor causative of movement at all levels from the atomic to the universal or cosmic. Without movement there is no life. Scientifically we measure heat in terms of temperature and we admit total absence of movement only at Absolute Zero temperature or minus 273°C. The energy implied in the notion of movement is called in the Veda: Fire and heat or warmth, that 'pervades the whole universe and being manifested as lofty Viṣṇu preserves life' (*R̥V*, X; 1, 3) while Agni is the 'augmenter of food' (*l.c.*, 4); in other words, Agni as energy or heat is the cause of growth of living beings even those that are apparently cold, or that have the same temperature of the environment, which are all living beings except birds, mammals and some chemiosynthesizer bacteria and blue-green algae, the Cyanobacteria.

Within the laws of *r̥ta* it is 'Agni who knows, who fixes rites and seasons' (*R̥V*, X; 2, 3). And again it is 'Agni who corrects our faults and failings' (*R̥V*, X; 2, 4) and reminds 'man weak of mind' to perform the sacred acts at the right season invoking each God at the proper time and in the proper manner (*R̥V*, X; 2, 4-5). In other words, it is the knowledge and wisdom of Agni which guide agricultural practices, including irrigation, ploughing, sowing, harvesting and post-harvest treatment of the earth's produce; he guides hunting and harvesting of wood, herbs and timber; he guides the mind and every act of everday life. As the one who sets the seasons, the calendar on earth, he is the one who knows when the herds should be taken to the high pastures and when they should return to the village. All acts have to be undertaken after appropriate propitiatory rites are performed to attune man with *ṛta*, according to Lord Agni's instructions, since 'he knows, he dwells in *ṛta*'. Cooperation of the Gods has to be secured and man's confidence in himself has to be strengthened to generate determination, discrimination and steadfast appropriate action throughout his lifetime. Man's actions are regulated by the law, the ecological principles applied 'with wisdom' to the various environments in which he lives.

Agricultural, pastoral and general living practices would have been different in the various places occupied by the migrant Indo-European tribes, but social and family rules and habits tend to be conservative. In fact, most ancient habits concerning intimate family life have remained unchanged to this day in orthodox families, specially the habits relating to the impurity of women at certain days of the menstrual cycle and after delivery when she is specially vulnerable to infectious diseases and other ailments; the traditional care of pregnant women and newly born babies is biologically wholesome; mother and child are specially treated with appropriate massage, food, anointing, fumigation specially during the peri-natal period. For instance a decoction made from *nīm* leaves (*Azadirachta indica* or *Melia indica*) is used for vaginal ablutions as disinfectant after delivery and in the cure of minor venereal diseases; where the *nīm* is not available, decoctions of *Salix* (willow) bark and leaves are used in the same manner. Fumigation of women after delivery and making the puerperal woman squat over fume-generating burning plants 'purifies' practically by disinfection of parts of the body at a time when those organs are in need of special attention and they also create peace of mind and a feeling of well-being also through its symbolic power.

Ancient man learned the laws of nature empirically, from experience and practice which, allied to his power of discrimination, enabled him to improve steadily on his interaction with nature without transgression but according to ecological principles. Sacrifices and rites attuned to *ṛta* acquire ecological validity.

Much of the *AV* is directly related to the use of many different plants, some of which still bear nowadays the same name and use. Important among the plants was the *kawa*, the 'all-curing plant' that continues to be used in *Āyurveda*, together with other closely related species as ingredients of a large number of different preparations. But one is repeatedly reminded that all acts of preparation are necessarily ritualistic and that Agni, giver of force, power and strength, is present at all Vedic rites (*AV*, II; 17 1-3) because Agni 'understands immortality' (*AV*, V; 30, 14); many rites are performed for practical purposes only, but all entail elaborate rituals and require the participation of Gods. Agni's blessings are invoked for success, for wealth and prosperity, for progeny, to conjure diseases, against sorcerers, demons, enemies, *bhūtas*. *Bhūta* is a word usually translated as ghosts and goblings though it is used in the *ṚV* and the *AV* for all 'beings' and *bhūta* is the spirit of each being (*AV*, I; 32, 1, 2). In *AV*, V; 24, 2 Agni animates even *bhūta*, he is invoked against witchcraft, savages, thieves and niggards, against snake poison (*AV*, X; 4), and he is also invoked to burn down the enemy and consign falsehood to the flames, he is even invoked against bad dreams (*AV*, XVI; 6, 9); he is finally called upon to make imprecations of all sorts (*AV*, X; 5). Agni puts everything right with energy as the great purifier he is. The third of the five ecological elements, the *mahābhūta*, is fire which is the link between the material and the immaterial, between earth and water on one side and air and void on the other.

The Vedic culture was pragmatic and could not have been otherwise, the philosophical speculations of the sages pursued at the same time two main streams, the abstract or speculative, and the pragmatic or the applications of knowledge and understanding to everyday life. 'The purifying one (Agni as energy) entered into the green ones (plants)' (*AV*, X; 8, 40); the

AV discriminates and shows the use of many more plants and animals than the earlier *R̥V* does, and it also describes some technicalities.

The importance of the *pīpal* was mentioned above. It symbolizes life and recycling of life and immortality through its ever expanding capacity of putting forth new roots that eventually coalesce into a trunk. The ever fluttering leaves of the *pīpal* is evidence that the Maruts play with them and among them, at times they rest there; the *pīpal* is usually evergreen and lives for centuries, almost indefinitely and is considered to be masculine because is grows as an epiphyte on other trees, preferably the *śami*, considered to be feminine. The name of specific medicinal plants is sometimes kept secret, but several diseases and their remedies are described in detail and unmistakable terms, for instance malaria (*AV*, I; 25, 4 — *AV*, 22, 10); spotted fevers, hepatitis or jaundice, leprosy, epilepsy, parasitic animals, specially worms (*AV*, II; 32, 3) and all minor common diseases. Even plants to promote hair-growth and virility are mentioned in *AV*, IV; 4. The plant against fever is said to be born on mountains and to be a companion of *soma* (*AV*, V; 4); it probably is the willow from which salicilic acid, the basic component of aspirin, is extracted. Later health and medical knowledge were codified in a comprehensive body of knowledge pertaining to health, the *Āyurveda* and the *Yogasūtra*.

Plants are also used in practices of sympathetic magic, against witchcraft, against evil spirits and super-human foes and exorcisms were often performed by fumigation. Disease causing bacteria and organic particles bearing viruses are invisible to the naked eye; in this sense they are harmful spirits that could not be seen but undoubtedly exist and can be destroyed by fumigation. Many useful plants are specifically mentioned, like sugar cane (*AV*, I; 34, 5), grapes, the hemp and many others, some as yet scientifically undetermined. The forest tree is repeatedly eulogized for his heroic power or as the one who relieves from the demon.

Fire, the third of the five basic elements, is associated to earth where plants grow, to water and air that are needed for the preparation of extracts by boiling and distillation, by fumigation and by mixing with cooked food. Agni is described at times as 'flesh eating' (*AV*, XII; 2, 42) of which two readings can be made: fire destroys fever by preparing medicines and second, the dead body is cremated by fire and sublimated into nothingness. The second reading is obvious in those hymns where fire is mentioned in the context of the performance of funeral rites, while the first reading seems to be intended when dealing with aspects of cures of fevers in general; Agni destroys fever, but as fever (heat) it also can destroy the flesh. Lord Agni indeed walks in all directions.

Besides the invigorating effect of fire, water is indispensable in the preparation of medicines, none however would be effective without the power of *mantras* recited or chanted by the sage and his disciples during the preparation process. Finally, since spiritually and ecologically everything is related to everything else, several other Gods are also invoked, most important, besides Agni, being Savitṛ that in my opinion is the personification of the abstract idea-concept of Life. Sarasvatī or knowledge and Brahmaṇaspati (*AV*, IV; 6), the Lord of Prayers, are also present in the preparation of remedies and medicines as well as the Aśvins.

Agni and water are essentials of life: 'waters are possessed of glory in the plants'. Agni is the divine perceived but not fully understood life-process that cannot take place in the absence of water. Life or the essence of life was and continues to be mysterious and unlike the global water cycle that is factually, figuratively, symbolically and practically described in the *Ṛ̊V*, the *SV* and the *AV*, life and the absence of life, as we know it, are not often spoken of openly. The termination of life of the body or death on the contrary is often spoken of and discussed in its many aspects, as well as the opposite of death, which is birth

(Filippi, 1997). Death is recalled with respect and in a manner comparable to the manner in which all manifestations of life are discussed, because death is the beginning of a new life. When does a circle start or finish? All the points that make a circle are sacred, so even are the different stages of the cycle of birth, life and death, not only because they are expressions and manifestations of Lord Agni, but perhaps as much because they are mysterious and remain essentially unexplained. They are the unknown of the after death, hence faith, religion and the theory of *karma* take over. The spiritual importance of Lord Agni who as fire sublimates everything, is clear; cremation of dead humans was a custom introduced late, the ancients most probably burried their beloved ones after death; as the Kalash, Kafirs and Dards still do; also *sādhus* and *saṁnyāsīs* even nowadays are not cremated. Cremation is not ecologically wise in an overpopulated world, though it is advisable from a sanitary and hygienic point of view. At a spiritual level cremation means liberating the soul from the body fetters, it means sublimating the material part of the individual, it means making the spirit immortal and identified with Agni, the universal energy. Cremation immortalizes the deceased precisely because it leaves no or very little material remains that are usually consigned to running waters, so that the cycle may be perpetually renewed materially as it is spiritually.

In fact, it is Agni who 'guards our bodies with ever watchful care' (*Ṛ̥V*, X; 4,7) also because body temperature is an indicator of health or disease. Agni is eulogized as physician and maker of remedies (*AV*, V; 29,1). In his mysterious interactions with life Lord Agni has also much to say about the functioning of the mind; 'free the man possessed by a demon' (*Ṛ̥V*, X; 161, 162), and Agni is also requested to cure tuberculosis or consumption of the body and many other bodily disorders, including leprosy and infectious maladies. Good health is taken as the normal condition, loss of health is loss of the normal law and therefore disease is often taken to be the result of a curse.

Agni and water are givers and sustainers of life, they are 'affectionate mothers . . . givers of all, givers of life' (*Ṛ̥V*, IX; 2), they have healing power (*Ṛ̥V*, X; 137), but 'most excellent are waters . . . most excellent is Agni . . . praised is the lightning cloud' (*Ṛ̥V*, I; 161). It is evident that the *ṛ̥ṣis* understood that the elements work together, there would be no life in the absence of any of them; no life is possible without the cooperation and interaction of each element or, as we would say today, without the participation of all and every ecological factor. Further the *ṛ̥ṣi* extrapolated from the life of the individual, to the life of the Āryan society as a whole, later to become the Indian society at large. It is also made clear that the whole is the 'most excellent', that each part plays its role excellently and that the whole cannot function without the adequate function of all the parts, in this case: fire and water. The whole, whatever it is, cannot function if *ṛ̥ta*, the universal cosmic law and order, is not observed and followed obediently. Soul and body are the Fire and Water pair that enables life to go on (*Ṛ̥V*, V; 11, 9) and Varuṇa's magic 'puts fire in the water' (*Ṛ̥V*, V: 85, 2) figuratively as well as physically as body heat and swamp fire. Incidentally, this sentence was often misinterpreted and at best considered to be foolish by the learned scholars, while it clearly refers both to natural phenomena and to the **fire of life** or life energy, that cannot express itself in the absence of water. Common fire is the next indispensable ingredient for a better living process: 'Agni accept with flames' (*AV*, V; 29, 15).

As mentioned, the global water cycle was fully understood by the ancient *ṛ̥ṣi*, beginning with the endless flow of water into the sea that remains unaltered; then 'water vapour ascends to heaven' (*Ṛ̥V*, VIII; 41, 6-8; 42) and 'Varuṇa is the large hidden ocean who envelopes the world with his robe (of humidity)'. The burst of the monsoon must have been a striking sight, with the percolation of water in the soil and the emergence of springs and sources of water not available in the plains. The frequent lightning and copious rain following days on end of dense cloud cover would naturally have been linked to mighty Indra, whose thunderbolt is light and thunder in one. In fact, there are good descriptions of the monsoon in hymns to Indra.

Clouds are important for people spending most of their time in the open; Parjanya, the cloud, is often remembered and one simile is biologically very expressive. He is requested to drop on earth the semen (*pānī* or water is a word that can be used as well as *bīja* or seed, as a synonym of semen) of father sky that generates fecundity in Mother Earth (*R̥V*, VII; 101, 102). The famous and usually misinterpreted and misunderstood hymn to the frogs (*R̥V*, VIII; 103) is a marvellous piece of good biological and ecological insight. *R̥ṣi* Vasiṣṭha shows accurate knowledge of climatic and meteorological events and in this particular case also of the biological and seasonal cycles of different species of frogs, each with its own peculiar mating call. The 'unexplained' verse: 'cow bellow and goat bleat . . . and green and spotty (frogs) have vouchsafed us treasure. The frogs that give us cows in hundreds lengthen our life in their most fertilizing season' is a poetic rendering of a correct observation: good rains breed frogs in plenty since the tadpoles feed and grow in waters, and they are of different species, the green and the spotty. 'O Varuṇa . . . let the frogs . . . croak along the water courses' (*AV*, IV; 15, 12-14). The hymn also contains a good description of the female frog spreading out the four legs for reproduction; this is the posture she assumes to receive the male's *amplexus*. Good monsoon rains breed many frogs as well as good pastures and contented grazers such as cattle, horses, goats and sheep that will be healthy and productive. This is how plenty of frogs are a good omen for the next season. The hymn is very clear and not at all obscure, as most commentators would have. Unnecessary far-fetched interpretations are only secondary possible meanings if at all. Frogs are also a symbol of fecundity in pre-Colombian American cultures, specially in Central and South America, and they also play a significant role in the shamanistic practices of the Turkish people of the Altaï region.

The most important bio-physical-ecological aspect of water is that it is indispensable for Agni as the fire of life to become operative. Agni born in heaven is at home in water, he forces himself in water and becomes wood, cattle and their produce. The frequent appellation of fire as the grandson of water is not only due to the fact that living matter, twigs and wood included, cannot be produced without water, but also to the fact that fire or heat-energy is necessary for the current biochemical reaction of the life processes to take place. The appellation of fire as *Tanūnapāt*, or son of himself, indicates that energy generates energy, that heat and food generate life-energy in the same manner as movement generates heat. Mental processes such as thought, meditation, concentration or *tapas* also cause an increase in body temperature.

Water, however, is not only the chemical compound H_2O that we call water. Even in contemporary parlance **water** is a synonym of any **liquid**, inclusive of medicines or semen. Soma Pavamāna is often described as flowing like a liquid or fluid (*ṚV*, IX; 30 1 — *ṚV*, IX; 44, 4 — *ṚV*, IX; 45, 6).

Although the Veda are revealed Truth and do not contain detailed descriptions of the processes or methods followed for the acquisition of knowledge, some technicalities find their way in a more or less disguised manner in many hymns, even in the *ṚV*. Formulae, recipe or techniques are only given symbolically and obviously could be understood only by the initiated disciples who would have had the benefit of observing the acts of the *guru* and the *ācārya*, listening to their teachings and assisting them in the preparation or manufacture of whatever it was (*ṚV*, IX; 71 *et al.*) the master was doing. Instructions include what would appear to be magic incantations that may well be procedural formulae or recipes. The whole process was accomplished by chanting, the sound and rhythm vibrations being an important element for the success of the process of conferring power to the maker and the made. There is a meaning in every gesture, in every act and in every *mantra*. The meaning can be objective, intellectual for memorizing or spiritual to influence the psyche, the mind and the spirit. The power infused in the preparation of medicines is either transferred to the user or will destroy the cause of the illness; 'may he enriched with prayers come soon and early' (*R̥V*, IX; 93, 5).

To quote only a few of the decriptive lines: 'Soma roars as he passes through the tail of the sheep' (which is the woollen sieve) (*R̥V*, IX; 43,5), in fact, fermentation generates foam and sound (*R̥V*, IX; 75, 4) and the sieve was made with the wool of the sheep's tail. Many uses of *soma* — or many different products — 'may go many different paths' or may be used in many ways (*R̥V*, IX; 78, 2). The change in colour of *soma* during the various stages of preparation (*R̥V*, IX; 78, 96) may indicate the preparation of dye stuffs many of which are indicator dyes, meaning that they change colour according to the pH or the oxigenation of the solution. A common example is the preparation of indigo, another is antocyanine that turns from pink to red, blue, violet as the flower first blooms, becomes mature and finally senescent; during the life-cycle of the flower the pH (acidity/alkalinity ratio) and oxidation level of the cell sap is what change and are the cause of the colour change of the flower, of indigo or of other chemical species. In the preparation of dyes, the sequence and tone of the colour change indicates the correct undertaking of the usually elaborate process.

Different local populations and tribes knew well the natural products of the land. There is a long list of natural chemical products including dyes, medicines, psychotropic drugs, poisons, pain killers; they knew the properties of food, fibers and building materials, but it is not my purpose to discuss this here. I would rather refer to the exhaustive publication of plant, animal and mineral products having medicinal properties included in the *India Materia Medica* by K.M. Nadkarni.

Throughout the Veda we sense a deep respect for life, the

most mysterious of all magics under whatever form it appears. Life is an important **manifestation** and **expression** of God, second perhaps only to Agni 'giver of life' (*AV*, II; 29): there would be no life without Agni. Throughout the history of mankind and perhaps the pre-history as well, man looks up and inwardly when he thinks spiritually and about God and all that is good. The flames of fire are always turned up, as are the branches of the trees. 'Vanaspate may you whom the sharp hatchet has brought for great auspiciousness, grow up with hundred branches, with thousand branches may we raise to greatness' (*ṚV*, III; 8). Thus the practical Vedic people recognized the presence of God in everything in the universe, including in the tree that they were about to cut down and they used everything in the best way possible, after the offerings were made and sacrifices conveyed by fire to all the Gods, by Agni Jātavedaḥ, the all knower.

Everything is sacred by virtue of its own nature because energy pervades everything, thus the lofty tree is worshipped as well as the humble grass on which we sit and the one that helps ignite the fire; all and each one play their role in the cosmic symphony. Artifacts made by man, from the humble clay pot to the mighty chariot or, later, the great temples as well as the idols that represent Gods and are a late development, have to be sanctified by appropriate sacrifices because they are a part of nature though only secondarily so and through man's hands and mind. Vital breath, *prāṇa*, has to be infused in the idols at the most crucial moment of the ritual which is the sacrificial process itself. Materials are taken from nature to make things but as a new form is created for a new purpose, life has to be transferred to the new object from the whole from which the material was taken. Polynesians, the great navigators, had a similar behaviour: they invoked the spirit of the tree about to be cut for building their canoes, specially the large travelling double canoes, then they ritually transferred the spirit of the tree to the finished craft, requesting its good offices to direct them in their migrations across the ocean and before embarking in their long distance sea voyages. Appropriate sacrificial rites have to be performed to abide by *ṛta*; it is dangerous to fall out of step or out of the appropriate vibrations of the law that governs the universe.

An interesting aspect is how the presence of thieves is taken for granted and in a matter of course manner (*ṚV*, VII; 55, 3); maybe it is far-fetched to see an ecological wisdom in the way people living in remote areas consider thieves and brigands, for instance in Tibet. Ecologically, however, this reveals an acute observation of the facts of nature: predator species of animals such as carnivores are needed for the maintenance of the ecological balance of multi-species ecosystems; diseased, old, weak prey are weeded out by the carnivores who feed on them, while the gifted animals who run faster or who find better ways to escape the predators or to find shelter or who know how to defend themselves, will be spared and in turn will generate healthier and better equipped offsprings. Likewise robbers are to be found in all human communities, but they are specially institutionalized, so to say, in sparsely populated areas at the outer margins of those parts of the world where man lives more easily without having too much effort to keep alive. They occupy an ecological niche that needs to be filled, human brigands and *ṭhugs* take the place of animal carnivores, they do not eat flesh but take goods which are matter, and money which is energy and thus provide for recycling of matter and energy of the human population in areas where there is very little local production. Thus, as visitors, invaders, traders or caravans pass by, they bring to deserts, both geographical and social deserts, the essentials for survival that are not produced locally, so they have to be traded or stolen or both.

Life is difficult to define, as a concept or idea, but is experienced as a *status quo*. Life is felt, is recognized, is lived and perceived when it leaves the body and stops being, but not when it begins. A hibernating bear, a leaf, an egg-cell fertilized or not, curds, any plant or animal are all living beings even if life is not readily discernible from movement or heat; these creatures will be seen to be alive when the bear warms up and moves out of its winter torpor, or while the leaf remains green, the egg-cell of plants and animals divides and grows into an embryo. Plants and animals grow and reproduce while life is present, but when it stops, green plants become yellowish and putrefaction sets in dead plants and animals alike. Life is mysterious and all Gods are involved in the life processes directly or indirectly; if they were not, they, the Gods, would not exist. The great and mysterious aspects of life are inherent in Brahmā, whose consort Sarasvatī is knowledge because there can be no knowledge without life, or, as Descartes put it: '*Cogito ergo sum*', (I think, therefore I exist). Agni is vital energy, Savitṛ is the glory of living, of the life-giving Sun, he is the Hope that daily rises anew after the fears of the dark night. I believe that the idea and concept of life was personified in Lord Savitṛ, and on this I will return later on.

Soma exercises power over the human body and mind. Soma **liberates** the instinctive and intuitive perception, a process **facilitated** by drinking special substances and Soma could represent the non-empirical, non-experimental, the unexplained or **revealed** aspect of the understanding of natural phenomena. The ancient *ṛṣi*s must have realized that there are means of perception and communication other than those usually perceived and performed by human sense-organs, as for instance telepathy. Soma was probably taken as one of the means to achieve supra-sensory perception. Soma is glorified and exalted. Incidentally, the contemporary counterparts of telepathy are radio and television, these are means of communication the existence of which the ancients, innocent of the knowledge of electro-magnetic waves, sound transmission and electronic devices, might have guessed existed from observing the behaviour of animals. The orientation and migratory habits of animals who always return 'home' safely, the orientation and communication among insects, as for instance the honey bees that were well known, the synchronized behaviour of herds of wild animals such as deer, were observed facts that must have puzzled the minds of the ancients who then talked of vibrations. The mysterious means of communication and orientation of animals was translated in the folklore as 'animal speech' and animal wisdom; all the animals of the *Pañcatantra* speak and exhibit great knowledge, they are cunning, both good and bad. In fact, elephants, whales (unknown to the Vedic man), individuals of herds of hoofed animals communicate by ultrasounds to which man is deaf. Naturally the ancient perceived those manifestations of life and, unable to explain them otherwise, resorted to the *asu* or magic power of Varuṇa. At present we have ways and means to measure ultrasounds and other vibrations which are not perceived by human bodily sense-organs and we are amazed at the intuition of the ancients who did not have these instruments and machines. We speak of 'vibrations' when we 'feel' unexplainable communication. For instance when we meet a person for the first time, we may have unexplainable feelings or reactions of sympathy or antipathy; such feelings are usually mutual and only mean that the individual vibrations do not agree; some places are congenial, others are not. In fact, sympathy means having a common pathos (emotion); antipathy means having opposite pathos. Congenial means having similar, or mutually agreeable reactions (genius means an immaterial being or spirit, like the *jini*).

To this day there is no *exhaustive* explanation of how migratory species of animals such as mammals, birds, reptiles, fishes, insects and many others, can navigate through air and sea over widely distant geographic places and return with pinpoint accuracy to their birth or nesting place. We know that some animals, for instance pigeons, can sense and are guided by electromagnetic waves; many mammals sense ultrasounds, such as whales, dolphins, elephants, bats and polarized light is perceived by insects and crustaceans and can be perceived by man under forced special situations. It was Lazzaro Spallanzani of Galileo's shcool who made the first scientifically recorded experiments with bats showing that even when flying in total darkness they can avoid objects not thicker than a string; only about three centuries later it was proved that bats have a radar-comparable navigational system for eco-location that enables them to fly safely in total darkness. Orientation by pheromones, by shock or thermal waves or by humidity and barometric pressure sensors is common among flying and swimming animals which move in a three-dimensional system or space; but though these devices were explained scientifically only as late as the twentieth century, they must have been guessed or perhaps even recognized by ancient man. Myths that refer to animal intelligence and 'speech' are common all over the world and they are often similar among many people of very different cultures. The unexplained remained in the realm of *māyā* and the myth of the stolen cows, for instance, besides probably reflecting one or more historical facts, is also a symbol of the 'hidden knowledge' that should be given to man for his benefit, since 'our sires of old who knew the footsteps, found light and retrieved the cattle from the mountain' (*R̥V*, IX; 97, 39); 'drinking of this that finds the light' (*R̥V*, IX; 108, 2). Soma and some practices like *yoga*, specially *rāja-yoga* and meditation give mental power and understanding and strengthen the body.

Air and Ākāśa

A few words about air. Air is recognized as breath of life, *prāṇa*, of all living beings, including fire that cannot exist without air (*R̥V*, X; 151, 4), and also plants and animals that cannot exist without air. The recurrent word *bhūta* indicates all beings and being alive means to have a spirit, therefore whether material or immaterial or just air, *bhūta*s have a real existence.

Air as wind can become dangerous (*R̥V*, VII; 89) and should be propitiated specially in the open plains and in the mountains, where wind can become highly destructive. Strong winds may uproot even the lords of the forest, they may contribute to trigger landslides and avalanches causing the formation of dams across rivers and impoundments of waters behind them, they extinguish home and camp fires and may incite forest and grassland fires to rage. Terrifying winds speak a language of their own understood only by ghosts, goblins, fairies and maybe by a few among initiated men. But natural elements are ambivalent and Vāyu may also be beneficial as when he brings rains. Clearly, as later said the Buddha, the middle path is the best, not too much and not too little of everything. The peasants of my home country pray to St. Anthony when there is an excess of something, such as rains requested during spells of drought: 'troppa grazia Sant Antonio' (too much grace, O Saint Anthony), please do not give us too much anything, even grace! In general way, however, the cloud bearing winds, or the Maruts, are welcome (*R̥V*, I; 167-169), which is natural in monsoonal areas where all nature thirstly awaits the rains after long months of drought.

Air and water are means for the transmission of vibrations, visible and invisible, measurable or not, physical or mental (*R̥V*, I; 171) that produce sound, heat, motion and emotions. Other means of communication among men or between man and his environment depend on sound, music, rhythm, cacophonies that are all vibrations lying at the root of transmission of information and the offer of devotion. One of the great merits of the ancient sages is to have detected the visible as well as the invisisble forces, waves or vibrations that fill the air and the void: *ākāśa*. Sympathy and antipathy between persons arise frequently even at the first meeting; maybe they are an expression of such feelings that cannot be rendered by words. We usually rightly say that domestic animals instinctively know if a newcomer is good or bad or indifferent, if he is a friend or not, if it likes them or not and they behave accordingly. What is true of today's cows and dogs must have been true of their progenitors who lived with the Vedic man; animals' instincts rarely make mistakes.

The importance given to the syllable ॐ, which is the sound vibration *par excellence* which precedes all others in time and importance, was recognized to be so great that it could not but set life in motion by putting man on the *same* wave-length, so to speak, as the Gods.

Finally about the physiology of meditation. In recent years there has been much scientific research on different aspects of supernatural perception and achievements; this is no place to recapitulate the literature on the subject, suffice it to say that it is now well known that the amount of **dopamine** in the blood increases during motion and action. Increase of body heat during *tapas,* meditation and intensive mental activity, or just the concentrated will to increase body temperature, may bring about altered states of perception that can be induced also by natural chemical compounds produced in the brain. These have effects comparable to those produced by some psychotropic drugs. Chemical substances closely related to opium and its derivates, the so-called **brain opiates**, have properties similar to those produced by the poppy plant: opium, and they also bring greater resistance to pain. Yogic methods achieve insensibility to pain, voluntary increase in body temperature, voluntary control of heart-beat and many other feats, including expanded mental power.

From the observation of means of communication, the pathways of which could not be detected directly by human sense-organs, man sought to experience the same during episodes of deep meditation or trance (*R̥V*, IX; 18, 1 — *R̥V*, IX; 20, 3); Mitra. Varuṇa's perception 'with the eyes of the mind' (*R̥V*, VIII; 25, 9) is mentioned. It could be that the study of transmission of something intangible through an intangible medium, *ākāśa,* produced the remarkable idea *ākāśa* as void, that is comparable but not exactly the same as ether in ancient and medieval Western philosophies. The concept of *ākāśa* in turn must have led to the remarkable concept of *śūnya* or void or zero which is the greatest feat of ancient abstract thinking. Zero has no intrinsic value but may acquire any value according to its position, including its position in any number; it is a direct logical development of the philosophical concept of *ākāśa*. The void, or nothing, can acquire any value at any time and place, if duly used. The concept of *śūnya* represents a remarkable leap forward from philosophical **theory** to philosophical **practice**, arithmetics in this case. The perception of *ākāśa* as one of the five fundamental elements of the universe is a much more subtle matter than the perception of earth, water, air and fire. It is a perception that goes into the abstract, much beyond the understanding of life and is the recognition of the much that the Vedic man and we do not know about the processes of the universe.

Practicalities

Some further aspects of the application of theoretical knowledge to practical pursuits can be mentioned here. Health was seen as the normal state, the maintenance of order in the body of man and animals as well as in the body of nature. Health is the law, ill-health is disruption of the laws that govern natural forces, due to ageing, a curse, witchcraft or poisoning. Ill-health is physiological and ecological imbalance; disruption of order and law, it causes biological and ecological imbalance, impoverishment or degradation of the patient, be it man, animal, plant or the environment. Degradation causes poor pastures, wear and diseases in animals, decrease in productivity, all of them causes of migrations in search of new pastures. When no direct cause and effect relation was found either for the diagnosis or the cure, magic had to be resorted to; magic of course works very well for mental patients or hypochondriacs. Only healthy animals could be offered in animal sacrifices (*AV*, III; 29) to the Gods, which is a hygienic practice of respect to Gods and to the humans who would later consume the offering. A whole hymn (*AV*, III; 28) is dedicated to avert the ill-omen of twins born to cows. In rural Europe the habit persists of destroying twin calves of different sex because 'they bring bad luck' and because in many places they are believed to be the offsprings of a cow possessed by a demon. The biological truth of this story is that the male of a pair of calf twins of different sex is what in English is called a 'free-martin'; it is a poorly defined male calf with all the characteristics of an intersex. At present we know the cause of the anomaly: it is due to hormonal imbalance that results from the mixing of the bloods of the placentas of the female and male twin embryos. Obviously, efficient herdsmen as the Vedic people were, they would have been horrified by such a freak, hence the label of 'Bad omen'.

Sacrifices had to be made to Lord Agni who sustains, maintains and controls *r̥ta*; logically, when disorder sets in, Agni is invoked to restore order. As Vd. Baghavan Dash (1975, p. 8) says: ' . . . all the active or productive aspects of *pariṇāma* or evolution, at the macro- and micro-cosmic levels are due to *rajas* or energy' . . . 'Agni, according to the Sāṁkhya system'. And Agnī is the 'kinetic factor at all levels of nature' (*l.c.*, p. 22). *Āyurveda* also recognizes different aspects of Agni, but to discuss this is beyond the scope of this study.

Interestingly Lord Savitr̥ is invoked to keep away disease and in this context also the mountains, the pressing stones and the herbs who shed juices are taken together (*R̥V*, X; 100 8); ecologically this makes sense since the mountains give the pressing stones, the medicinal plants used for different purposes, including the preservation of health, and most important of all: pure mountain water and air. Both water and air are incorporated as ingredients in the process of grinding the plants to prepare medicines.

Man interferes with the environment because basically man is not only a doer, but also a maker; the two combined produced man the tool-maker, the craftsman, the engineer, the artisan, the architect, the priest, the medical man. The pleasure that man derives in making things, the usefulness to everybody of what a few can make is stated clearly: 'Atharvan first by sacrifice made man confident; for this skill the Bhr̥gus were esteemed of all the Gods' (*R̥V*, X; 92, 10) and Agni Narāśaṁsa, the praise of man, Agni of all men, plays a decisive role (*l.c.*, 11). There is no doubt about the antiquity of fire, in fact, fire has made man: **Man. Man** became what he is now by the use of fire for implementing different technologies.

In Vedic mythology Tvaṣṭr̥ represents the technologies themselves and the ability needed for the correct manufacture of objects that are born from science and that are in turn generated by the understanding of *r̥ta* or the dynamics of natural and man-made systems. This is what techniques are.

The production of fire by attrition of the *araṇi*s represents the sacredness of the process and the need to follow the rules. Significantly Trita, a very ancient Vedic God, guides a priest, Agni, in the process (*R̥V*, X; 115). The uses of fire for different purposes are listed (*R̥V*, X; 115-122) where 'these sages found what lay remote and hidden . . . from radiant Dhātr̥, Savitr̥, Viṣṇu, Agni, Bharadvāja who brought the *Br̥hat*' . . . 'They found with mental eyes the earliest *Yajus*, a pathway to the Gods, that had descended'; this is a good description of how knowledge and consequently the ability to make things was acquired. This includes all knowledge, spiritual, religious, factual and techincal as well as scientific, that all contributed to the development of man.

Fingers are poetically described as the 'glittering maids' (*R̥V*, IX; 65, 1) not because, as some translators have said, or perhaps not **only** because of gold rings, but principally because fingers do so much and so well. 'See, all is done with these hands' is a common saying always expressed with great pride.

From the point of view of technical aspects of the *R̥V*, the *Maṇḍala* IX dedicated exclusively to Pavamāna-Soma (Agni-Soma) indicates the importance given to mental power as related to technical skills (*R̥V*, IX; 36, 3). Material and intellectual wealth make an indissoluble pair (*R̥V*, IX; 31, 1), as well as mental power and skill on one side and glory on the other, or intelligence and wealth (*R̥V*, IX; 32, 6). All the while Pavamāna-Soma 'purifies . . . and sends the Gods who strengthen law' (*R̥V*, IX; 42, 5). Law in this context also means the rules of how to do things correctly to achieve an end.

At a later time Indra's power supports science and technology to ensure livelihood for man (*R̥V*, X; 112, 8): 'In genuine wrath thou (Indra) looseneth the mountain (landslides) that opened the cave (where the *Paṇis* had hidden the stolen cattle) so that the *brahman* easily found the cattle'. In other words, according to this hymn, the king must be encouraged by men's prayers, instructed by the learned and protected by the Gods: significantly the cattle had been stolen from the Lord of Prayer, Br̥haspati. These are ecological laws applied to human society.

Finally, towards the end of the *R̥V* several verses refer to the means to preserve a functional society: in *R̥V*, X: 113, 5 the three powers that regulate society are linked together: Varuṇa's *māyā,* Mitra's law and Indra's sovereignty. A strong spirit of communality pervades the *R̥V*, the *SV* and the *AV*, hence the creation of *saṁghas* and the recurrent recommendation of **harmony** among people (*AV*, VI; 74) and, I would add, between man and all nature. Food cooked by Agni Vaiśvānara ritualistically is recommended to unite people who have been separated by guilt or obligation (*AV*, VI; 119, 1, 2); Vaiśvānara, the Pacific will also ensure begetting offsprings.

The hymns attributed to *r̥ṣi* Viśvāmitra, mostly in *R̥V*, III, are in general very practical, while the hymns by *r̥ṣi* Vasiṣṭha in *R̥V*, VII tend to be spiritual and devotional, though they reflect a very good knowledge of nature and also teach many practical aspects of everyday living. The personalities of the *r̥ṣi* can be outlined from their hymns.

Talking of technicalities I would end by recalling the joyful mood of *R̥V*, VIII; 1, that contains a detailed description of how *soma* is pressed to extract the juices, how these are filtered and later collected in three earthen pots, the *droṇakalaśa*, for the preparation of the beverage. The description in fact matches closely that by Robertson of the preparation of wine from grapes that the Kafirs make ritualistically and it also matches the description given by Lièvre and Loude for the preparation and consumption of grape wine by the Kalash. Fermentation is described happily as the voice of Soma and the description of how water oozes out of burning wet logs as 'the water that rests in Agni' (*R̥V*, VIII; 102, 14). While the sound of Agni is joyous one can easily imagine the happy sounds coming from the hearth and the bonfires on the commons during festivals, specially the winter solstice series of rites and festivities.

The natural elements: fire, wind, water, air, seasons, birth, growth, old-age and death of plants and animals, reproduction and reproductive cycles, floods, landslides, avalanches, earthquakes and intellect are all expressions of the divine and they all fall within the realm of the external law and order, *r̥ta*, or, alternately, its temporary disruption or disorder. But on the whole, the R̥gvedic hymns extol life and the joy of living, according to each one's *dharma* (*R̥V*, VIII; 35, 13), or duty.

In conclusion we may say that the sages were fully conscious of their duty to transfer the knowledge that they had acquired to other men; 'the ancient names are brought to us by the songs of the poet who is a sage by wisdom, with the mind of a seer and the actions of a sage' (*R̥V*, IX; 96, 16-18). Thus, practicalities are not forgotten: 'Purify the elixir through the filter'! (*R̥V*, IX; 97, 39-40); but this could also be read: 'Clarify your ideas through thinking, observing and experimenting' so that you may live a healthy life.

The wise man first comprehends the light of God in his heart.
Then with three, the mind, the speech, the deeds purifies the soul.

By his own nature he further makes himself most excellent and contemplates on earth and heaven.

R̥V, III; 26, 8
(SS and SV transl.)

With three purifying strainers he (Agni) purified the sun
with his heat the thought, discovering the light.
The mightiest treasure he produced by the powers of his own nature,
then he looked over heaven and earth.

R̥V, III; 26, 8
(transl. Max Müller and Oldenberg)

5

Lord Agni and Fire

Agni revealer of Śruti to mortal men
and giver of wisdom . . . *Ṛ̥V*, I; 31
(from SS & SV)

O Agni, be unto us of easy approach
as a father to his son:
Stay with us for our sake . . . *Ṛ̥V*, I; 1, 9
(from Griffith)

AGNI as God is unborn (*Ṛ̥V*, I; 67, 3) or is 'the first born', he is the institutor of worship (*Ṛ̥V*, IV; 6,1); he is the one who knows mysteries and does wonders (*Ṛ̥V*, I; 77); he rises anew in ancient fuel, which can be read: he is always renewed in or by ancient wisdom (*Ṛ̥V*, X; 4, 5); and Agni himself declares his universality (*Ṛ̥V*, III; 26, 7). Agni is universal and always existed since the beginning of time, since the sound ॐ happened and put in motion all vibrations. Lord Agni is not just common fire. Agni is the Lord of fire and he is 'fireness' in fire (*Ṛ̥V*, I; 12, 6), 'by Agni is *agni* inflamed', or we would say: Agni gives vitality and energy to knowledge. Angi is the essence and divinity in fire, heat and energy. Significantly all the *Maṇḍala*s of *Ṛ̥V Saṁhitā*, except the VIIIth, open with a hymn to Agni and the *Saṁhitā* as a whole opens and closes with praises to Agni. All the hymns of *Maṇḍala* IXth, including the first, are dedicated to Soma-Pavamāna and can be read as addressed to special aspects of the dual divinity Agni-Soma.

Agni as common fire is born spontaneously or can be kindled by man for instance by friction of the fire sticks, the *araṇis*. Agni as God is father of the Gods and as common fire he is their son (*R̥V*, I; 69, 1). As God Agni is observer of 'heavenly laws of Gods and (as fire) of mortal men'. He is giver of 'wisdom that prolongs our lives' (*R̥V*, I; 94) in time and quality. As God **and** common fire he is destroyer of evil (*R̥V*, II; 8, 5) and 'Agni is continuously to be found in fire' (*AV*, IV; 39, 9). '*agni* bring Agni to the sacrifice' (*R̥V*, I; 44, 8) in other words: *agni* fire (who art the means to an end) bring Agni God (who art the knowledge or truth, an end in itself), to the sacrifice (that men offer to Gods)". Hence the worship of Fire by Hindus, Zoroastrians, Vedic and pre-Vedic man. In fact, we see fire, in one way or the other: if not actually worshipped, the *de facto* present, represented, invoked or just remembered in all cultures; in Christianity the Holy Spirit is represented by 'tongues of fire'. Fire as light has only recently been substituted by cold light, but fire is nevertheless still present in the mind of man physically as light, and conceptually as energy. Fire is the light of wisdom brought by reason.

The evolution of the concept of Agni as a non-personalized God is clear in *R̥V*, IV; 1, 11; where he is said to have 'first appeared as footless and headless . . . in the home of **Holy Order** . . . to fulfil the sacred law of worship (*R̥V*, IV; 1, 11-13) . . . (*l.c.*, 18) . . . . now all the Gods abide in their dwellings . . . brightly beaming Agni, the herald'. Worship is and can be performed at all times because Agni first appeared after all vibrations were set in motion. In other words, the 'home of holy order' means *r̥ta* whose home is the whole universe. Agni is the visible, tangible expression and manifestation of the universal energy that maintains the cosmos in order.

Agni as father and mother of mankind (*R̥V*, VI; 1, 5) belongs to all men as Agni Vaiśvānara; he is expressed as being one with Varuṇa and Mitra (*R̥V*, VI; 3, 1) and is requested to give the astronomical readings for the sacrifice (*R̥V*, VI; 2, 3), because he is invoker and inspirer of the univeral rites (*R̥V*, VI; 1, 2). The Bharadvāja hymns repeatedly identify Agni with the Sun, which may indicate the habit of noting the position of celestial bodies to mark the calendar or otherwise make astronomical observations. In other words, man could not exist without Lord Agni or apart from him.

S.P. Saraswati and S. Vidyalankar (1977, p. 423), derive the word '*Agni*' from अग = first and the root नी = to lead, thus they interpret the word *agni* to mean 'the one who is involved first', the 'foremost leader'. They further recall that he is Vratapati (Lord of vows), that he makes everything part of himself and that he is also a drying agent. The importance given to the drying power of Lord Agni is significant. Agni is said to dwell in waters, which is true, as mentioned elsewhere in this book, because Agni is present in water as energy. The ecological role of *agni*, common fire, as a drying agent is of great importance for people living at a time when emerging agricultural practices required crops to be well dried for preservation over the wet season and winter humidity. The fire of the sun or the fire of fires specially lit for the purpose is necessary, to this day, to dry up the grains for preservation in earthen pots. The earthen pots themselves were initially sun-baked and only later they were baked in kilns for which fire was again needed. It may also be recalled that hay or grass when humid may ignite spontaneously and putrefaction also generates heat. In the mountains grass and hay for fodder is usually kept hanging from trees where they dry quickly after rain or snow and are beyond reach of the cattle; this is preferable to keeping them in closed quarters where they are not immune to rot or attack by rodents.

Dayananda (acc. to SS and SV, *l.c.*) has Agni as the Supreme Lord, venerable, adorable, omnipresent, respected by the learned and glorified by divine texts and sacred lore. Agni is the most brilliant (powerful) master of the intelligent mind. According to Sri Aurobindo (*l.c.*) Agni is Godwill and according to the same author (*l.c.*, p. 425), '*hotaram* is . . . the destroyer of *daityas*, a synonym of Agni Jātavedas'. The usual rendering of the term Jātavedas is 'omniscient'. These meanings are all interrelated, because being omniscient, Agni Jātavedas has the wisdom to discriminate good from evil and as a *hotṛ* he has the power to destroy evil. Originally 'Agni was the only immortal and later the other Gods received immortality from him'.

ṚV, I; 1, begins with the invocation, laudation (Griffith), worship and magnification (Max Müller) of Agni the adorable Lord, divine, high priest and Creator, keeper and sustainer of cosmic order, the one who works through and feeds eternal laws, who is fed with offerings of *ghī* and who sustains all that is light and luminous by night and mornings. He is immortal. He is the source of affluence, vitality and of interrelated knowledge and prosperity (*ṚV*, I; 147), he is the protector of the cosmic sacrifice of creation; he gives and accepts and he is indeed Truth itself. In terms of contemporary science we would say that Agni is energy and matter, because he is capable of interchanging the two.

'Agni is the first among immortals . . . he shall to mighty Aditi restore us' (*ṚV*, I; 24, 2). Agni is also Viśvacarṣaṇir (*ṚV*, I; 27, 9), which means: well known to all. These seem to me, especially *ṚV*, I; 1, to be perfect descriptions of the root-idea and initial concept of God, and they well express the need and urge that man has to worship God. Agni thus becomes the all-pervading energy, or 'Soul' (*ṚV* I: 146, 1) 'that is sunk in the lap of all that moves and moves not . . . and is ever youthful' (*l.c.*, 4). Agni is praised as the source of inspiration (*ṚV*, I; 22) 'may he conduct the Gods hither', where Gods stand for all that is good, including knowledge. Agni is also requested to bring the spouses of the Gods, including Agnāyī (*ṚV*, I; 22, 9; *l.c.*, 12), which is one of the very few times when she is invoked. In fact, Agni appears often to be rather neutral than masculine or feminine; here it appears as if a gender had been given to Agni, as the husband of Agnāyī, almost in retrospect and out of necessity, because all the other Gods bring their spouses with them.

Agni's face is turned everywhere (*Ṛ V*, I; 97, 6), ancient, wise, (*Ṛ V*, II; 3), the source of prosperity, material as food, intellectual as glory and spiritual as bliss. The sacrificial fire is nourished with *ghī* so that Lord Agni, therefore different from fire itself, may bring nourishment to man. Agni is the performer of sacrifice and the means that leads the seeker of knowledge or Truth. As the Hotṛ he is Truth personified and 'gloriously great'. As Aṅgiras, Agni is the giver of all the good that is in him such as Truth which of course derives from understanding; he is dispeller of ignorance (*Ṛ V*, I; 74, 3) and is again worshipped as dispeller of night and darkness, synonyms of fear and ignorance. Agni is the one who brings light at the beginning of the day. 'Agni in the darkness of night or dawn and of the mind' (*Ṛ V*, I; 1, 7). Knowledge is the means of our preservation (*Ṛ V*, II; 5, 1) and Agni is eulogized as the radiant, the sustainer of *ṛta* and he is approached and worshipped in all humility with the most touching prayer:

> Lord be unto us of easy access as a father to his son.
> Stay with us for our sake.

Lord Agni also plans for the future, by blessing 'women with children' and 'with motherly intelligence' (*Ṛ V*, X: 80, 1) and he instructs the bride to be vigilant over the domestic fire, the life and human reproductive cycles. Lord Agni leads the bridal procession while Lord Savitṛ, the Vivifier, gives away the bride (*Ṛ V*, X; 85, 8-9). *Ṛ V*, X; 85, 40, is interesting in that it mentions Agni as the third husband of the bride, after Soma and Gandharva, while the fourth is the human husband, who is in turn separately and previously prepared for married life. This can be interpreted thus : the future bride goes through a long period of preparation and training with the purpose of developing as an excellent wife, mother and carrier of tradition to the future generation. As a child the girl child is 'wedded' to 'Soma' from whom she learns the home sciences, how to lead a wholesome and healthy physical life, how to prepare food and medicines and in fact the Aśvins come as wooers; the girl is taught how to bring up children who are inevitably always present in joint families (*Ṛ̥V*, X; 85, 42). To this day the importance and authority of *dīdī* or elder sister in the inner family world is second only to that of the mother, and *dīdī* replaces mother whenever necessary, with full authority. 'Soma' will also instruct the girl about intimate family remedies and matters as well as kitchen habits and hygienic practices in general. Then Soma hands the young girl over to her second 'husband', *Gandharva* from whom she will learn recitation of the oral tradition, myths, chanting and music. Finally the future bride is 'handed over' to her third 'husband', Lord Agni at the time when she is biologically ready and prepared to become a wife and mother. It is Agni who hands her over to her human husband after she has been fully educated and when she is apt to assume all the responsibilities of a woman, the lady of the household. 'Agni has given her to me for the sake of children and wealth' (*Ṛ̥V*, X; 85, 41). The bride, fully conscious of her role, will bring happiness and prosperity also to 'our bipeds and quadrupeds' (*Ṛ̥V*, X: 85, 43, 44) and 'let her husband become the eleventh son' (*Ṛ̥V*, X; 85, 45). This indeed is a good poetical rendering of the four stages of womanhood: education and training, learning of tradition and rituals, physiological readiness for matrimony, consummation of the marriage. Even the Gods make oblations to Agni who is the moving energy of the physiological aspects of the life of animals and all mankind (*Ṛ̥V*, X; 88, 4, 9) and no marriage rites are complete without the circumambulation of the sacred fire. In *AV*, XIV; 1, 9 this is summarized thus: 'Soma was the bride seeker, both Aśvins the wooers; Savitṛ̥ gave Sūryā (the daughter of the Sun god) to her husband'.

There is no better expression of the early formulation of the concept of God and Agni as first God than the cornerstone of the *Ṛ̥V*, the very first hymn. It clearly expresses the idea of God as a consequence of the human quest for intellectual, spiritual and practical knowledge. God is he who answers the many hows and whys of his child. God Agni is the fire that possesses the seeker after Truth, he is the inner spiritual fire (*ṚV*, I; 58, 1) ; he is the truth of everyday's life as well as **The Absolute Truth** (*ṚV*, I; 145, 5) and the law of nature and of natural philosophy; Agni thus becomes the reality sought in religious and metaphysical speculations. As the human father teaches his son, God Agni at a higher level is invoked to enable the understanding and to disclose the truth that is above and beyond the common man's immediate grasp. The greatness and unrivalled beauty of this hymn lies exactly in rendering the agony of man in his fever to learn, to participate consciously in the drama of nature, which is the same as the fire of *tapas*. This can be understood as the *ṛṣi* saying: 'Take me — God Agni — take me as far as I can comprehend in spite of my human limitations' . . . . 'thou who liftest men to immortality' (*ṚV*, I; 31, 7). Agni is both God and the expression and manifestation of God related to the intellectual and spiritual quest, but at the same time Agni is also *agni*, common fire.

Agni is one, yet many (*ṚV*, I; 127, 5) and 'gives mental power to him who sings the sacred song' (*ṚV*, I; 151, 2); thus he is defined also as mental power (*ṚV*, I; 77, 3). Agni is the clearer of the path. Physically, fire clears the forest path and intellectually and spiritually he clears the path from ignorance (*ṚV*, I; 94). Fire as 'bright red flames' gives strength to others, as for instance the Maruts (*ṚV*, I; 64, 7). Agni Vaiśvānara, as benefactor of all men (*ṚV*, I; 98), takes care of the whole universe; pervades all plants and vegetation and is Truth as the fire of understanding. In *ṚV*, I; 95, 7 he is said to 'stretch his arms with might as Savitṛ', because Lord Agni as energy itself is also the energy of life.

Common Fire

Different aspects of fires and their ecological roles are described (*ṚV*, I; 95); a clear distinction is made between fires kindled by man and fires that 'God have kindled' (*ṚV*, VII; 1, 22) that clearly refer to natural fires. Natural fires occur everywhere. In swamps, *apāmnapāt* could be swamp fire or methane produced by anaerobic fermentation of organic matter at the bottom of swampy waters. It ignites spontaneously upon reaching the surface of the water when bubbles come in contact with the oxygen in the air. Also phosphorescent organisms in the sea present in their billions may 'put the sea on fire'; fire erupts spontaneously as bush and savannah or forest fires, that are kindled by the decomposition of organic matter or are ignited by lightning. Two positive aspects of fire must have been recognized at about the same anthropogeological time: fire for heating and drying and fire for cooking. Forest fires leave behind them roasted carcasses of animals and surely very early primitive man learned empirically that cooked meat is more digestible and nutrient than raw meat, one reason being that raw animal fat is hardly digestible while heated fat is more readily digested and absorbed; in addition ashes would have provided some salt that could otherwise have been deficient in the diet of very early continental man. With time, roasted meat gave way to boiled meat, even more nutritious and digestible. It is clearly recognized (*R̥V*, VII; 7, 7—*R̥V*, VII; 42; 6—*AV*, IV; 35—*AV*, XII; 3, 24) that cooking increases the value of food, see also *R̥V*, IX; 66, 19 and *R̥V*, IX; 72, 9, where it is said that agni is sent down to us with food for vigorous strength and 'measure thou forth . . . splendid ample strengthening food, O Pavamāna'. The use of fire for warmth and dryness brought with it the need to either store away fire as embers or to develop the ability to kindle fire anew. A small percentage of early men lived in natural caves where storing fire and keeping wood near to dry it up for later use would have been an easy task once the observation of cause and effect had been achieved by some perceptive elements of the human community. Storing away twigs, dry grass and branches of trees for later use may have been one of the first methodical plans made by man.

Difficulties however were great for those ancient Hominids living in the open and worst of all for those living in wet climates or during the rainy season. Underground hearths, containers made of stone or hard wood to keep the embers may have been an early answer. Terracotta containers came late, when pottery was developed: 'a receptacle for agni' is mentioned in *R̥V*, I; 140, 1. Large numbers of perforated terracotta pots of different sizes and shapes are to be seen at the National Museum in Delhi coming from the very early strata of the Harappan and earlier civilizations; similar ones are even now used for carrying and storing embers and light.

How to make a fire was a crucial problem. Again we may imagine the most gifted among early men, much before the Harappan or any other ancient civilization, sitting and observing what nature does. Man would have tried to reproduced good Mother Earth's ways: either produce heat by letting grass fermentate in some corner of the cave or under some tree or fallen log or under a little stone hut made by man himself or he might otherwise have tried to make sparks to ignite some dry leaves or grasses. The technique used would depend on the local climate and season. Flint stone lighters are widely used all over the world to this day in humid and wet places where matches, a recent invention, are useless; or in remote areas where matches are a luxury quickly consumed and finished. Kindling a fire by attrition of two pieces of wood would have naturally followed; the *araṇis* are frequently mentioned directly or through metaphors throughout the Veda, always with great respect and devotion. In conclusion, man learned that he could do what lightning does: he could ignite dry twigs and he could, by striking some stone against another or by using meteoritic iron: 'beget the fire between two stones'; 'Indra destroys the devil of ignorance which obstructs the path of virtuous thoughts as the lightning burns a tree' (*R̥V*, II; 12, 3 —*R̥V*, II; 14, 2). Kindling fire by rubbing dried sticks against one another became the ritualistic way of kindling fire. The surest practical way, however, would be to use intelligence to plan and not let the fire go out. To this day most rural people keep embers under cinders always burning. The sacrificial fire itself is ignited from the home fire.

The Ṛbhus, said to be descendants of Aṅgiras are, in the Vedic context, the pursuers of knowledge who attained physical, mental and spiritual glory through their good deeds; they have a share in the sacrifices to the Gods (*ṚV*, I; 20, 8). Aṅgiras, one of the first *ṛṣis*, is said to have composed many hymns of the *ṚV*; he was ancient enough to be considered a *prajāpati*. His name can be derived from the same root as Agni and he is invoked as 'God of fire' and 'fond of sacrifice'. Later myths have him born of the mouth of Brahmā, the Creator. **All** his wives or daughters have names of **ideas** or **qualities**. Aṅgiras is associated with Atharvan who is one of the most ancient *ṛṣis* who was also reputed to be able to make fire and offer sacrifices. The Āṅgirasa and the Ātharvana are respectively descendatns of Aṅgiras and of Atharvan and are frequently mentioned together as Atharva-Āṅgirasa. They are expert in matters concerning ritualistic and technical use of fire. Later legends attributed to them supenatural powers and immense technical ability such as to rival the magical powers of an ancient Atharvan called Dadhīca. The *vajra* was fashioned by Dadhīca and this legend, that would have a core of truth, obviously indicates the early use of fire to make metal instruments and weapons of 'magical' quality and power.

From *ṚV*, X; 67, 2; it is clear that the Āṅgirasa or fire priests were descendants of the brave and divine sages who first performed the sacred rites; in the hymns of praise they are requested to recite for posterity, reflecting correctly the 'inner' recondite meaning and upholding the intelligent way of doing things.

Agni as God, as the expression of God related to intellectual and spiritual quests, and agni as common fire and the uses to which it can be put, is again in my opinion expressed in the Vasiṣṭha hymns (*Maṇḍala* VIIth). Many technicalities are taught by *ṛṣi* Vasiṣṭha, as for instance the purification of organic matter, presumably food, wood and animal hides by fumigation; Agni, the black-bannered God, can be used to produce smoke, which is a common technique used for disinfection in many cultures. Fumigation is also part of the *gṛha-praveśa* and marriage rites. Among the Kalash, the Kafirs and the Dard of the Himālaya-Karākorum ranges and the South-Siberian Turks of the Altaï mountain regions, fumigation is used as a purifying agent for disinfection of homes and stables and as a routine practice, specially when they are visited by infectious epizootic diseases (Lièvre and Loude, 1990, pp. 50, 57, 72, 203). Fumigation by burning incense and branches of resinous trees and shrubs like the juniper and odoriferous roots and grasses, are also widely used to induce trances and for shamanistic and divination purposes; they are also a common practice in the rituals of many faiths. Burning sulphur, pyrethrum and its derivatives is commonly practised to keep mosquitoes and other insects away, an important practice, since malaria may have been one of the single most important diseases of ancient times all over the world. Consuming food prepared through the good offices of fire and smoke is still a sacred, almost daily ritual practice. We do not owe our food only to Mother Earth and it would not be available in good form without the action of Agni-God as the energy of life and life-processor and agni-fire as food processor. This is another example of the cooperation of several Gods for a single purpose; in fact, no ecological factor can act in isolation. Fermentation is a natural process used for purification of organic substances and one that requires the cooperation of several elements. The vats in which fermentation takes place are made of wood of the *pīpal* tree 'made strong by iron, *ayas*, nails, (*ṚV*, IX; 1, 2); iron here could mean metal in general. The fermentation process and all natural principles are mentioned as Soma-Pavamāna, that is 'everything and all Gods' (*ṚV*, IX; 5). Soma, the juices with a thousand powers (*ṚV*, IX; 42, 3), permit participation in cosmic affairs (*ṚV*, IX; 10, 8) and are the 'divine elixirs of penetrating insight' (*ṚV*, IX; 12, 7-9). Soma dwells in the hills (*R̥V*, IX; 18, 1) and Soma-Pavamāna 'graspest all things with thy mind and purifies thyself with thoughts . . . as such find us fame' (*R̥V*, IX; 20, 3). Agni and Soma are mind thoughts (*R̥V*, X; 19), thoughts that can be put into practice as techniques for different purposes.

Common fire is often represented as Indra (*R̥V*, II; 11, 1 *et al.*) and eulogized with terms comparable to those attributed to Agni. The identification with Indra suggests that common fire and its many uses were quite distinct in the mind of the *r̥ṣis* from Agni God.

Among the ecological aspects we find Agni by day as the sun's energy and by night as the home fire and the camp fire. Maybe it is also recognized that energy is always present even if not visible. Agni as creator and sustainer of life initiates the cycle with the photosynthetic process which is the production of organic matter in green plants thanks to water, mineral salts as nutrients and energy provided by sunlight; in several different contexts (*R̥V*, V; 44, 1) we are reminded that this is how life is created though the details of this 'magic' could not be explained. Fire is represented as kindled by Tvaṣṭr̥'s daughters as the ten fingers moving the *araṇis*. Agni also has many cosmic and ecological roles to play, as sacrificial fire (*R̥V*, I; 95, 3), as astronomical fire, as the sun who sets the seasons; fire is latent in waters and water is indispensable for life, including for producing combustible material such as wood; Agni is swamp fire or methane and finally Agni is the energy that moves the water cycle (*l.c.*, 10); fire is also used to burn away dead grassland to promote the sprouting of fresh grass and in a host of other ways. Agni as sun marks diurnal and annual cycles and early man was impressed by nature's recurrent cycles of time. Perhaps the only unidirectional aspect of time that he must have perceived was the process of ageing of all that lives. The Sun, the prime giver of life on Earth, is an expression of Agni as energy and of Savitr̥ as Life and Hope; the sun sends his vivifying rays downwards while fire on earth sends flames upwards; Agni is the go-between, the messenger between man and Gods, he sublimates the offerings made by man to the Gods and in return gives the imponderables: life, thought and energy. Nothing in this world would be possible without Agni: 'O Agni, thou on whom all other fires depend' (*R̥V*, VIII; 19, 33) in accordance with *r̥ta* which in the present context is all the ecological principles on earth. Rituals and the proper pronunciation and intonation of the *mantra*s are the religious expression of the true knowledge perceived and transmitted by the ancient *r̥ṣi*s.

Thc Aśvins arc related to the physical life of the body, as such they are closely associated both with Agni as God and *agni* as common fire; 'let the fire divine bring oblations to us again' (*R̥V*, X; 24, 4, 5) that can also be read as an allusion to the preparation of decoctions, infusions, and artifacts. Meat was usually consumed after boiling as is still the habit among the Kalash and Himālayan and Karākorum people in general: the Aśvins are requested to 'churn out the fire' (*l.c.*, 4). We can easily visualize the *r̥ṣi*s and the *ācārya*s who came after them, preparing food and decoctions ritually and studying their effects on man and animals. Purification and concentration of extracts 'fifteen fold' to prepare 'strong juices' by fire is indicated in *R̥V*, X; 27, 2. All of these are habitual processes practised in *Āyurveda*. While the material preparations are done by fire, songs and incantations and therefore sound vibrations accompany the process (*R̥V*, VIII; 35). 'The Aśvins coming from the east may bring plenty of food and medicines' (*R̥V*, VIII; 5, 31 *et al.*). The *dāsa*s or earlier inhabitants are specifically mentioned as knowing better food and better medicinal plants of a rich flora and fauna previously unknown to the newcomers (*R̥V*, VIII; 9).

From a biological point of view, man is a diurnal animal guided mainly by sight. Light is the main requirement for man's orientation; at night, fire is the natural substitute of the sun's rays. By day, light from the sun, who is an expression of Agni, enables man to go about his business; Agni is represented in the sky by Sūrya and is honoured as such (*R̥V*, X; 7, 1-3). Therefore Lord Agni is the one who illumines man by day and by night, physically and metaphysically as well as symbolically. Lord Agni enables man *to see*. Agni is implored to come out of darkness (*R̥V*, X; 1,1) as the one who subdues the gloom and fear of night (*R̥V*, 1; 143, 3—*R̥V*, X; 1,2) while 'Soma teaches the secret names of the Lord', perhaps by super-sensory perception.

Lord Agni-God

'O Agni . . . . through all thy fiery glow purify this prayer of ours . . . cleanse us with thy own cleansing power, purify me on every side . . . Savitr̥ God by both of these libations and purifying power (material and spiritual) purify me on every side'. Savitr̥ appears here fully in his role of Vivifier, Impeller, the personification of Life and Hope, because thanks to the heat and energy of fire he can maintain or restore health and life and he can give hope for the future. In conclusion, it seems obvious to me that Lord Agni is the path to knowledge through understanding (*R̥V*, I; 72); he stimulates the need to perform noble deeds (*R̥V*, I; 79, 9); Agni is therefore both the means to perform rites and knowledge itself; Agni enables man to take the appropriate action deriving from understanding. By meditation **vision** is enhanced: 'eyes that Soma gives' (*R̥V*, I; 139, 2).

Lord Agni in its fearful mood as anger and wrath and as destroyer of Rudra, received a different name: Manyu (*R̥V*, X; 83, 84) whose main duty is to destroy enemies.

The closing hymn of the *R̥V* is also dedicated to Agni (*R̥V*, X; 191) and shows a fully evolved concept of God. Lord Agni is now, in the present tense, the maifestation and trustee of the socio-political structure of the Āryans. The hope is expressed that man may have learned his lesson and that human beings may be able to unite for the welfare of all. Agni, God, is the power needed to ensure that this will take place, he enjoins men to 'assemble speak together; let your minds be of one accord. As ancient Gods unanimously sit down to their appointed share'. These terms are typically those of an evolved, well formed and mature religion that reflects a well structured society. Here Agni is the most ancient of the overlords, the wisest, the one who has the keys to the **Absolute Truth** as well as the keys of human truth. Agni has knowledge as well as power to impart that knowledge and guide and direct those who should disseminate that knowledge. Agni the mighty one, is the one who obtains all that his friends and worshippers require and he is requested to bring to man **all Gods** as he is enkindled. Thus at the end of the *R̥V* we find Agni as a fully developed totipotent God, no longer just an idea of what was perceived and of the much more that is not yet understood by man. Agni is the one who can direct the thoughts of **all** those assembled for worship; he can make them of a common mind and purpose; Agni more than an individual God has become a social and political God as well, though he has retained the exclusive quality of being **the ONE** worshipped in the Assembly. Man may learn his lesson and may human beings be able to unite for the well-being of all.

Agni has grown from being **Knowledge** to the personification of **Wisdom** itself. Agni is requested to 'make us sinless in the sight of Aditi, the original human mother, the one who cannot be divided, she who is free from bonds' (*R̥V*, IV; 12, 4) who is here invoked as the primeval giver of mental and spiritual humanhood. Agni is acclaimed as the guide, teacher and the one who helps men who have become 'weak of mind, of feeble understanding'... 'then the prudent discerning Agni worships the Gods ... in season' (*R̥V*, X; 2, 5). In other words, man recognizes his short-comings and to compensate for them he establishes rituals. Lord Agni illumines the path of eternity and of infinity, the **Space/Time continuum**. Thus Agni satisfies man's desire for fame and immortality, while Prajāpati is the first human father, whose antiquity is lost in time, who is as ancient as the beginning of man and 'the one who instituted the Vedic sacrifice'.

'Agni understands immortality' (*AV*, V; 30, 14); the *ṛṣis* of course knew that immortality of the body is impossible, but they postulated that immortality of the spirit, which is the energy and heat of Lord Agni that resides in the human body while alive, could be attained. In fact, through the enunciation of the *śruti* the *ṛṣis* themselves attained immortality in the minds of men and in mythology as the constellation of the *saptarṣi*, that points to the north. They taught men how to reach the goal of immortality by participating in the rites (*ṚV*, VIII; 44, 30) and praying to 'prolong our lives' (*ṚV*, VIII; 48, 3): 'we have drunk *soma* and become immortal; we have the light of God discovered'. The powerful effect of sound vibrations is also taken to 'give kinship with the Gods' (*ṚV*, IX; 10, 8); as well as the exhilarating power of *soma* and the enhancement of man through sound and thought. Rituals duly performed help to make man and all the nature of this world one with the universe, hence the conclusion that all is sacred. Would this be the great mystery of all Mysteries? Would it be the beginning of esotericism which is at the root of the secrecy of religions that are entirely revealed, if at all, only to the selected few? (*ṚV*, VIII; 44, 28 — *ṚV*, X; 85, 3) . . .'and let this man, God Agni, be with thee the singer of the praise: be gracious, holy one, to him'. In fact, these particular hymns are a good example of how philosophy of science becomes religion through the belief and faith in God who is the only omniscient and omnipotent. Hence the need to perform rites and rituals, to utter prayers and to be initiated. To rituals and prayers always new details are added to improve on their efficiency (*ṚV*, VIII; 45, 1); 'kindle the ritual fire to purify your heart'. In the *Vālakhilya* hymn XI (*ṚV*, VIII; 59, 6) it is said that 'God gave to the *ṛṣis*: revelation, thought and power of song'.

The meaning of the first and last hymns of the *ṚV Saṁhitā* (*ṚV*, I; 1 — *ṚV*, X; 191) is direct, concise and clear. Though rendered with slightly different variants by different commentators, the basic meaning is the same in all of them. There is no misunderstanding about what the two *ṛṣis* of the hymns at subsequent times had in mind and what it was that they had seen with the eyes of their mind. In comparing the two hymns, the evolution of the basic concept of the primordial God Agni into a well established, powerful and generally acknowledged God at the end of the *Saṁhitā* leaves no margin to doubt. These two hymns are explicit and only one interpretation with no double meaning is possible. This interpretation is that at the beginning only Agni is worshipped, eulogized and prayed to with the full consciousness and firm belief in the power and greatness of the idea of God who is Truth and Knowledge: 'Agni fill me with splendour' (*R̥V*, I; 23, 24). Later the concept of God is extended to other ideas and powers, but Agni remains omnipresent and omniscient (*R̥V*, I; 27, 2). At the end of the *R̥V*, Agni is a social God with polity and political power.

The dual divinity Indra-Agni is worshipped as wealth: Indra, and as rays of wisdom: Agni; while the vital breaths are the *śruti*. The physical counterpart of this allegory is the need of air for respiration (*R̥V*, I; 112, 4) and combustion; hence fire is described as the son of father wind and of mother sticks, the *araṇis*. Accordingly there are three types of fire rituals and oblations: (1) with food presentation and presence; (2) with *ghī*, for the sublimation of matter into spirit, and (3) for purification of dwellings and preparation of medicines for the body and the spirit. Agni is master of three worlds; physical, mental and spiritual (*R̥V*, I; 146, 1) and extends over **Time and Space**. **Time and space**, in reality, are one, or rather, two that merge into one another as a continuum.

In the Christian culture, St. Francis of Assisi who also lived in close partnership with nature, in his 'Chant of all Creatures' (*Cantico delle Creature*) sings:

> Praise to you, my Lord, for brother fire
> by which you illuminate the night and
> he is beautiful, jocund and strong.

To St. Francis fire is 'joyful, beautiful, and strong'; in the *R̥V* fire is 'vigorous and loud voiced'. Throughout the Judaico-Christian, Graeco-Roman, Druidic, Vedic and Hindu-Buddhist tradition, fire trials were common as 'divine judgements'. At present, fire walking is reputed to be safe only for the pure at heart. Fire has always been used to punish or test virtue, to destroy enemies and give supernatural powers to such as can manipulate it, such as the alchemists of medieval and Renaissance Europe. Flames of fire are seen as a halo around Gods as Saints of all religions (Vannucci, *Fire and Marksmanship*, 1995).

The dual divinity Indra-Agni appears to indicate the recognition that man is the sum total of physical power (Indra) and mental and spiritual power (Agni); a significant representation is 'O resplendent Indra-Agni (wealth and power), I looked around longing for weal' (*R̥V*, I; 109, 1, 2 *et al.*).

The most common epithet by which Agni is greeted (*R̥V*, I; 1 *et al.*) is 'adorable' but others are also frequent (*R̥V*, I; 127, 1, 2) such as 'divine keeper of truth and cosmic laws, luminous, resplendent, shining, giver and acceptor'. He is eulogized as messenger to the Gods and the one who brings the Gods to the sacrifice; he sits at every rite (*R̥V*, I; 14, 11) intermediate between men and God, he is the ancient (*R̥V*, II; 3, 1) and ever young.

Fire in agriculture and in everyday life as dispeller of humidity, fire as drier of green and wet firewood, animal hides and pelts, grains, is as important as fire giver of light and heat and fire for cooking. This is manifest in both the *R̥V*, I; 140 and 141 where Agni the priest is lauded for his use in agriculture and even more so in the *AV* where it is obvious in the repeated importance given to the *araṇis* and to the dried grass that receives the first sparks. Technicalities about the use of fire are given in some detail among other places in *R̥V*, III; 3. In the present context what should be pointed out is that the technicalities and practical aspects of dealing with and using fire are not to be confused with Lord Agni, though they come under the same name.

The repetition of the same adjectives for different Gods and the fact that most of them are in turn worshipped as '**the** Greatest', '**the** Mightiest', **the most** Wonderful, **most** Lovable, **most** Adorable, **most** Luminous and so on has created confusion in the mind of translators who cannot see how each and every God can be the Greatest. This is best explained by the reply given by a mother who was questioned about how could she truthfully and honestly write to each of her many sons: 'My **dearest** one'; the mother replied: 'Each son is truly the dearest'. This answer that all mothers will find natural and self-explanatory suggests the notion of a 'collective Absolute', a syncretism of all and everything that is one of the infinite characteristics of the Godhead. However, the frequency of superlatives in the Veda has often been mentioned as lack of consistency, or lack of will, intention or competence of the seers to draw a clear picture of the Vedic Religion; it has also been taken as a result of their inability to draw rational theories and to formulate a consistent religious doctrine. Ecologically speaking, however, since everything is related to everything else and since under different situations and at different times it is one or the other **ecological factor** that is the overruling or decisive one, it is as if a particular God or ecological **factor** is the one who does, i.e. the factor that is preponderant and is the regulatory element under the particular conditions and purpose being considered. It is ecologically correct to eulogize, address and consider as topmost different Gods under different contexts of place and time. Each God occupies a particular ecological niche, hence each factor or each God is addressed in turn as '**the Greatest**' because he is **de facto** the greatest, or the determining factor, or the most important factor at the particular time and place and situations, both natural and man-made. It must be made clear that most Gods are ideas and determining factors, but not the natural phenomenon itself.

The complexities and interactions of nature's ecological principles is also rendered in the multiplicity of meanings of single *stotras*, which again is an ecologically valid approach because every natural phenomenon is acted upon and in turn reacts to many different environmental variables at the same time. Ecological factors (from the Latin verb: *facĕre* = to do, to make; *factor* = the one who does, who orders) are the elements or impinging forces. Indra at times cannot be easily differentiated from Agni (*R̥V*, I; 15, 3) and from the sun, Sūrya, by the epithets addressed to them but it is clear from the context of the hymns that they are different personalities, different principles, different Gods or deities, different factors, different determinants. Thus I believe that we can safely conclude that most Gods of the Vedic man, as reflected in the Veda, mostly represent definite concepts rather than natural entities.

There is a great similarity also in the approach to Agni and Indra. Indra is the **King** of the Gods and as Dandekar has convincingly shown (1997), he would have been a successful chief of the Āryan tribes in their eastern migrations and occupation of Saptasindhu; in fact, the word **King** is more a human than a godly title. The deification of such a great leader is natural and God Indra has retained a number of purely human attributes and weaknesses. Leader of men and leader of Gods in battle, conqueror of lands and people, giver of wealth, God Indra is one who is typically not the deification of a concept, but the deification of a great man who was a giver of material benefits. Indra is also termed resplendent, noble, beneficial, glorious and of supreme intelligence, Indra brings light and form (*R̥V*, I; 6,3) to men as well as material wealth through his ability and valour in conquest. The thunderbolt and the lightning powers of Indra are more related to what in French would be described as '*foudre de guerre*' (lightning war-power) and his attributes are more generally linked to battles, wars and conquests. He is the great Lord, but is neither the primordial nor the supreme God, he is said to give light and life to the mind (*R̥V*, I; 6, 1) as the rays of dawn (*l.c.*, 3, 5), the one who brings wealth and is of adamantine justice (*R̥V*, I; 7, 2). But there is an important difference between Indra and Agni; Indra **is made** a

God because of his great deeds, while Agni is God by virtue of his own nature, because he is understanding, truth, knowledge and the immortality to which man aspires. Agni resides in the human mind, as part of the cosmic energy. Indra (*R̥V*, I; 8) brings fame, victory and power and the conqueror's land and riches to man, Indra is a deified myth based on the historical facts of the descent of the Āryans to the sub-continent. Agni in contrast brings the Gods as the 'willing ones' to man and he brings down himself (*R̥V*, I; 44, 8), Agni is the one who burns the bad things (*R̥V*, I; 12, 5), he is the sage, the purifier, just and good. Agni is described as 'our messenger (to the Gods)' (*R̥V*, I; 12) and he is source of inspiration, spiritual fire (*R̥V*, I; 21, 3), the *hotr̥*, the wise, master of wealth: intellectual, spiritual and material. Agni is bearer of oblations, much beloved, whose ordinances are true, resplendent, chastiser of mischievous people, sage lord of the house, guardian of virtuous peoples, ever young and ancient at the same time, purifier and with always renewed, always young splendour along with the wisdom of antiquity.

Agni is known from time immemorial (*R̥V*, VIII; 75, 1) and is invoked to bring forth valiant men and food: material, intellectual and spiritual, as 'food for thought'; he is the giver of joy and gives room, for instance by clearing the forests by fire (*R̥V*, VIII; 75, 11). Agni is seen as manifested in nature's glories and as a source of nature's gifts, while Indra is the distributor of man-conquered wealth. Agni, the enlightened and giver of enlightenment is called Jātavedas, the all knower and the great *asura* rich with magic power (*R̥V*, V; 12, 1 — *R̥V*, V; 15, 1). The dual divinity Indra-Agni associates Agni and Indra because, in a way, they complement one another.

Agni has a few distinctive appellations that are exclusively his; such as Tanunapāt or son of himself (*R̥V*, I; 13, 2 — *R̥V*, I; 142, 2 *et al.*) because fire is lit by fire and the concept of God implies that God **is** but cannot be generated by any other entity. Another significant appellation is Narāśaṁsa, the praise of man

(*R̥V*, I; 13, 3 *et al.*), or the one who shows the way (*R̥V*, I; 18, 9); Agni Vaiśvānara as beloved of all men because he gives supreme knowledge as well as practical usefulness that provides man with better goods, better implements and better weapons. Agni also gives brave men, brave warriors who will be the means by which Indra will become the great conqueror and king. Agni is the one who prepares the sacrificial food which in turn can also be interpreted, I believe, as 'the understanding necessary to attain **wisdom**', because knowledge is the food of the mind; 'where on the *barhiṣ*, the sacrificial grass, immortality is beheld' (or: can be reached, *R̥V*, I; 13, 5) and where the gates of *r̥ta* are opened to the mind (*R̥V*, I; 13, 6). Witnesses to this are Ilā (nourishment), Sarasvatī (flowing waters) and Mahī (the great one, *R̥V*, I; 13, 9) who are givers of comfort for body and soul. Tvaṣṭr̥, the skillful architect, and Agni are invoked to be present (*R̥V*. I; 13, 10) for the understanding and use of nature. Throughout Agni is the directing intelligent mind; as the *hotr̥* he ensures communion with the Gods, he is always the lord of the house and always kindled anew with lively flames.

The idea of God in early man would have been a mixture of wonder, fear and interest to obtain help, support and practical benefits. Agni is both intangible as God and utilitarian, as fire. Agni as everything else has multiple manifestations and plays many roles; he is character and mind purifier (*R̥V*, I; 13, 1) and also, as fire, the means to clean infected wounds, purify the house and stable and burn away all pollution and disease; fire is used for smelting and purifying metals from their ores, to make steel and extract active plant substances by crushing, boiling and distillation (*R̥V*, I; 36). As purifier *par excellence*, Agni is present in the house fire and at all Vedic sacrifices, he brings physical and spiritual food (*R̥V*, I; 31, 11), Agni God and common fire are distinct (*R̥V*, I; 26, 7): 'may he be our dear household Lord . . . we with bright fires be dear to him' (Griffith transl.) or 'may the Lord of men . . . be dear to us and may we also be dear to our Lord by our spiritual favour (SS and SV transl.); in *R̥V*, I; 36 'the ancient' may be Lord Agni and the 'young one' the newly kindled fire. But either as God or as common fire, Agni is everywhere and always present, unborn as all-pervading potential energy, or born by friction (*R̥V*, I; 67) or otherwise manifested. Repeatedly the creative power of Agni Vaiśvānara is invoked (*R̥V*, VI; 9,3 *et al.*).

Fire has been a boon to man (*R̥V*, II; 1, 2) who recognizes (*R̥V*, 26, 8-10) that the 'Gods adored with brilliant fires have granted precious wealth to us. So with bright fires we pray to thee' (Agni) . . .'with all thy fires find pleasure in this our sacrifices and this our speech, O son of strength' (Griffith transl). 'Blessed by you men with spiritual fervour imbibe the best of your qualities; may they use them to help mankind' (*l.c.*). 'O. . .venerable God, source of strength, may you with your life giving energy. . . guide us with sacred wisdom (*R̥V*, I; 31). This vividly conjures the image of the beginning and evolution of the thought of Agni as God, the one who is frequently mentioned as the original God 'the best and earliest Aṅgiras', 'a God among Gods' and where the mythology in support to the statement follows: 'Agni, revealer of the *śruti* to mortal men and giver of wisdom'.

The magical aspect of Lord Agni may have been represented by the mythical being unclearly described as a 'divine horse' (meaning, I believe, **power**) called Dadhikrās or Dadhikrāvan to whom fire hymns are dedicated (*R̥V*, III; 20 — *R̥V*, IV; 38, 40 — *R̥V*, VII; 44) and 'from whom came the gift in early times'. Dadhikrās has been identified by commentators with the morning sun, which cannot be correct since he is '**compared**' and '**likened**' to the sun, **not identified** with it. In fact, Lord Agni as God is never fully understood (*R̥V*, V; 19, 1).

Fire is red and yellowish and to this day red is an auspicious and well liked colour and ochre-yellow or red is the colour of the robe of *sādhus* and *lāmās*; at *Holī*, red is the most widely used colour and, of course, it is the colour of the bride's attire. Agni Vaiśvānara is the friend of man (*R̥V*, I; 59) in that he is not aloof (*l.c.*) and he is always at hand to help man as lord of all bounties, plants, animals, and minerals (?), literally what is mentioned is: 'riches in the mountains', which could be mineral ores. The Aravalli hills were mined for copper ores as far back as C-14-dated more than 3000 years BP, and 'sustain man as deep planted pillar'. As common fire, Agni exists (*ṚV*, IV; 33-37) to satisfy the Gods with hard work with the approval of the great ancient architect Tvaṣṭṛ. The legend regarding the deft-handed Ṛbhus is very old and the Ṛbhus themselves are deified humans associated with the Ādityas and experts in 'the ancient sacrifices'; the hymns related to the Ṛbhus and to Tvaṣṭṛ by sage Vāmadeva are indeed pure science and technology in poetic form.

Maybe a word would be in order here to further distinguish between Agni as fire, that indicates strength, Agni as Sūrya that indicates energy, and Agni as Śakti, that indicates power, as can be deduced from the context of the hymns of the *ṚV* that taken together constitute powerful internal evidence.

In conclusion, Fire appears as heat, light and flames and as 'other fires' (*ṚV*, I; 59, 1) including other forms of energy such as life processes and basic technologies. The living body is warm, the sick body is hot and the dead body is cold. Cooked food is better for the health and makes stronger people, the tip of sticks can be hardened by fire and fired pottery is harder and lasts longer than sun-baked earthen pottery or bricks. Accordingly I tried to find out whether there is in the Veda: 1. discrimination between fire and Agni; 2. evidence of the use of fire in science and technology; and 3. mention of the antiquity of Agni as God.

1. Discrimination between common fire and Lord Agni: the omnipresence of Agni is repeatedly stated and the omniscience of Agni Jātavedas is a recurrent theme; consequently, as discussed above, Agni **Is** God, the primordial God (*AV*, III; 20, 21) differentiated from common fire that was made Agni Vaiśvānara. On the other hand, common fire is a manifestation or an

expression of Lord Agni and this is also the Zoroastrian viewpoint. As fire, Lord Agni has many ways of expressing himself, but fire for technical purposes is respected and eulogized through the Ṛbhus.

According to Schuré (1899), the great scholar of esoteric traditions, Agni is the first born among the Gods, the lord and generator of sacrifices, the conveyor of all mystical speculations, he has sacrificed himself as his object, he generates other Gods, organizes the world, produces and maintains universal life and is a cosmogonic power. It seems to me that though not in the correct chronological order, Schuré describes the 'career' of Lord Agni, from his first birth as God in the mind of early man to the Jātavedas of the Veda, and the energy/matter concept of modern physics.

Common fire is natural phenomenon and is used in many ways as 'he who travels in various directions'; in fact, man mastered the art of making and using fire in many ways since hundreds of centuries ago. Physically Agni burns, spiritually he destroys evil thoughts and intellectually he provides for acquiring and keeping knowledge (*ṚV*, I; 79). But Lord Agni as spiritual fire (*ṚV*, I; 19, 2) is beyond complete comprehension and perfect mental representation. The name of the God and of common fire may have remained the same, but the concepts of Lord Agni encompasses much more than just common fire. He is terrific (*ṚV*, I; 19, 5), both benevolent and protective and agitator of major forces such as clouds, rains, oceans (*ṚV*, I; 19, 8) and like Savitṛ, among other means, he expresses himself through Sūrya.

Finally the dual aspect of Agni God and *agni* fire is clear in *ṚV*, I; 99, where Jātavedas the all knower is invoked to 'consume as fire the wealth of the enemy and as God to carry us through grief and troubles as a boat across the river'. Fire destroys the forest, but also clears the way for agriculture and pasture land; he protects as a guard and is inspirer of sacred actions and promotes prayers. Agni lies in the innermost core of the heart (*R̥V*, I; 145, 5) where the soul resides, but man depends also on common fire for practical purposes of everyday life (*R̥V*, I; 150).

2. Evidence of the use of fire in science and technology: internal evidence in the Veda shows that the knowledge of the origin and the use of fire by Vedic man and by the other men with whom they came in contact, was lost in the ancient past. I mentioned above the triple meaning and triple nature of the Vedic language. Two such meanings are usually easy to perceive, one is material and the other spiritual. The third or divine and esoteric meaning is meant exclusively for the education of the initiated few. It is spelt out as mnemonic series of catchwords rather than explanation of a subject that would have already been discussed orally at length during the period of teaching and indoctrination of the *śiṣyas* by the *guru*. The esoteric meaning is subject to different interpretations and may have been formulated differently by various commentators, philosophers, scholars and translators. It must be noted that even where purely technical uses of fire are intended, Lord Agni is invoked before any major, or minor, enterprise is undertaken. This practice is quite natural since there is no distinction or rift between sacred and profane. The fundamental concept of the Indian tradition that everything is made sacred by the omnipresence of Agni God, is ecologically valid; fire and God Agni and their respective ecological roles are perhaps nowhere else described as well as in *R̥V*, I; 65 to 73, specially hymn 67.
3. The antiquity of Agni: very early (*R̥V*, I; 31—*R̥V*, I; 189)

> fire-worship was instituted and already in the *Ṛ̥V* it is recognized as an ancient practice (*Ṛ̥V*, I; 36, 4 — *Ṛ̥V*, I; 96, 1-3 — *Ṛ̥V*, 127, 10). Agni is said to be the 'first to come among the divines'; Agni is 'the **early Aṅgiras**, a God and God's auspicious friend' and 'the sages were born after thy laws, active in their wisdom' (M. Müller transl.). Earlier commentators (MM. and Oldenberg, 1895, p. 53) saw (*Ṛ̥V*. I; 60, 1) reference to the celestial **and** terrestrial birth of Agni, who was brought to Bhṛ̥gu and Mātariśvan as well as reference to the mythical ancestors, the *ubhayāsaḥ* who first established the sacrifice to Agni.

In *Ṛ̥V*, I; the expression of Agni through Sūrya had already matured fully in the Agastya hymns and at the end of the *Saṁhitā* (*Ṛ̥V*, X; 183, 3) Lord Agni is well established as the giver of life and energy and **He** expresses himself 'in plants and herbs, in all existing beings I have deposited the germ of increase. All progeny of Earth have I engendered, and sons in women who will be thereafter' (transl. Griffith).

I would refer back to Dandekar (1979a) who draws attention to the spiritual aspect of the Vasiṣṭha hymns and who sees the origin of *bhakti* in the powerful addresses of the *ṛṣi* to Varuṇa. Dandekar also shows that the *asu* or significance of Varuṇa can be understood as the 'one who possesses magical power'. It is possible to perceive a strong belief in absolute monism throughout the *Maṇḍala* VIIth of the *Ṛ̥V*, where Agni personifies knowledge, abstract and practical, and Varuṇa personifies the unintelligible and unexplained aspects of the universe; for this reason Varuṇa operates through his *asu* and is magic itself. Vasiṣṭha firmly believes that 'no secret can be withheld from your knowledge'; (*Ṛ̥V*, VII; 61, 5) in a hymn addressed to Mitra-Varuṇa, the practical/theoretical pair, the direct and indirect knowledge, the day-to-day reality of the world in which the *ṛṣi* lived, but the *ṛṣi* also believes in the ultrasensory reality that he sensed as the power of Varuṇa, which is above man's comprehension.

It is possible to render most, or much of the VIIth *Maṇḍala* in plain bio-ecological terms, since 'men in deep thought engendered glorious Agni' (*R̥V*, VII; 1, 1) . . . Lord of the homestead . . . to be honoured in the home forever (*R̥V*, VII; 1, 2) friend and granter of wealth and wisdom (*l.c.*, 1, 5) far seeing (*R̥V*, VII; 4), wise and generous, **who has allowed man to seize him.** The words indicate the gratefulness of the thinking man, the scientist who becomes one with God, which **is that** which he has understood. Further the '*r̥ṣi* is to bring help to men' (*R̥V*, VII; 26, 5) from what he has understood. However, at this stage the identification of man with the Godhead is qualified, because only the **consecrated fire** is **Agni God**.

The syncretism of the Vasiṣṭha hymns lead to a naturalistic monism that pervades Indian philosophy and the Indian way of thinking and living that culminated with Ādi Śaṅkara. Much later in Italy it found expression through Giordano Bruno who expressed comparable ideas of a general, all-pervading, naturalistic pantheism. An example of the inter-relationship that the *r̥ṣis* saw in all aspects of nature is expressed in *R̥V*, VII; 12, 13 where 'Agni, thou art Varuṇa and Mitra; Agni is the great God that comes from all directions' and has all meanings and values; Agni is eulogized as the enlightener of all, who has filled heaven and earth with his energy and knowledge. Agni taught how to pray and gave practical advices as well.

The first hymn of the third *Maṇḍala* (*R̥V*, III; by *r̥ṣi* Viśvāmitra) can be read as the evolution of Agni from fire and sun into food; it also indicates growing complexity of rituals that develop to satisfy the striving for perfection and the desire of man to always surpass himself. Perfectionism in this case aims at more and more powerful worship of Lord Agni and the acquisition of magical powers. It is the same *furore* that struck Michelangelo Buonarroti who left his masterpieces unfinished and his body exhausted because he could never reach to the level of perfection that his own super-ego demanded, nor could he attain the beauty of the works of the God in which he devoutly believed. The achievements of giants like *ṛṣi* Viśvāmitra, *ṛṣi* Bharadvāja, *ṛṣi* Vasiṣṭha or Michelangelo Buonarroti were not by them considered to be achievements; they considered them only as a partial unveiling of *ṛta*; they were always unsatisfied with their own work and were tormented by a feeling of failing and falling short of their high ideals; almost a feeling of guilt, of being unworthy and unable to muster the perfection that they demanded of themselves but that they saw only in God.

It is not only in India or in the Āryan or Indo-European world that fire is an omnipresent reality. To this day man-made fire is kept to honour and be honoured in homes and places of worship, by people of many cultures and is often taken as manifestation of God.

However, as an after-thought, a sad remark: when man learned how to make fire, he likened himself to God as he conceived it; then, as the apprentice sorcerer that man is by nature, he become afraid of his own creation and had to propitiate it 'at Ilā's holy place'. The beginning of man's pride is evident in *ṚV*, I; 95, 9: 'O fire divine, kindled by us. . .' and in *ṚV*, I; 127, 8 where fire is called 'the guest of man'. Rituals therefore had to be developed also to appease man's own fear and to request boons. With time, inevitably, rituals became more and more complex: 'may we improve the rites with new performance' (*ṚV*, I; 31, 8) and finally, they may become an end in themselves (*AV*, XIX; 43, 1); 'O Agni thou wast born for our purpose' (*AV*, I; 7, 6).

In another context Dandekar (1979a, p. 7) proves that rituals came later and younger members of the Vedic pantheon are more prominent in Vedic rituals than older Gods such as Agni or Savitṛ themselves.

Undoubtedly Vedic man perceived that all light on Earth is the outcome of combustion, which is fire or Agni in his many different manifestations. Agni expresses himself also as enlightenment of the spirit and of the mind. The light of perception and understanding are a result of Agni as energy. The cold light produced by phosphorescent animals such as fire-flies or fire-beetles, is the exception rather than the rule. Man the Inventor was able to invent cold light, also called tubelight, only as late as the twentieth century and that too, as the result of a practical joke.

In conclusion, all light and warmth, far or near, directly or indirectly, comes from Lord Agni. Vedic man saw no other light.

By thee, O Agni, Varuṇa who guards the law, Mitra and Aryaman, the Bounteous are made strong;

For as the felly holds the spokes, thou with thy might pervading hast been born encompassing them round.

ṚV, I; 141, 9 (transl. Griffith)

Agni was born the first of all, like Sūrya lovely with his light; with lustre these have spread abroad.

ṚV, VIII; 7, 36 (transl. Griffith)

6

Lord Savitṛ, Life and Hope

Let no one here debar me from enjoying the
golden light which Savitṛ diffuses
He covers both all-fostering worlds with praise
even as a woman cherishes her children.
*Ṛ*V, III; 38, 8

In Ṛgvedic times there probably was no differentiation between the spiritual and the intellectual, as there was probably no differentiation between knowledge and truth. Truth was knowledge and intellectual was spiritual. This is one reason why ideas could be as concrete as what we now call 'real' and this is also one reason why I believe that abstract ideas, or ideas/concepts and deified ideas would have preceded the personalized forms of anthropomorphic divinities. It is what in brief I stated as 'philosophy precedes religion'. Thus, coming back to my initial proposition that the ancient-most God or Gods are personifications of ideas/concepts, I see Savitṛ as the very ancient characterisation of the abstract concept of Life, 'the Life in living', the **it** that makes **living beings** a category apart. As 'fireness in fire', the idea of 'life in living' once it was conceived, must have been one of the most bewildering thoughts man ever had.

Savitṛ the God is often mentioned in association with Bhaga, a deified man, the Āditya who brings good fortune and therefore gives Hope.

It appears logical to speculate that early man must have wondered frequently over the magical miracle that is life, and the generation of new life. First as an idea of something that exists but is intangible, like the energy and the power of fire, then as a concept of something that makes a body different before and after death, the wonder of **living** and the concept of **life** must have developed into the concept and characterization of Savitṛ. The concept of Hope is implicit in the concept of Life; 'for my protection I invoke the golden handed Savitṛ' . . . 'praise the water offering, O Savitṛ' . . . 'we call on him . . . on Savitṛ who looks on men' (*Ṛ̥V*, I; 22, 5-7). The concept of Life is different, unique and means more than the concept of just being alive, or the concept of energy or life-energy. Agni is the energy in nature, but this is not the same as the concept of Life, which is the essence of living. Agni is powerful and strong in his physical aspects (*Ṛ̥V*, I; 94, 12), he can sooth the wrath of Mitra, Varuṇa and the Maruts, because they are all dependent on him, and he intercedes for the natural forces of water, earth and air to protect man; in other words the powerful Agni is to be invoked for protection against the unleashed fury of nature against which puny man is helpless, but Savitṛ who is always gentle and not particularly strong is otherwise extremely powerful since he is that something, the indescribable life-principle that uses the energy and power of Agni to generate and maintain life in living beings. Early man recognized that the life principle is the same in all living beings. Without the active presence of the 'life principle', Agni himself would be unable to create and sustain life. It is abundantly clear that 'energy' is one that moves the cosmos in its different aspects, including the world we live in; this energy is equated with Lord Agni, the essence of fire; only Agni can protect man against himself, but only Savitṛ can impart, create and sustain life and only he can put in motion what can move, including astral bodies who are imbued with a life of their own, the explanation of which is inaccessible to earth-bound man.

Savitṛ as the essence of being alive, controls and directs living beings; in other words that undefinable, non-material, unbound principle that makes a living being different from a dead body, is Savitṛ. Savitṛ is compared to a mother, the original human mother Aditi, who is the unbound, unfettered who vivifies, stimulates, regulates movement and life processes. Savitṛ similarly impels life processes and the act of living in the right direction and of course he is in direct association with *ṛta* that is all law and order of the cosmos, inclusive of the law of all matter, ways and means that make life possible. Savitṛ in the Gāyatrī *mantra* is associated to, but is not identical with Sūrya who is at the root of the web of life on Earth. 'Of Savitṛ the God, the sapient *asura*, we crave this great gift which is worthy of our choice' (*ṚV*, IV; 53, 1 — transl. Griffith).

Savitṛ is the personalization of the concept of the most impressive magic, the one that makes the act of living possible; he is the concretization of the very difficult to understand and impossible to explain idea of **Life**, that, unlike fire, man is unable to create. **Life** is a riddle that man has been unable to solve to this day in any of its multiple aspects. Life may well have been seen as an act of magic of *asura* Varuṇa and Savitṛ himself would be imbued with Varuṇa's magic power of *asu*. Life is the most precious possession of man, hence the golden hue, the golden hands and arms, the golden tongue, the **multiform** golden and bright chariot of Savitṛ and his association with the golden Sūrya. The chariot that carries Savitṛ has an infinite variety of forms and is bright as life itself. Sūrya is then an expression of Agni, the mediator for the realization of life that begins on earth with the photosynthetic process, active only in the presence of light.

Savitṛ endowed with great *asurya* raises his golden arms, he is motion and life in motion and he distributes these powers among all beings. The 'gesticulation of the God is . . . typical of the great world magician producing his magnificent magic'

(Dandekar 1979a, p. 25) which, as I see it, is **Life**. By the movements of arms and fingers Savitṛ infuses life, at dawn night is sent away to await his arrival (*ṚV*, I; 113, 1) and he, Savitṛ awakes all diurnal animals and man while he puts to sleep the nocturnal animals, the process is reversed at dusk when Savitṛ puts to sleep diurnal animals, men and green plants and awakens nocturnal animals, thus completing the most basic cycle, the day-night cycle. Savitṛ, the God true-minded (*ṚV*, I; 73, 2), also puts to rest, temporarily and permanently when he spells the end of living and the advent of death; 'for thou art might to produce and lull to rest the world of life . . . ' (*ṚV*, VI; 71, 2).

Savitṛ has a well marked personality within the Varuṇa philosophical complex, as discussed by Dandekar (*l.c.*, 1-27) and guided by my stated biological bias I concluded that the beautiful mysterious figure of God Savitṛ is the personalization of the idea of Life and Hope. God Savitṛ is the Enlivener, Vivifier, Supporter, Impeller, Luminous; throughout the Veda the aspects of Savitṛ as motion are emphasized, and life is motion. I see Varuṇa encompassing all magic, all the *asu*, all that in the universe is not understood or explained by man and I see Savitṛ as the abstract idea of Life; Savitṛ represents that aspect of Varuṇa's *māyā* that refers to the presence of all life on Earth and that he, Savitṛ, as the Grand Stimulator and Vivifier, 'puts in motion'. Savitṛ the Lord is Life itself, and Hope, represented by Bhaga, his regular associate: 'may Bhaga and Savitṛ send us forth', for instance *ṚV*, V; 42, 5 — *ṚV*, V; 82, 1 — *ṚV*, VII; 38, 1.

As mentioned above (Chapter 3) magical powers are invoked and become necessary to represent mentally those phenomena that are not otherwise obvious to the intellect and as Dandekar points out, Savitṛ transcends the limitations implied by the nature of Sūrya and, I would add, of all other Gods with whom he has been identified at one time or the other by different commentators.

The perception of the existence of an imponderable, invisible, barely perceptible **something** that now we call 'life' and formulation of the idea of life as a moving principle or acting idea, the formulation of the working concept of life is an intellectual feat as great as the formulation of the concept of *ākāśa*, or later on, the concept of *śūnya* or zero.

Savitṛ is as much the life principle in men, women and children as he is the life principle in all animals and plants as well as in the unseen, but well manifested in their effects, living things that multiply and turn milk into curds or cause the fermentation of plant juices; they all grow, multiply and generate something similar to themselves.

According to Dandekar, the word Savitṛ derives from the root *sū* (to stimulate, to vivify) and 'the activity suggested by the root *sū* is very often characterized by some form of mystical or magical power' . . . '*sū* denotes . . . some form of magical underlying a sort of magical charging' (Dandekar, *l.c.*, p. 23). Savitṛ therefore is not only the stimulator, the Vivifier, the Initiator, but he is also somewhat mysterious, as life also is. The Vedic approach to and representation of the mysteries of life is logical; the mysteries of living and dying have been a constant preoccupation of all men at all times. Undoubtedly life is the greatest of all magics and mysteries and one of the most direct concern ever.

Dandekar (*l.c.*) published a thorough study of Savitṛ and convincingly showed that the 'essential nature' and 'personality of Savitṛ is only an aspect of Varuṇa', that 'the movement of Savitṛ's hands and fingers is particularly emphasized by the Vedic poets' . . . and that 'Savitṛ of the *ṚV* is a representation of Varuṇa in his special gesture as commandant and the magician of the world, a gesture which is easily the most impressive and at the same time the most expressive of the essential personality and nature of that God'. However, it appears to me that Savitṛ is more than just a representation of Varuṇa; he has a reality of his own as the grand Vivifier and since only Savitṛ can 'put in motion' or give life, he must be the essence of life itself.

I should like to point out that essentially my reading does not differ from the interpretation given by Dandekar; all the references that the master quotes agree also with my reading. The latter, however, adds one more dimension to the description of the personality of the Great Savitṛ. My interpretation expands the God's attributes and characteristics: it expands the meaning and concept as the life principle itself which pervades all those components of the universe whom we recognize as 'living'. My reading upgrades, if I may say so, Lord Savitṛ to be the **essence of Life** itself. In the reading of this biologist, Savitṛ is first and foremost the Vivifier, the one who gives life, because it is he who is **The Life-principle itself**; Savitṛ is therefore the source of Life, the same life that he ceaselessly regulates. Each line, each verse of the Veda bear literal, intellectual, spiritual, mythological, symbolic and figurative meanings, all of them valid, specially when dealing with such complex a phenomenon as Life; thus, none of the possible readings necessarily invalidates earlier readings that were 'decoded' with different 'keys'. I have used a bio-ecological key.

Dandekar (*l.c.*) also showed that Savitṛ is a very ancient God; he is associated with the older Gods and can be traced back to the proto-Āryan ideology; Savitṛ is not, as some authors supposed, a newcomer to the Vedic pantheon. This conclusion confirms my opinion that the original God or Gods are born of abstract ideas that evolve into concepts that later become anthropomorphic and are finally encompassed in the religious canon by rites and rituals. 'The Wise One arrays himself in every form: for quadruped and biped he hath brought forth food' (*ṚV*, V; 81, 2).

All Gods are alive, hence they cannot resist Savitṛ's will.

Savitṛ, genderless like Agni, perhaps combines the attributes of both sexes because the act of living, the essence of life and the physico-chemical processes that sustain life are sexless and irrelevant of sex-attributes; living is a magic in itself, exclusive and never duplicated, accordingly I see that Savitṛ 'includes and transcends the distinctive figures of all these Gods' (Dandekar, *l.c.*, p. 15). Sūrya visibly and physico-chemically puts life to work through photosynthesis, while Savitṛ is the subtle, imponderable principle that, among infinite other acts, also makes real, enacts photosynthesis. Savitṛ enables Sūrya and Agni to promote the life processes that can be gauged, for instance growth, maturity, reproduction, senescence. Sūrya is seen correctly as light, Agni as heat or energy in general (*ṚV*, X; 114, 1) while Savitṛ remains indefinable: 'O much praised vital principle, O Savitṛ' . . . 'when the adorable Lord . . . mounts high . . . then bipeds and quadrupeds and the flying birds in the fulfilment of their ambitions are set to their tasks' (*ṚV*, VIII; 27, 12 — SS and SV transl.) or: 'May this God Savitṛ, the Lord, the offspring of waters, pouring down his dew be gracious' (*ṚV*, VI; 50, 13).

God Savitṛ as the Enlivener is associated to water and air, or wind, *prāṇa*, without which the life-principle cannot express itself nor become a concrete reality; life cannot be put in motion or exist without water and air (*ṚV*, II; 38, 2). Water is offered to Sūrya with cupped hands when greeting him at sunrise, and Savitṛ drives away immaterial evil spirits and he is sinless.

In a comparable manner we may conclude that Lord Savitṛ can give and withdraw life of living beings; he is the **it** that makes a living body different from a dead one, the **it** by which Lord Agni can act, the **it** that generates, sustains and destroys life; (*ṚV*, I; 150, 1). 'Most gracious God who brings to life and lulls to rest, he who controls the world, what moves not and what moves, may he vouchsafe us shelter — Savitṛ the God — for tranquil life, with triple bar against distress' (*ṚV*, IV; 53, 6). 'Full of wisdom . . . the

God stretched out golden arms that he may bring forth life' (*R̥V*, VI; 71, 1).

Savitr̥ is often described in terms of life-cycles (*R̥V*, II; 38, 4 — *R̥V*, III; 33, 6) such as circadian rhythms or the awakening after night's rest; he controls and separates time intervals and the duration of cycles and parts thereof, like the seasons and day and night . . . 'the night obeys Savitr̥' and he is called when the soul is ready to depart.

As life-order Savitr̥ is praised and, significantly in the same hymn (*R̥V*, I; 22, 9-12), Agni is requested to bring the spouses of the Gods and heroes, who are individually named and who, evidently, indicate the feminine role in the perpetuation of human life. In other words, thanks to the energy of Agni and to Savitr̥'s magic, life can be maintained and regenerated through feminine power and intervention. But, since there can be no life without water 'rich in wealth', water is also invoked (*R̥V*, I; 22, 14) in the same context. Waters or liquids hold all medicines and hold, potentially, the energy of fire (*R̥V*, I; 23), 'waters' include semen. Savitr̥'s association with Agni is clear (*R̥V*, I; 95, 7) and the latter is said to 'stretch his arms (flames) with might like Savitr̥'.

Savitr̥ the God true-minded (*R̥V*, I; 73, 2) has also an ethical aspect since he is said to make man sinless, which means disease-free, and therefore man should not become a hazard or handicap to his family and the society at large; the expression of making man sinless can also be read as an encouragement given to man to use life properly. Illness and poor health were regarded as punishment for transgressing *r̥ta* or as the result of a curse that might have been well deserved. The sun is Savitr̥'s *sūryāśmi* and he is mentioned as Varuṇa's eye. Savitr̥ bestows immortality to the R̥bhus for their good deeds (*R̥V*, I; 110, 3) and to meritorious men (*R̥V*, IV; 54, 2, 5-6) while Varuṇa guards the immortal world of the non-living. Savitr̥ binds living beings with the laws that control and regulate all the cosmos from the movement of the celestial bodies, believed to be alive because they move, like Sūrya himself and which are all included in *ṛta*, to the invisible creatures that make curds and other foods.

When man conceived the idea/concept of Life, the pair Life/Hope was born, because Life engenders Hope, hence the pair Life/Hope, or Savitṛ/Bhaga. As an old saying goes: 'While there is Life, there is Hope'; hope in every sense, including hope of further understanding.

Finally I would recall that it is Sāvitrī, daughter of king Aśvapati, a name that is probably a symbol of all Āryans, who outwits Yamarāja himself and causes life to return to the dead body of her husband Satyavān, the truthful.

The reading of the hymns dedicated to Savitṛ bring to the mind's eyes the image of puzzled *ṛṣis* thinking about 'what is life'? — 'what keeps it going'? — 'by what magic does it develop and evolve'? — 'is being alive the same in what moves and moves not'? — 'what is this **it** whose absence spells death'?

> *Savitṛ God who looks at every creature*
> *laying to rest the immortal and the mortal*
> *. . . he, Savitṛ, gold-handed Asura, kind leader*
>
> ṚV, I; 35, 2 and 35, 10

> *For thou (Savitṛ) at first producest for the holy*
> *Gods the noblest of all portions, immortality;*
> *Thereafter as a gift to men,*
> *O Savitṛ, thou openest existence, life succeeding life.*
>
> ṚV, IV; 54, 2 (transl. Griffith)

7

Conclusion

Contemporary and Vedic Expression of Ecology

THE word 'Ecology' is a relatively recent addition to the scientific vocabulary; it is not much older than about 100 years. It literally means the 'science of the house'. More specifically, Ecology is the description and analysis of the structure and function of the environment in which living beings exist and of which they are a part. The interrelationships of living beings among themselves and with the environment as well as the laws that govern these processes and interactions are the subject-matter of ecology. The environment in which biological species live includes both living and non-living things, therefore all the factors that influence the existence of life and reproduction of plants, animals and microbes are the object of ecological studies.

Andrewartha, *et al.* (1954) defined ecology as the study of the distribution and abundance of individuals of biological species. Obviously the presence or absence and the number of individuals of any species at a given place and time is the result of the sum total of the positive and negative factors that favour or prevent the life and reproduction of that particular species at that particular place and time.

How did ancient man perceive the relationships of cause and effect of living beings among themselves and with their environment? Present-day ecology goes into details of physical, chemical, biological, socio-economic, climatic, geographic and other aspects of these relationships and interactions; how far did **Ṛgvedic man** progress towards identifying these relationships? Did man in those far away days develop a methodology adequate to analyse processes and to apply the results of the analyses to practical purposes? How far did man go in altering the functioning or dynamics of natural ecosystems? How was the socio-economic structure of the community of man influenced by climates and ecological features and how did he react to them?

From the previous chapters it is clear the Ṛgvedic man did not formulate ecological or any other scientific theory in the contemporary sense of the word 'scientific theory'. The question is, did he perceive the principles on which scientific theories were later based? How much was his culture influenced by the different environments that he occupied?

The answer to these questions is that he did study the environment, that he drew practical conclusions from his studies and that his culture was, as all other cultures, strongly influenced by his environment. Indeed he reacted to it by developing a way of life systematized down to the minutest details of the daily activities and habits of the individual, of the community, of man's participation in the cosmic drama and in his religious beliefs and life. The fundamental questions that ancient man put to himself would have been related to what we now call matter and energy, matter in general and energy as power; to man's place in nature; to life, death and disease; to immortality and the means to satisfy his own needs. With time also questions such as 'where am I', 'who am I', 'where do I come from' would lead to philosophical and religious speculations. However the first observations and lessons that man learned from nature would have been related to what we now know to be the fundamental questions of the present-day science of ecology; they were matters of survival importance, related to matter and energy, to space and time, to life and hope.

The single most important ecological principle is that of 'competitive exclusion'. According to this principle two biological species cannot occupy the same ecological niche indefinitely; this is where enters the concept of space and time. This principle was first formulated mathematically by Volterra (1926, 1928) and later elaborated biologically by Gause (1934, 1935), Hutchinson (1959, 1961), Margalef (1956, 1958a, 1958b), Odum (1971) and other ecologists, including myself. Ancient man could not be aware of the subtle reason why two species cannot co-exist indefinitely in a limited space and time under constant environmental conditions, though he could easily see that two material bodies cannot occupy the same place in space at the same time. Matter and energy are more readily understood than space and time. Man perceived life as a constant struggle and as such it is often mentioned in the Veda and in the Avesta. However, it would have been difficult to perceive that each individual and each species lives in an hypervolume where the vectors representing ecological factors unremittingly change in magnitude and direction. The ecological niche concept is better understood as an idealized hypervolume of conditions formed by an infinitely large number of vectors that endlessly change form and dimensions. Another reason why this would be difficult to perceive is that unending changes in the magnitude and duration of ecological factors cause both a short-term and a long-term variability of the environment of each and all ecological niches at all times. Uninterrupted and continuous changes of every ecological factor along time is perceived as movement and growth, phenomena of which ancient man was well aware of, as he was also aware of the continuous change and evolution of everything. In this sense the *ṛṣis* and all ancient thinkers would be, in contemporary ecological terms, ecologists of the Andrewartha school since they would see the changes of the distribution and abundance of individuals of the different species in space and time, even without knowing or understanding how this would happen and what would be the underlying causes.

Ancient man would be aware only of the end-result of the dynamics of ecological factors of which he would otherwise be totally ignorant.

The main conclusion of the theory of competitive exclusion which is mathematically correct, would seem to be empirically false, unless we realize that constant actions and reactions take place between an infinitely large number of ecological factors. The whole is extremely complex and unless we undertake strict scientific analyses, we would perceive only the end-results but not the details. Laboratory experiments under strictly controlled conditions have repeatedly proven the theory to be correct, but its empirical aspects were the only ones that early ancient man could in fact see and sense from his own participation in the dynamics of the world around him.

In fact, Vedic *ṛṣis* saw harmonious movement everywhere; they saw constant changes within the harmony of nature and this they interpreted as the law and order of the universe, *ṛta*. It is in this sense that celestial bodies, rivers, forests and living beings, move around and grow and reproduce and thus participate in the universal life and movement. Matter and energy are everything down to the atomic levels; it is the interaction of the two members of this couple that originates life and maintains it. This active and effective principle man saw in Fire, Lord Agni. He recognized it in the five *mahābhūta* or elements of existence: earth (solid matter), water (liquid matter), air (subtle matter), fire (energy) and *ākāśa* that is the other side of the coin (void, non-existence, the opposite of matter).

The ancient *ṛṣis* put to good use the knowledge of nature gained through empiricism and experimentation as well as that borrowed from other cultures. By and large the use that the *ṛṣis* made of nature, of good Mother Earth and of water, the cleansing one, was wise. Large-scale degradation of the environment by over-exploitation was avoided thanks to the small number of human beings that was then well below the carrying capacity of the ecosystem; also some forms of management of the environment were developed through irrigation, forestry practices and animal husbandry as well as agriculture. The deep respect for the Life Principle personified by Lord Savitṛ and inherent in all living beings, made man one of the many knots of a very complex web, rather than the centre of a universe created for the use and benefit of man himself, as vouchsafed by later creeds. Man saw himself as one of the many elements of the life web; though to his own eyes he was the most important of all he did realize that he had to attune himself, his behaviour and his actions to the eternal laws of the Universe, this is man's *dharma*.

The attitude of identification of ancient man with the world around him as taught by the ancient *ṛṣis* is evident in the Veda: it reflects man's perception of the structure and function of nature or what we would now call the ecological aspects of the many different environments colonized by man.

Vedic man expressed his knowledge through songs of praise to the Gods; modern scientists express themselves through theories and proved or unproved hypotheses.

One of the most striking aspects of the Vedas is the *ṛṣi's* passionate endeavour to **understand** which transpires throughout the *Ṛgveda*. Understanding, in the thinking of the ancient sages, was not limited to a quick overview of whatever matters or phenomena they were studying — Vedic sages considered understanding as the '*raison d'être*' — the scope of their life on Earth. For the purpose of understanding, the sages sought knowledge by all means; they rationalised their observations seeking the relationships between cause and effect of everything that happens in nature, including human beings; but, when no clear-cut explanation was found, they resorted to mythical representations to record their knowledge as far as it had been possible for them to go, given human limitations. Patient and methodical observations over many years and many generations led them to recognize *ṛta*, the Law and Order of the

Universe, as **the** existence, **the** fact, **the** *status quo* established and governed by the greatest of the ancient gods: Varuṇa. Varuṇa is the Governor or, as Dandekar says, the Administrator of *ṛta*. Varuṇa governs by holding invisible fetters, the *pāśa* that regulate material and ethical worlds of all living beings. In contemporary terms, we would say that Varuṇa's fetters are the laws of physics, chemistry, biology and ecology that determine, limit and regulate *ṛta*. Varuṇa's spies are the researchers and philosophers who unveil *ṛta*, make scientific discoveries, and bind them into hypotheses, theories, principles and natural laws that can, more often than not, be expressed in mathematical terms. *Ṛta* is Truth — the Absolute Truth — unveiled by observation, and logical deductions that lead to knowledge. Knowledge leads to understanding that goes as far as the human mind can go. Ethically correct behaviour is the fruit of logical thinking.

The obsession with understanding *ṛta* that governs the Universe, thus became an exercise in logics and mathematics — logics in its purest form. Mathematics is the abstract, precise and accurate expression of logics that apply to all fields of knowledge, as is evident in all systems of Indian philosophy. The need of both precision and accuracy for logical thinking, resulted in the invention of the **zero**; in visualizing infinitely large numbers, in numerical series, the decimal system and the basic postulates, hypotheses, theories and laws of arithmetics, geometry, algebra and other branches of mathematics, physics and astronomy. Similarly, logical thinking leads to ethics; unethical behaviour is always illogical. Logical thinking also leads to grammar and syntax, syllabic scripts, metric poetry and music, hence it leads to the concept of harmony and *dharma*. *Dharma* is seen as the result of logical thinking applied to individual and social behaviour. Logical thinking also evolved into the punctilious details prescribed for the performance of the *Śrautasūtra* with the purpose of integrating man in time and space.

Evidently, Lord Varuṇa, the great God of Vedic man, emerged as the very powerful and wise Governor responsible for the individual and collective obeisance to the mathematical rules that govern and maintain the cosmos, hence the role played by astronomy (astrology) in the Vedic *ethos* as in all great cultures. Mathematics can be seen as an abstract series of concepts derived originally from the observation of nature and all phenomena that created and continue to regulate the universe. Thus followed the conviction that the cosmos emerged from an original state of nothingness, of void or, others believe, from a primeval chaos; finally order was achieved and, like the zero, order is a mathematical concept and expression.

Similarly, to the sages of other evolved cultures, the *ṛṣis* strived to find man's place in the universe, hence the formulation of individual and collective *dharma* for the many different members of mankind. *Dharma,* an abstract concept, later personified, is the fundamental ethical law that governs all of us; it is Reality regulated by the Great *asura* Varuṇa. In addition to ethical *dharma* however, there is material reality which also influences behaviour : this is day-to-day living behaviour that is determined by the environment in which we live. These are the ecological constraints imposed on all living beings, man included: they are called Varuṇa's fetters, the *pāśas* that act through subtle, often imponderable and concealed means. Human behaviour is therefore governed by the *dhārmic* code of behaviour, which is the ethical factor on which is superimposed the physical reality of daily living. These are the ecological determinants, or ecological factors figuratively described 'Varuṇa's', spies, guards and all other subordinates to the great Administrator of *ṛta*: Varuṇa.

Dharma has basically remained unaltered over the many centuries because all human beings under any circumstances have basic ethical obligations towards themselves and others that are inherent in the nature of man: it is the 'humanness' in man that makes man different from animals — or rather, should make rational man different from irrational beings. Or, can all living beings be divided into two categories, rational and irrational? But that is another question.

The moral obligations of man are fundamentally the same in all cultures, as for instance the written and unwritten laws regarding perjury, theft, murder, incest and so on. Historically, however, what happened with the wandering Indo-European tribes over the centuries is that at successive periods in time they found themselves living in different environmental conditions and in contact with different people with whom they had to share the same resources. The *dhārmic* principles originally promulgated by the 'forefathers', the 'ancients', the *r̥ṣis* had to be gradually adapted to changed and changing material living conditions brought about by changed environments and an evolving and developing material culture. This is evident, for instance, in the myth relating to the three R̥bhus brothers who were capable of making objects so perfect as their elder, Viśvakarman himself was unable of making.

Different modalities of *dharma* evolved according to the various functions of the sexes, the age, the occupation and profession of people at different times and places. Recommended and accepted human behaviour inevitably became the composite of the basic human ethical *dharma* plus the ecological constraints and requirements imposed by environmental realities such as foods, raw materials, evolving agriculture and domestication of new plants and animal husbandry, on the changing human socio-cultural type of life.

The foresight and wisdom of the ancient seers was to allow for the flexibility necessary for survival of the people while at the same time sustaining the traditional ethical *dharma* — unaltered, represented first by one of the Ādityas : Aryaman. The fundamental *dharma* as for instance in relation to Truth, to mental, bodily and spiritual cleanliness and hygiene, to marital, family and filial duties and rights and so on, have to a major extent remained unchanged because they are sound basic principles attuned to *ṛta*, the eternal Law and Order of the Cosmos.

Dharma is ethical; physical behaviour is ecological—*dhārmic* principles will always be *Sanātana Dharma*, because to a great extent it is wisdom personified.

A comparison with the epic of Gilgamesh is significant at this point. Gilgamesh, the legendary king of Uruk, partly human and partly divine, was forgotten with time, with the rise and fall of kingdoms and cultures because what he sought was impossible, non-realistic, *adhārmic*, unethical according to *ṛta* that is unchangeable because it is what **IS**. Gilgamesh sought immortality of the body. He followed his own ideas rather than the universal Law, which was known to the elders of his kingdom. *Ṛta* is what IS, even if known under different names and connotations; it is universally valid and cannot be changed by man, only by time. Gilgamesh failed in his quest: his name and struggle were forgotten in the course of time because they were *adhārmic*, and did not conform to the natural law and order that governs the living and non-living world.

To the *ṛṣi*, the elders, the 'ancients', mathematics was the reality of everything everywhere as revealed by the movements of the celestial bodies down to the infinitesimal small, as revealed by astronomy, numerology, the poetic metres, music, and as expressed in the number of *ślokas*, in *yantras*, in the construction of the *vedī*, of the sacred enclosure, of the temple, the house and much more. Everything was measured, every *yantra* has a meaning — later Śiva-Naṭarāja was represented contained in the *śrīcakram* with 6 or 43 triangles and none other. The Cola bronzes are eternally fascinating as they are a later materialization of mathematical language, ideas and representative symbolism. In this manner the great Śiva-Naṭarāja who had put life in motion is constrained by geometric imperative: *ṛta* has rules for everything.

Nobody can escape his *dharma* though ecological constraints influence his *karma*. *Dharma* however reigns supreme.

Part II

Introduction

IN Part I, I showed that while contemporary scientific research established the foundations of ecological theory on which rational use and management of nature must be based, the ancient Indian sages, the *ṛṣi*, had already established the foundations of an ecologically sound way of life some three to four thousand years ago, or earlier. The ancient traditional Indian way of life was objectively correct, rationally sound and ecologically valid. The 'Indian way of life' has been tested by time and has survived to this day, but it is swiftly being eroded away by human population pressure, or the excess of individuals of one species: *Homo sapiens*. Man is the consumer *par excellence* who in fact gives very little to the environment, except exploitation, excreta and other wastes, many of them noxious or not recyclable. The world population of *Homo sapiens* is at present already larger than the carrying capacity of the planetary system of Earth.

A radical difference between the Indian cultural tradition and the Western traditions is that the Indian cultures, and we could generalize for much of Asia, seek wisdom, while the Mediterranean and European cultures in general have traditionally pursued knowledge as the **summum bonum** to which man can aspire. Amongst all traditions and all men, knowledge has frequently been used unwisely forgetting that knowledge without wisdom may become very dangerous indeed. In fact, the concept of *asura* in post-Ṛgvedic times, is that of a creature with much knowledge and power derived from knowledge, but no wisdom: arrogance having replaced wisdom. We have under our very eyes the mixed blessings of genetic engineering as applied to medical practice, agriculture or pharmaceutical production, some of which are potentially capable of great feats, including that of altering demographic patterns. Man likes to play God, but how safe is it?

In the present work I try to analyse a few selected hymns of the *R̥gveda* from a purely biological point of view in an attempt to discern the knowledge of the *r̥ṣi* and how they applied the wisdom derived from understanding the implications of that very knowledge, to the pragmatic pursuits of everyday life.

The methodology that I adopted is the same as in my earlier book, namely using a biological key to 'decode' the verses, and seeking internal evidence in the Vedas themselves. Admittedly the stanzas may have more than one meaning, for instance spiritual meaning in addition to, or superimposed on, the biological meaning which is the one focused here.

I have also tried to understand the *saṁskāra*s related to these hymns and I tried to find the logical *nexus* between the rites, the observation and the understanding of all nature, including the cosmos as seen by human eyes from planet Earth. I found that the logic of the rites and of the rituals is coherent with the facts of nature. The unveiling of *r̥ta* is based on logical thinking.

As Dandekar pointed out, many of the rites and much of the rituals are not intended to be a 'copy' or 'repetition' of natural phenomena; they should rather be seen often, but not always, as the expression of some sort of 'sympathetic magic' that would enable man to participate in the phenomena of the cosmic order or *r̥ta*, and in those of all worldly nature. The existence and interaction of all forms of life, within nature's own rules, is seen as the best guarantee of eternal presence of man in the world as it is in the present, coming from the past and going into the future. Consequently participatory rites and rituals are means to an end; the sacrifice is a means to acquire eternal existence and become immortal. The law of *karma* is, from this point of view, derived from the conviction that man can be integrated in nature's cycles, where nothing is ever lost in time or space, provided man attunes himself to the cosmic law, *ṛta*, that regulates all in all and that is the expression of the Absolute Reality, or Absolute Truth, the *Brahman*. In this sense the *ṛṣi* did achieve immortality, which is one of thinking man's ancientmost and eternally persistent desire. Appropriately enough the names of the *saptarṣi* were given to the fixed stars of the Great Bear. Immortality becomes a synonym of liberation from 'Varuṇa's fetters'.

Most of the *saṁskāras* or Vedic sacrifices, are meant to show the way in this direction and also to achieve integration of the world within oneself with the world outside the self. This is, I believe, an important point of Advaita Vedānta with all its intellectual, spiritual and psychological implications.

The first hymn analysed here from these points of view is widely quoted, excessively maligned and misunderstood; it is **about** — and not **to**, as usually quoted — the frogs, *maṇḍūka*; which is *ṚV*, VII; 103. Western commentators in general consider the comparison made between the annual life-cycle of the frogs with the annual rites performed by the brāhmaṇa as being odd or astonishing: Louis Renou uses the word: *singularité*; others considered it downright derogatory. Needless to say, however, the profound bio-ecological wisdom shown by this parallelism, not 'comparison' or 'assimilation' as often repeated, shows perspicacity in understanding nature, wisdom in ritualistic rendering, and pragmatism in the use of the understanding developed from the knowledge acquired by observing nature. The rituals, therefore, have to be made appropriate to the place, the time and the purpose. The stated purpose here is the perfect integration of man, particularly the *yajamāna* or sacrificer, and his wife, with all nature, including the universe, as represented by the deities of the seasons.

The second hymn is to the wedding of Sūryā, daughter of the

Sun God: Sūrya; it was said to be a patchwork of inputs made at different times. It is shown here to be a very ancient hymn formulated with a very definite purpose in mind: the celebration of the sacredness of marriage, though it is probably true that repetitions and additions were entered at later times, probably to reinforce or clarify the original arguments. In this hymn only the most ancient Vedic deities are invoked for guidance and protection. Rather than a hymn to the 'ideal bride', as often stated, it is a song that not only celebrates the institution of marriage, but also gives guidance and instructions for the education of the bride and bridegroom and for their joint life as responsible adults. The hymn is also a guide for correct behaviour not only during the wedding ceremony, but even more so for the consummation of marriage as a preparation for a healthy life of partnership and friendship. With characteristic candour the *ṛṣi* talks of intimate matters such as defloration and sexual intercourse which are dealt in greater detail in the *Gṛhyasūtra*. Hymn *ṚV*, X; 85 has much the character of a behavioural and social guide, the profound social meaning of which goes much beyond its literally obvious phrasing.

The third hymn is to Araṇyāni; it is one of the shortest in the whole *Ṛgveda*. It is dedicated to the one that 'tills not yet has stores of food': the Lady of the Forest. The importance of this aesthetically and poetically extremely beautiful hymn, lies in that it focuses on the importance and sacredness of the forest, and in the meaning and value it has for the daily life of the people. The forest is apparently good and bad, but those who recognize and respect its intrinsic value will experience that the Lady of the Forest as the forest itself, is a real mother to human beings. We can easily imagine this song and similar ones being chanted by weary villagers to invoke protection and to reassure themselves when entering the recesses of the jungle where mysterious forces, not always friendly to man, are always present and moving around. This beautiful song has a powerful psychological component for the benefit of simple villagers and all human beings.

The fourth chapter is on the personalities of Indra and Varuṇa. They are seen here from the perspective that Indra represents the material reality of migrant Āryan tribes who conquered and finally settled in Saptasindhu, and that Varuṇa, the greatest and one of the ancientmost gods of Vedic and pre-Vedic man, represents immaterial reality. Indra, according to Dandekar (1997), is 'one who won his divine suzeranity through his own powers' while . . . 'Varuṇa, the administrator of cosmic law, also came to be represented specifically as the god who enforces moral order within the human community'. In my opinion Indra is a great war-lord deified because of his great exploits, while Varuṇa is the greatest god since the beginning of time, because of his intrinsic nature.

Finally Appendix I refers to the contribution made by Eng. T.B. Swaminathan to the general discussion that followed the session that I chaired on 11 January 1997 at the International Conference on Sanskrit and Culture, held at Trichur, Kerala. The discussion centred on the relevance of Vedic studies to present-day lifestyles. The final word of wisdom was given by T.B. Swaminathan who kindly condensed his teachings with the text on 'The Carpenter and Pythagoras Theorem', included in this volume.

Appendix II refers to my views as a naturalist/ecologist on the latest discussions on the identity of the *soma* plant as expressed by Kashikar and Dandekar.

Before closing this Introduction, I should express my gratefulness to the India International Centre, New Delhi; to the Indira Gandhi National Centre for the Arts and to the Bhandarkar Oriental Research Institute for the constant use of their libraries and to the staff that spared no efforts to assist me in my studies. I am further specially indebted to Dr. Uma Chakravarty, for spending the major part of ten days, and much exchange of correspondence, revising and correcting my often faulty Sanskrit quotations and for many interesting dicussions.

The book by Nath (1996), and specially those by R.N. Dandekar and by U. Chakravarty, published after I had written this Second Part, proved to be particularly useful to crystallize my thoughts on the two great figures: God Varuṇa and Adhirāja Indra.

To all these and many others I offer my thanks and requests for corrections and additions; the text would certainly be enriched and improved by constructive suggestions, inputs and discussions.

1

Maṇḍūka, the Frogs

ṚV, VII; 103

ṛṣi Vasiṣṭha Metres: *Triṣṭup; Anuṣṭup*

संवत्सरं शशयाना ब्राह्मणा व्रतचारिणः ।
वाचं पर्जन्यजिन्वितां प्र मण्डूका अवादिषुः ।। १ ।।
दिव्या आपो अभि यदेनमायन्दृतिं न शुष्कं सरसी शयानम् ।
गवामह न मायुर्वत्सिनीनां मण्डूकानां वग्नुरत्रा समेति ।। २ ।।
यदीमेनाँ उशतो अभ्यवर्षीत्तृष्यावतः प्रावृष्यागतायाम् ।
अख्खलीकृत्या खितरं न पुत्रो अन्यो अन्यमुष वदन्तमेति ।। ३ ।।

saṁvatsaraṁ śaśayānā brāhmaṇā vratacāriṇaḥ ।
vācaṁ parjanyajinvitāṁ pra maṇḍūkā avādiṣuḥ ।। 1 ।।
divyā āpo abhi yad enam āyan dṛtiṁ na śuṣkaṁ sarasī śayānam ।
gavām aha na māyur vatsinīnāṁ maṇḍūkānāṁ vagnur utrā sam eti ।। 2 ।।
yad īm enām̐ uśato abhy avarṣīt tṛṣyāvataḥ prāvṛṣy āgatāyām ।
akhkhalīkṛtyā pitaraṁ na putro anyo anyam upa vadantam eti ।। 3 ।।

अन्यो अन्यमनु गृभ्णात्येनोरपां प्रसर्गे यदमन्दिषाताम् ।
मण्डूको यदभिवृष्टः कनिष्कन्पृश्निः संपृङ्क्ते हरितेन वाचम् ।। ४ ।।
यदेषामन्यो अन्यस्य वाचं शाक्तस्येव वदति शिक्षमाणः ।
सर्वं तदेषां समृधेव पर्व यत्सुवाचो वदथनाध्यप्सु ।। ५ ।।

anyo anyam anu gr̥bhṇāty enor apāṁ prasarge yad amandiṣātām ।
maṇḍūko yad abhivr̥ṣṭaḥ kaniṣkan pr̥śniḥ sampr̥ṅkte haritena vācam ।। 4 ।।
yad eṣām anyo anyasya vācaṁ śāktasyeva vadati śikṣamāṇaḥ ।
sarvaṁ tad eṣāṁ samr̥dheva parva yat suvāco vadathanādhy apsu ।। 5 ।।

गोमायुरेको अजमायुरेकः पृश्निरेको हरित एक एषाम् ।
समानं नाम बिभ्रतो विरूपाः पुरुत्रा वाचं पिपिशुर्वदन्तः ।। ६ ।।
ब्राह्मणासो अतिरात्रे न सोमे सरो न पूर्णमभितो वदन्तः ।
संवत्सरस्य तदहः परि ष्ठ यन्मण्डूकाः प्रावृषीणं बभूव ।। ७ ।।
ब्राह्मणासः सोमिनो वाचमक्रत ब्रह्म कृण्वन्तः परिवत्सरीणम् ।
अध्वर्यवो घर्मिणः सिष्विदाना आविर्भवन्ति गुह्या न के चित् ।। ८ ।।

gomāyur eko ajamāyur ekaḥ pr̥śnir eko harita eka eṣām ।
samānaṁ nāma bhibhrato virūpāḥ purutrā vācaṁ pipiśur vadantaḥ ।। 6 ।।
brāhmaṇāso atirātre na some saro na pūrṇam abhito vadantaḥ ।
saṁvatsarasya tad ahaḥ pari ṣṭha yan maṇḍūkāḥ prāvr̥ṣīṇaṁ babhūva ।। 7 ।।
brāhmaṇāsaḥ somino vācam akrata brahma kr̥ṇvantaḥ parivatsarīṇam ।
adhvaryavo gharmiṇaḥ siṣvidānā āvir bhavanti guhyā na ke cit ।। 8 ।।

देवहितिं जुगुपुर्द्वादशस्य ऋतुं नरो न प्र मिनन्त्येते ।
संवत्सरे प्रावृष्यागतायां तप्ता घर्मा अश्नुवते विसर्गम् ।। ९ ।।
गोमायुरदादजमायुरदात्पृश्निरदाद्धरितो नो वसूनि ।
गवां मण्डूका ददतः शतानि सहस्रसावे प्र तिरन्त आयु : ।। १० ।।

devahitiṁ jugupur dvādaśasya r̥tuṁ naro na pra minanty ete ।
saṁvatsare prāvr̥ṣy āgatāyāṁ taptā gharmā aśnuvate visargam ।। 9 ।।

gomāyur adād ajamāyur adāt pṛśnir adād dharito no vasūni ।
gavāṁ maṇḍūkā dadataḥ śatāni sahasrasāve pra tiranta āyuḥ ॥ 10 ॥

Translation

1. They who lay quiet for a year, the brāhmaṇas who fulfil their vows,

   The frogs have lifted up their voice, the voice Parjanya hath inspired.

2. What time on these, as on dry skin lying in the pool's bed, the floods of heaven descended,

   The music of the frogs comes forth in concert like the cows lowing with their calves beside them.

3. When at the coming of the rains the water has poured upon them as they yearned and thirsted,

   One seeks another as he talks and greets him with cries of pleasure as a son his father.

4. Each of these twain receives the other kindly, while they are revelling in the flow of waters,

   When the frog moistened by the rain springs forward, and green and spotty both combine their voices.

5. When one of these repeats the other's language, as he who learns the lesson of the teacher,

   Your every limb seems to be growing larger as ye converse with eloquence on the waters.

6. One is cow-bellow and goat-bleat the other, one frog is green and one of them is spotty.

   They bear one common name, and yet they vary, and, talking, modulate the voice diversely.

7. As brāhmaṇas, sitting round the brimful vessel, talk at the Soma-rite at Atirātra,

   So frogs, ye gather round the pool to honour this day of all the year, the first of rain-time.

8. These brāhmaṇas with the *soma* juice, performing their year-long rite, have lifted up their voices;

   And these Adhvaryus, sweating with their kettles, come forth and show themselves, and none are hidden.

9. They keep the twelve month's God-appointed order, and never do the men neglect the season.

   Soon as the rain-time in the year returneth, these who were heated kettles gain their freedom.

10. Cow-bellow and goat-bleat have granted riches, and green and spotty have vouchsafed us treasure.

    The frogs who give us cows in hundreds lengthen our lives in this most fertilizing season.

(transl. Griffith, 1889)

Commentaries

Stanza 1—To begin with, the parallelism between the behaviour of the frogs and of the brāhmaṇa is established. It will be followed by the parallelism between the frogs and other beings. The parallelism refers to the behaviour of both frogs and brāhmaṇa in relation to the annual solar cycle. It is made clear further on (7, 8, 9) that it is the 12-month year of the solar revolution that is meant, since the seasons are regulated by the solar year rather than by the 13-month lunar year.

The brāhmaṇa may voluntarily observe a vow of silence practically or symbolically for one year (or: since last year; or: for one season) but the frogs are inevitably compelled to observe the yearly cycle of droughts and rains; if frogs did not hide in their underground holes during summer, they would dry flat because of the thinness of their skin that does not protect them against desiccation.

Frogs 'disappear' under cover out of ecological compulsion which they cannot avoid; the brāhmaṇa observe a vow of withdrawal through spiritual compulsion or reasoned religiosity. What is emphasized here is the difference between the appropriate behaviour of an animal that is moved by instinct rather than reason, and man who is primarily moved by reason and by his power of discrimination that permits him to draw correlations of cause and effect that guide him through life.

Parjanya, the rain cloud, brings God-given rain equally to the frogs who revel in water and to the brāhmaṇa who have also suffered from the dry heat of summer. Rains bring back to active life aestivating frogs confined to their digs during the hot pre-monsoon period as well as to man exhausted by the heat.

This is a hymn by sage Vasiṣṭha and the *Nirukta* refers to the myth according to which Vasiṣṭha himself on one occasion resorted to praise Parjanya to call for the fertilizing rains. As the frogs applauded the sage, Vasiṣṭha in turn praised them thus: 'O frog join me. O swimmer invoke rains. Float in the middle of the pond, having spread your feet'. Whether this is really the origin of this hymn or not, sage Vasiṣṭha had obviously attentively observed and interpreted the causes and effects of the behaviour of frogs. May then the behaviour of the brāhmaṇa be equally meaningful and successful.

The translation and interpretation of this hymn by SS and SV (v. VII, p. 2801 *et seq.*) emphasizes the fact that all beings, even 'lowly' animals like frogs and high learned brāhmaṇa, are all bound to nature's cycles and phenomena that are usually called Varuṇa's fetters, as mentioned also in many other hymns. We should however notice that there are no 'lowly' or 'higher' animals or living beings in the Vedic tradition; they are all *bhūta* or '**beings**', though later commentators introduced the designation of 'lowly' to forms that are still in an early stage of biological evolution on Earth. The bondage of man to the cosmic law or *ṛta* is well expressed as Varuṇa's fetters and in fact even twentieth-century man in spite of his scientific knowledge, his technical achievements and matter of fact arrogance is ultimately still dependent on the forces of nature. These manifest themselves through climates, catastrophes, normal development and natural processes and events good or bad, constructive or destructive. SS and SV also show their understanding of surrounding nature as they literally translate the 'skin on the bottom of a dry pond' as 'water skin' which is comparable to a dry leather bag used to carry water. They further note (*l.c.,* p. 2800) that in the *AV* (IV; 15, 14) the frogs are invoked thus: 'O frog join me, O swimmer invoke rain, float in the middle of the pond having spread your feet'; they note the onomatopoetic use of the terms *majuḥ* and *gomayuḥ* of cows and *vagnuḥ*, the croaking of frogs and *ajamayuḥ*, the bleating of goats; the latter, they say, are as happy with the approach of the rains as with the approach of their calves. The *ṛṣi* further compares these sounds with the inarticulate cries of joy of a child at the approach of his father. SS and SV are not shocked, as Renou, Max Müller and others were, and do not find insulting the comparison made by the *ṛṣi* between different living members of the same ecosystem, such as men, frogs, goats and others. SS and SV show a knowledge of the biology of frogs and remark that a very appropriate comparison is made between the chanting of the priests at the night long *Atirātra* ceremony and frogs who croak throughout the night. All living beings exemplified here by frogs and brāhmaṇa are found to observe the *gavam ayanam* or 'God's appointed order' as the term is understood by Sāyaṇa.

Thus, the parallel between frogs and brāhmaṇa is clearly spelled:

- they aestivate throughout the year, they croak when Parjanya brings fertilizing rains;

- they **praise**, **greet** each other, they **rejoice** and make **merry**, they are **satisfied** and **decorated** and they find their **life in water**;

In a similar manner the brāhmaṇa:

- take note and observe the yearly cycle of seasons;
- they praise the Gods loudly and rejoice at the arrival of rains since, like with the frogs, there is life in water;
- they take a vow of silence for one year, such as the frogs that kept quiet in their holes for one year (or, better: since last year's wet season);
- as the frogs start croaking also the brāhmaṇa engage in rituals that cannot but be appropriate for the season. We could notice here that later, in a somewhat changed culture, India still commemorates appropriately the changing seasons and the seasonality of rains in many ways, including with different musical *rāgas*.

Stanza 2 — The accurate power of observation of *ṛṣi* Vasiṣṭha is not directed only at living beings; the inanimate components of the environment equally come under his scrutiny 'for the sake of understanding'. Thus *ṚV*, VIII; 103, 2 begins with an objective description of the mud at the bottom of the dried up pond that he realistically compares to the dry 'water skin' as the leather water-bag was then called; this is further compared to the dry skin of a thirsty animal, which is exactly how the dried up mud usually looks before the rains set in. But when the floods of heaven come, suddenly the waters become alive again; the symphony of the different croaking sound of several species of frogs becomes in a sense comparable to the happy lowing of cows with their calves beside them. As the grass is growing fast and the cows rejoice and will produce more milk after the rains have come, similarly the frogs can come out of their aestivating digs with renewed joy of living and with a loud optimistic voice.

This stanza expresses well the fundamental meaning of the hymn: the recognition that after the trial of the dry months comes the reward of the rains, according to the rules of *ṛta*. All nature thrives as the recurrent season of plenty sets in. To this day it is common to see people happily go outdoors and rejoice at the first rains after the bursting of the monsoon.

Stanza 3 — The *ṛṣi* goes on to describe the renewal of life, the shrivelled, dried out thirsty frogs that can at last make merry 'meeting and talking to one another' and there can be no greater joy than that of a child meeting his father. Thus the comparison is here more specifically turned to human beings in general as the children will loudly express their happiness at the coming home of their father. A beautiful image to convey the understanding of the pleasure that frogs, taken as a symbol of nature at large, experience at the arrival of the life-giving heavenly waters, or return home of the father after a day or a season of work.

Stanzas 4, 5, 6 — From stanza four onwards the observation of the *ṛṣi* is more pointed and detailed; it acquires a more general ecological significance, although it remains focused on the frogs.

These are described as 'varying', or as we would say zoologically, as belonging to different species distinguished by their colours and by their 'voices'. The voice of the frogs, their croaking, is the species-specific mating call of the male frog. In ecological terms, the species-specific 'voice' is the ecological niche that is typical of and occupied by a single species. In a way the 'voice' is one of the items encoded into the 'identity card' of the particular species of frog. The female frog responds only to the 'voice' of the males of the same species and mates only with a male of her same kind, one who 'speaks her own language', which in this case is one of the elements of the ecological niche or ensemble of factors that keep each species distinct from all others. By this mechanism, several species of frogs can co-exist in the same body of water, without danger of hybridization between different species or lack of fertilization of eggs produced by a female mating with a male of another species. The mating call of frogs, like the pheromones secreted by many insects, specially moths and butterflies, is species-specific; by playing recordings of the male frog's calls, only females of the same species respond and congregate around the loud-speaker. As the *ṛṣi* says: 'as he who learns the lesson of the teacher'... where the great teacher is *vāk*, the Voice, the Word or Speech. Also birds, dolphins, whales, humans and others learn vocalization from the elders of the same species. Thus the *ṛṣi* points out that frogs of different species can happily share the same resource, or pool of water and all are equally benefited by the coming of the rains and the change of season. Much emphasis is put by sage Vasiṣṭha on this ecologically correct observation that different species can share the same resource or, in scientific parlance, several species can co-exist in the same ecosystem provided they occupy different ecological niches. In this case the ecological niche is reproductive isolation of species having slightly different environmental requirements besides having different croaking. In fact, two of the species described can be recognised as *Rana tigrina* that is large, congregates in and around ponds at the breeding season and is as voracious a feeder as it is a loquacious talker or singer. *Rana tigrina* owes its Latin scientific name for being spotted or speckled, as mentioned in the Veda. The other recognizable species is *Rana cyanophlyctes* which is the green one, very common, entirely aquatic and as described by the *ṛṣi* has the habit of skipping over the surface of the water or, in Griffith's translation: 'as ye converse with elegance on the water' and in SS and SV translation: 'when you eloquently converse, while leaping upon the waters'. As the *ṛṣi* says: 'they bear one common name, yet they vary'.

Vāk is also invoked, though not by name, when the *ṛṣi* emphasizes the importance of teaching: 'when one of these (frogs) repeats the other's language, as he who learns the language of the teacher'. Vocalization is learned from parents and siblings of all species of animals who emit sounds, even those that are not audible to man, as well as those that are audible to the human species.

Finally, growing fully developed limbs is a prelude to sexual maturity and the stage of reproduction and perpetuation of the species; a new biological cycle begins in tune with the seasons according to the laws of *ṛta*. *Ṛta* is not specifically mentioned in this hymn, but is implied and reminded in many other hymns of the same *ṛṣi*, because each act, each behaviour, all happenings of living beings and non-living things are regulated and cannot occur but according to *ṛta*, the law and order that governs the universe in its minutest details.

Stanza 7 — This again focuses on the parallelism between the behaviour of the frogs and that of the brāhmaṇa. The frogs are moved by instinct and the urge for survival and reproduction when they gather around the pond in the dead of night to honour the first rains. The brāhmaṇa similarly congregate at night around the vessel full of *soma* juice for the Atirātra rite that is part of the Soma Sacrifice, which is an act of reason rather than instinct.

This is the only place where the Atirātra rite is mentioned by name in the *ṚV* as it has come down to us. It suggests that particular importance is given to link the rite with the seasonal change of habits in nature, as is evident in the life-cycle of frogs who are living and breathing in water as tadpoles before metamorphosis, and who live and breathe in air after they metamorphose into frogs and grow stronger; when fully formed they extend their legs to swim, hence their limbs seem to grow; this is specially true of those species who float on the water. Obviously four important elements : earth, water, fire as heat and air are determinants of the bio-ecological cycle of frogs. Nature's own 'sacrifices' are duplicated by the 'sacrifices' conducted by the brāhmaṇa and the Atirātra reflects the observation of nature's sacrifices, by man. To be alive means going through an unending series of sacrifices, where sacrifice here means recognition and submission to *ṛta*; a participation in nature's sacrifices as a means to obtain cooperation of the Gods through 'sympathetic magic'. Sympathetic magic is taken here to mean that actually performing nature's rites is a form of participating in them. By performing similar rites, protection and immortality are sought. Sympathetic magic works on the principle that: 'I help you so that you can help me'. The Vedic man thus worked and lived with nature or, in today's terminology, we could say that he lived literally in harmony, in real resonance with nature. In fact, of all the ancient cultures, although modified by time and evolved and changed into religion, the Vedic culture and philosophy is the one that has survived longer; it is the Eternal *dharma* because it is ecologically sound and it is the one that will survive intact or almost so. It is ecologically sound because and so long as it obeys the laws of *ṛta*.

The brāhmaṇa sit all night long for the Atirātra rite; at the appointed time they make their invocations and chant their chants three times in the course of the night: after sunset, in the middle of the night and before sunrise; they sit around the vessel full of *soma* juice, which is a liquid purified by fire. The chanting thus coincides, or rather, follows and precedes the observation of the dipping and rising of the sun and the 'year long sacrifice' probably means that the observations were carried out daily, probably to determine accurately the time of the solstices and of the equinoxes. One is here reminded of the observations made by Alexander the Macedonian who said that the 'naked sophists' spent the day 'observing the sun' or spent 'all their time observing the sun'. The Atirātra rite may take a year long cycle to be completed, or 12 solar months, but the 'moonlit' night referred to in the text, indicates that one date was accurately fixed so that the lunar year would be corrected to coincide with the solar year. In other words, this is one more example of the scrupulous preoccupation of Vedic man with Time and with the accurate measurement of Time on Earth, that should be in harmony with astronomically determined astral time. The sacrifice would be invalid and inefficient if time was not determined exactly and elaborate purificatory and expiatory rites would have to be undergone if the purpose and efficiency of the sacrifice were not to be lost.

Identity of intention, coincidence of time, space and action (or the Aristotelic principles of the Greek theatrical 'magic') are the basic requirements for the performance and success of every practice of sympathetic magic that works through participatory strategy. Thus the croaking of the frogs coupled with the year-long observations of the brāhmaṇa are a sort of alarm clock set by man and regulated by climate and by the position of the astral bodies and the location of the observer on the surface of planet Earth. The frogs ring a double check to keep correct time! *Dvādaśasya*, or the 12-month year is mentioned in stanza 9 as God's appointed order.

Dandekar (1982, p. 316) very aptly says that magic is a 'method for increasing man's practical control over the world and thus has a great affinity to science. Magic is not a mistaken religion; it is mistaken science'. Elsewhere Dandekar (1979b, p. 23) again states that 'the performance of specific cultic rites was made to correspond with the rhythmic course of nature. Several sacrifices can be shown to have been intended as yearly rites for cosmic regeneration'. These statements fit perfectly with the words of this hymn and the rituals of the Atirātra sacrifice. I believe that many rites are not only intended as yearly rites of cosmic 'regeneration', of which there could be only one yearly, but such rites actually mark fixed points of reference; in other terms they mark fixes in the calendar that is then built around them. To this day people, not only Hindus, talk of so many days or weeks before or after such or other event or calendar fixes such as the solstices or Passover or Easter or the full moon of Phālguna. These fixes are determined in relation to one another because of the non-coincidence of the lunar and solar year during the revolution of planet Earth.

Stanzas 7, 8—The parallelism or analogy between the behaviour of the frogs and that of the brāhmaṇa is carried out one step further by comparing the sweating Adhvaryu priest who performs the acts and practical aspects of the sacrifice, with the work of the frogs which are now no longer hidden in their holes as during the hot dry summer months. Duties to be undertaken for living are laborious, it is not easy to live; the duties to observe *ṛta* are equally laborious; frogs and men alike have their share of work and duties. None can escape his *dharma* and *karma*.

Griffith points out correctly that the Atirātra sacrifice mentioned here is, according to Sāyaṇa, the *gavam ayanam* that lasts one whole year and begins and ends with the Atirātra rite. The Atirātra, among others, includes three different recitations during the night, as mentioned above; not every night, but special nights are chosen for this particular rite. Similarly different species of frogs replace one another over the night and may be identified by their own specific croaking.

There is no doubt that the timing for the Atirātra was calculated to begin with the solstice, most probably the winter solstice that usually marks the beginning of the year. Far from being lack of respect for the brāhmaṇa, as some commentators would have it, the comparison drawn between the frogs and the brāhmaṇa is a well calculated praise, since both, the learned men and the simple animals guided by biological imperatives, faithfully observe ritualistically the solstices and the equinoxes, the change of seasons and the coming of life-giving monsoon rains. Rains give life to the bodily existence while the sacrifice enlivens and immortalizes the non-material or spiritual existence.

The participation of the brāhmaṇa in nature's own rites goes beyond the repetition of rituals, gestures, invocations and recitations; the *yajña*, or ceremonial sacrifice proceedes from symbolism to symbolism. For instance the Atitrātra rite symbolizes the full yearly cycle of solar and lunar calendars; the *soma* juice, with emphasis on the liquid aspect of *soma*, also symbolizes water and is purified by fermentation that generates heat and is further purified by boiling with fire and filtration. Comparable purification rites are undertaken in the preparation of the *Haoma* rites mentioned in the *Avesta*; they have a striking similarity with those described point by point in the *Brāhmaṇa*s of the *ṚV*. *Haoma* is the Avestan form of the Sanskrit *Homa* and the Hindu *Homa* rite. Also lifting of the voice of both frogs and brāhmaṇa during the invocation, are a symbol of sound and it must be remembered that it was the vibration generated by the sound of the sacred syllable *AUṀ*, ॐ, that set in motion life on Earth, according to tradition. The croaking of the frogs re-awakens water-dependent life that was dormant but not dead and had ceased to manifest itself during the dry summer months. While performing the daily *sūrya namaskāra*, water is poured from cupped hands as an oblation to the rising sun, whose light must be seen through the water by the worshipper himself.

Stanzas 9, 10 — Men are admonished never to neglect the seasonal sacrifices. The frogs, like men, must observe the God-appointed order, *deva hitim*; the brāhmaṇa are specially bound to perform their seasonal duties from which none can escape. In ecological terms, all living beings are alike in that they are bound by Varuṇa's fetters and cannot escape having to submit to environmental constraints. Orderly succession of environmental events is part of the laws of *ṛta* and all who were scorched before the rains can now 'gain their freedom'; the frogs are liberated from their underground digs; they are liberated from 'remaining hidden' and men are liberated from oppressing heat. The same ecological factors impinge on the lives of all living beings. The return to active life after aestivation is loudly proclaimed by the frogs, each with its own voice. The last two lines of the hymn:

> The Frogs who give us cows in hundreds lengthen our lives in this most fertilizing season

were ridiculed and at best considered to be non-sensical by many Western commentators. However, whenever I enquired from Indian people, specially those from villages, what they thought of this simile, unerringly and unhesitatingly children and adults alike correlated the presence of many frogs with abundant rains, good pastures, numerous and healthy cows, abundant food and therefore a healthy long life for the people. The hymn means long life on earth and also long life in eternity through the appropriate rites, since in nature nothing is lost, nothing is created but everything is transformed. It indicates the preservation of life **and** of the means to sustain life.

Worship, prayers, meditation, *mudrās*, recitation and chanting are all technicalities and methodologies that enable man to concretize the purpose of the rites and rituals that empower him to participate in the life of the cosmos. Life is the most mysterious of *asura* Varuṇa's magics and it is conceptually represented by Savitṛ who is the 'essence' of the abstract principle and concept of life itself (Vannucci, 1994 & Part I above).

In Vedic mythological representation, rains are the seed of the sky which impregnate Mother Earth thus blessing all living beings with long life. The hymn clearly means that neither the frogs' chants nor the Atirātra rite are an end in themselves but they are only means to conquer the ultimate goal which is long life (Stanza 10), thanks to the sustaining power of Earth, and Eternal existence thanks to the power of the Sacrifice, *yajña*. In this case the Atirātra, which is part of the great Soma Sacrifice.

First and foremost the hymn is a celebration of the changing seasons and their regular return. It is one of the many consecrations of *ṛta*, the discipline that rules the universe. It is specifically and intentionally a description of nature's cycles and a glorification of the bliss of monsoon rains as exemplified by the biological cycle of frogs and by the rituals established by man to propitiate nature, to participate in *ṛta* that regulates the structure and dynamics or functioning of the cosmos. By the *yajña* and through the brāhmaṇa, man takes active part in the mysteries of the world of which he is a part and not just a spectator. The basic intention of many *saṁskāras* could be expressed as: let us participate fully in Nature' rites, because in so doing we will live fully, we fulfil our needs, desires and destiny and thus attain immortality; let us be one with the nature to which we belong so that nature may help us. Let us improve our health and fitness by participating in nature's own rites. The sages were not embarrassed in describing what they learned from the observation of the plants, animals and inanimate objects and things around them; they sought a comprehensive understanding of *prakṛti* or Nature, and of how it works; they realized that human beings must conduct themselves according to the laws of nature if they want to live and survive as individuals and as a biological species. The sages further realized that one way of achieving the eternal human desire of immortality was to participate in nature's cycles; the law of *karma* is a clear expression of one way of achieving immortality. In the case in point, frogs revive year after year with a different body, because their life-cycle is completed in the period of a solar year, but man renews and repeats his annual cycle of activities holding the same body year after year; man's lifespan, unlike that of frogs, covers many years; it is punctuated by the same natural cycles but hopefully knowledge and wisdom accrue with age.

By repeating symbolically the phenomena and processes of nature, not because he worships these phenomena in themselves and irrespective of whether he understands them or not, or whether he can explain them or not, man gains immortality because he recognizes and re-affirms through sacrifice that he is part of the same processes of recycling of nature that keep him alive. Man aims at 'immortality', hence the need to perform sacrifice. Sacrifices are not merely rites that sanctify or 'make sacred' common things or actions; sacrifices are rites that involve identifying oneself with nature, sharing and spending time together, they induce concentrated thinking and meditation, they involve spending energy and things so that material, intellectual and spiritual entities will acquire a higher value and become more efficient towards all and any sort of immortality, since material immortality, or immortality of the body, is of course, impossible. It is in this sense that oblations are given to Lord Agni who transforms the material into spiritual, matter into energy and in so doing acquires more power. The same concept is at the root of the belief in the transubstantiation of bread and wine into the spiritual body of Jesus Christ in the Christian Sacrifice of the Holy Communion, the Eucharistic Sacrifice.

Every rite or ritual involves also a certain amount of sacrifice; in fact just to be alive means to go through an unending series of sacrifices — sacrifices of all types. The word sacrifice is used here in its common sense of giving up something dear and also in the literal sense of making something sacred.

Immortality has been the dearest wish of most men since the beginning of the existence of Thinking Man. In one form or other it is found expressed in all cultures. It is a concept related to the concept of Fire. Agni the immortal is ever present as the heat of life, as the light of the sun that generates life, as the energy of living beings who reproduce other living beings similar to themselves, and who will exist eternally in the cosmos as universal energy. In the human species, much of paternal love is a disguised form of realizing the urge for immortality: the father's life continues and becomes everlasting through the life of his descendents: Mother's love is sacrifice rather than selfishness, it gives its all and is happy to pass away or step into a retiring shadow if necessary for the well-being of her children. In this resides the recognized power of the mother image to which the offsprings bow in faithfulness and hope.

An important aspect of *bhakti*, which is clear specially in the Vasiṣṭha hymns of the *R̥V*, is that the *r̥ṣi* prayed for knowledge, for understanding rather than for miracles; there was perhaps not so much devotion as obedience, submission to the law, discipline, the urge to understand and know *ṛta*. All the *ṛṣis* prayed not for granting miracles in themselves, but for the miracle, the grace of understanding. Immortality was understood as being one with, as sharing the great magic of existence, of life. In this sense immortality was achieved by the ancients, whose myths are alive to date. In all cultures where immortality of the body was sought, man was defeated. To cite only one very ancient example, I will recall the Saga of Gilgamesh, the classical rendering of which is from the twelfth century BC. The roots of the legend are various and are to be found in different cultures and languages from the Mesopotamian region and surroundings. The classical poem has come down to us from the library of the ancient city of Ninive in Babylon and is in Sumeric language translated by Pettinato (1992). The poem, engraved in terracotta tablets, relates the adventures of Gilgamesh, king of Uruk, and the roots of the legend are as old as the third millennium BC (2500-3000). All these ancient legends point in the same direction which is the quest for immortality that was the strongest desire of Gilgamesh who embarked in a perilous journey against the advice of his elders and peers. Obviously Gilgamesh failed in his hazardous quest: his body did not become immortal though his adventures did, as well as the admonishment he received.

Frogs

Amphibians are a class of vertebrate animals such as frogs, toads, salamanders, newts and others. They go through a complicated life-cycle and through many vulnerable passages from one stage to another. The cycle begins with the laying of eggs in water, watery foam or jelly. From the eggs emerge in due course of time the tadpoles which are entirely aquatic, have a swimming tail, no limbs, breathe in water and respire through gills, have no real teeth but only hook-like horny 'teeth' with which they scrape aquatic vegetation. Tadpoles are larvae which gradually metamorphose into the adult by resorption of the tail, the growth of two pairs of limbs, resorption of the gills and development of lungs, development of the osseus skeleton and of real teeth. Profound changes occur also in the nervous, digestive and excretory systems. The small frog or toad becomes carnivorous, grows to the full size of the species and develops reproductive organs, it breaths in air and acquires terrestrial habits until when it returns to water for reproduction. When adult, frogs usually mate at the surface of the water where they float easily by inflating their lungs and air sacs. The pairs remain joined for hours with the male keeping a tight grip on the female; this is called the *amplexus*. It helps to squeeze the eggs out of the ovary of the female and also helps the male to slowly pour the sperm or semen that fertilizes the eggs as they emerge from the female's body and are shed into the water. The eggs are kept in long gelatinous ribbons, masses of foam or other spongy involucres from where the tiny tadpoles will emerge at the end of the embryonic development period.

Frogs are highly sensitive to changes in the environment, including contemporary types of pollution, partly because they depend on different types of environment to complete their life-cycle, the aquatic and the terrestrial, which are successively water and air-breathing environments. Accordingly any environmental change that affects either the larval tadpole stage or the adult stage, threatens the survival of the whole population and of the species as a whole. Frogs are thus doubly vulnerable. At present the number of individual frogs of each species and the number of different species are decreasing sharply throughout the world due to pollution or changes in the environment or both, which affect one or the other of the morphological stages, either the tadpole or the adult. The narrow dependence of both stages on the environment precludes all changes of survival if ecological requirements are not met. Early man must have known this from observation, since in practically all cultures, including some tribal cultures of India, the frogs are much esteemed: they are signs of good luck and are sometimes totemic animals to whom even supernatural powers are attributed.

This is not the only hymn in the *ṚV* where the frogs are praised. They are mentioned briefly in *ṚV*, X; 166 and again in *ṚV*, X; 16, 13-14, where they are appropriately taken as an example of coolness. Verse 13-14 of the hymn to Agni (*l.c.*) describe the re-awakening of life, herbs, the lotus, grasses and other plants, after the coming of the rains on the places that summer or fire had 'scorched and burnt'. The frog, specially the female frog, is seen bringing refreshing coolness: '. . . may the earth cool again and . . . may this place be thronged with female frogs and give joy to the fire divine' (Agni); here the impressive fecundity of frogs is taken as an added good omen. In *ṚV*, X; 166, 5, man uses the frog as a symbol of conquest of solid ground. It reads:

> May I be highest having gained your strength in war, your skill in peace; my feet have trodden on your heads; Speak to us from beneath my feet, as frogs out of the water croak.

Viṣṇu

A digression on Lord Viṣṇu appears to be in order here. The origin of the concept of Viṣṇu as Preserver in the Hindu Trinity, can be traced to the early Vedas. In the Hindu Trinity, Brahmā is the Creator of life; Śiva is the Destroyer, or better, is the one who recycles life according to the correct observation that there is no life without death that in turn generates new life; and Viṣṇu is the Preserver of life and of the environmental conditions that make life possible.

The origin of the concept of Viṣṇu as Preserver of life on Earth is clear from internal evidence in the *ṚV* itself. This is based on the three strides of Viṣṇu whose steps regulate the movements of the sun and who was aided by the seven metres of the Veda to traverse the three worlds in just three strides. Similarly Indra was aided by the metres to conquer the threat and fear of insecurity, ignorance and death (*R̥V*, I; 22) or: night, darkness and cold. The metres are the means by which *śruti*, the revealed Truth, is formulated. Man benefited from these actions since 'mortal man when he beholds two steps of him who looks upon the light is restless with amaze. But his third step no one ventures to approach, not even the feathered birds of the air that fly with wings' (*R̥V*, I; 55, 5). Incidentally this and other verses are a clear indication of the care with which astronomical observations were made since very early times to determine the fixes of the sun's life. The movements of the celestial bodies are a sure indication that they are alive, even if endowed with a type of life different from that which is familiar to us on Earth. Viṣṇu is the one who measures the three regions; this world, the nether world and the celestial world.

As the Preserver, Viṣṇu also has something to do with immortality, thus he is the guardian of the loftiest station, upholding dear, immortal places (*R̥V*, IV; 3, 7).

The name Viṣṇu can be translated as 'the all-surrounding, all encircling, encompassing all' and he is also called *Evāyāvāḥ* in *R̥V*, I; 90, 5 and *Evāyāmarut* in *R̥V*, V; 87 and also *R̥V*, I; 90, 5. The meaning is that of one who is on his habitual way, who runs on his course.

There are only three hymns devoted exclusively to Lord Viṣṇu in the *R̥V*. They are *R̥V*, I; 154 and 156; *R̥V*, VII; 100. There are 73 hymns where Viṣṇu is either mentioned by name only, mainly in hymns to the Viśvedevas, or is mentioned at greater length and is often associated to Pūṣan, the very ancient pathfinder, guide of travellers, giver of prosperity and abundant food, who is therefore thus compared or joined to Viṣṇu himself (*R̥V*, VI; 49, 14). Viṣṇu is also associated to Indra, the Aśvins and Agni, respectively the overlord-king, the healers and the energy and heat of the universe. What is significant is that wherever

Viṣṇu is eulogized or his attributes are just mentioned, he is invariably the one who 'strode through the seven regions of the Earth' (*ṚV*, I; 22, 16) ; or 'the one of the mighty strides' or 'of the three steps' (*ṚV*, I; 90, 9 — *ṚV*, I; 154; 155 — *ṚV*, III; 54 — *ṚV*, V; 87, 8 — *ṚV*, VII; 99 — *ṚV*, VII; 100 — *ṚV*, VIII; 10, 2 — *ṚV*, VIII; 52).

Viṣṇu is he who speeds on (*ṚV*, II; 34), swift moving, bounteous (*ṚV*, VII; 40, 5), rich in food, milch cows, fertile pastures (*ṚV*, VII; 99, VII; 103). Viṣṇu is far striding (*ṚV*, IV; 3, 7) and he is found in three places (*ṚV*, VI; 12, 2).

Viṣṇu is the one 'who measured the earthly regions' (*ṚV*, VI; 49, 13) and who 'makes the regions broad for our existence' (*ṚV*, VI; 69, 5) and Indra/Viṣṇu who 'when fought the battle produced the three divisions' (*ṚV*, l.c., 8). Viṣṇu gives happiness (*ṚV*, VII; 35, 9) and bounty (mentioned at many places, ex. : *ṚV*, VIII; 25, 12 and 77, a *Vālākhilya* hymn). Viṣṇu is guardian of the future infant (literally and also figuratively as the New Year, in the context of hymn *ṚV*, VII; 36, 9) and is protector of his own supramost station, obviously the sky regions or heaven, in *ṚV*, X; 1, 3. Viṣṇu, Lord of the mighty strides, Śipiviṣṭa, is said to have measured spacious room for sacrifice by generating Sūrya, Uṣas and Agni (*ṚV*, VII; 99) and he is the lofty and bounteous ruling power (*ṚV*, VIII; 15, 9). Dandekar (1997) says: 'Viṣṇu must have originally been a god of virility and fertility'. The master bases his reading mainly on the etymology of the word *śipiviṣṭa* under which Viṣṇu is characterized in a few passages of the *ṚV*. According to Dandekar (*l.c.*, p. 31), 'the word *śipiviṣṭa* denotes an expanding, active male organ' . . . 'in confirmation of this hypothesis attention may be drawn on the Vṛṣākapi hymn . . . and the identity of Vṛṣākapi with Viṣṇu is proved by considerable literary evidence' . . . 'Viṣṇu's association with Sīnivālī, the guardian goddess of wombs' . . . 'and other epithets further support the concept of Viṣṇu as a fertility god from the popular religion of the masses of the common people'. Dandekar further states: . . . 'While granting recognition [to the gods of the popular cults] those poet priests took care to change the original character of those gods in such a way as to bring those gods, as far as possible, in line with the hieratic religio-mythological ideology'. Seen from this perspective it appears to me to be clear how and why in the *Ṛgveda* emphasis is put on the three steps of Viṣṇu, and how his personality grew to that of Regulator of the Seasons, according to *ṛta*, which is governed by Varuṇa. Thus the personality of Viṣṇu gradually evolved into that of the Great Preserver. Preserver of fertility and fecundity which are, in plants and animals, mainly regulated by the seasons.

Read in the language of the hymn to the *maṇḍūka* and of the Atirātra and Viśvajit ceremonies mentioned in the hymn and which are part of the *Soma-yajña*, all the references make sense as Viṣṇu being the one who measures and gives the time of the fixed points of the solar year on Earth: the solstices and equinoxes.

The *ṚV*, X; 15, 3 is a hymn to the Fathers. In it is said that 'I have gained son and progeny from Viṣṇu' and in *ṚV*, X; 184, 1; Viṣṇu is requested to give shape to the womb as Tvaṣṭṛ duly shapes the form, or embryo.

In *Maṇḍala* Xth of the *ṚV*, Viṣṇu is associated to Mitra who presides over correct observance of contracts and of judicial aspects of translations and is also a faithful observant of *ṛta*, the universal law of the cosmos.

ṚV, I; 154 by sage Dīrghatamas is particularly important in that it is dedicated to Viṣṇu who has measured out the universe with his three steps. It is a glorification of Viṣṇu's strides that separated sky, or heaven, from earth, the abode of man, and thereby created space for living beings and opened up the nether world to the ancestors. Viṣṇu also, it is stated, regulates the movements of the sun and with it and by inference, regulates the cycle of the seasons.

In the realm created and to this day preserved by the God's three strides, live all the creatures, all the *bhūta* or beings, to the ultimate end of the universe. The wish is expressed that man may reach the God's abode where there is plenty of all that is good; the abundance of spiritual knowledge and material goodness is inexhaustible (*R̥V*, I; 154, 6) and is poetically expressed as 'many horned and clever cattle'.

In the three hymns dedicated to Viṣṇu and from the several other places where he is mentioned, it is evident that emphasis is put on the three steps, the three strides, the symbolism of which is well known.

The Trivikrama *avatāra*, the dwarf myth, is a faithful representation of this aspect of Lord Viṣṇu. From internal evidence in the Veda and from later mythology, the three steps of Lord Viṣṇu are his main characteristic and glory. I would like to conclude that the personality of Viṣṇu as Preserver comes from the Vedic conviction — or revelation — that He is the Regulator, the Ordainer and Overseer of the travels — the transit — of the sun and therefore of the solar year and of the succession of the seasons, each bearer of its own products. Logically, Viṣṇu's consort is Wealth personified, Goddess Lakṣmī.

Viṣṇu is definitely not a personification of the sun, as many early commentators would have it. He is the measurer, regulator, and comptroller of the sun's movements and because of this He is the Great Preserver. He takes his bearings at the stations where the three steps are marked, which are the winter and summer solstices and the two equinoxes. The two equinoxes count as one because they are alike in space and relative time and because they are used since remote times to mark the place on the surface of the Earth where the observations are made. Viṣṇu is there — and here — and everywhere under the sun to oversee that *r̥ta* is faithfully observed regarding the solar year and man, who is to reap the benefits, is allowed to give participatory help in the process. Man helps and participates by chanting, at the right time, the same *mantras* that helped Indra to overcome fear, ignorance and death, and that helped Viṣṇu to regulate the course of the sun, in human terms. In so doing man can aspire to eternal life because he becomes part of the whole. Man should conquer, not beg for immortality. These concepts are clearly expressed in the R̥gvedic *Brāhmaṇas*.

These are also, I believe, the roots and origin of the personification of the concept of the Great Preserver, Viṣṇu the God who controls in space and time the yearly cycles and who teaches man how to observe, measure and fix time at any selected place (Vannucci, 1995 b).

Lord Viṣṇu showed to man that Space and Time are one as Matter and Energy are also one and interrelated. Matter and Energy are interchangeable and personified in Lord Agni. Time and Space are also interrelated and the Vedic *r̥ṣis* realized that man cannot find his place in the universe unless he measures places in relation to time and time in relation to place. This is the root concept of astrology and astronomy.

Frogs Elsewhere in the Vedas

Frogs are mentioned in the *AV* (*Atharvaveda*), in the *YV* (*Yajurveda*) and in the *Brāhamaṇas*. Of particular interest in this context is *AV*, IV which is in many ways an expansion of *R̥V*, VII; 103. It is more explicit and has beautiful description of the bursting of the monsoon. It refers to the rite performed to invoke rains, it describes the water cycle: beginning with the evaporation of water from the oceans it goes on to describe cloud formation and monsoonal winds that 'gladden the Earth', and finishes with the downpours or rain. It further describes how the waters imbibe the plants; the noise made by the troops of Maruts or winds, and the sound of the misty great bull or Indra; they all sound like pleasant music or songs and inevitably fertilize the Earth. The monsoonal rains brought by Parjanya are seen as the seed from Father Sky fertilizing Mother Earth; water is indeed *amṛta*, the godly nectar or ambrosia received from the sky. Agni Jātavedas, or omniscient Fire that here represents energy, particularly life-energy is associated to the waters and has become the energy within all plants. In fact, the rains come at a time when the weather is still hot, the days long and when there is plenty of light and sunshine; consequently plants grow fast and well. The magic of the great father *asura* Varuṇa does not manifest itself only by the awakening of plant life but animals also gain new vigour and energy, such as the 'spotted-armed frogs' that croak in the water (*AV*, IV; 12 — *l.c.* 13) and the herbivorous animals such as cows, goats and sheep. In conclusion, there too the comparison is made between brāhmaṇa and frogs quickened by Parjanya. In *AV*, IV; 13-15 the frogs are invoked to call the rains and to seek the favour of the Maruts. The she-frog is specially mentioned in her reproductive posture when she spreads the four limbs in the middle of the pond to receive the *amplexus* of the male frog of the same species. Different species are mentioned by name such as *khanvakha* and *khamakha*, while the female frog herself is called *tadurī*. This particular text of the *AV* clearly confirms the interpretation given above of the corresponding hymn of the *ṚV* (VII; 103).

The first stanza of *AV*, VII; 18, says: 'burst forth, O Earth; split this cloud of heaven; untie for us, O Dhātṛ that art master, the skin-bag of the water of heaven'. The second says: 'not heat-burned, not cold smote; let the earth of quick drops burst forth; water verily flow *ghī* for him; where Soma is, there is it ever excellent' (transl. Griffith). The equinoxes are obviously referred to here, when it is neither too hot nor too cold, both being alike the middle season, each between the two solstices, the summer and the winter solstice. Further, the parallel here is that the frogs and the Atirātra ritual mentioned in the *ṚV* are both true time markers; frogs mark the bursting of the monsoon while the night specified by the brāhmaṇa for performing the Atirātra marks the solstices (*viṣuvat*) as mentioned in the *Kauṣītaki Brāhmaṇa* (*Adhyāya* XVII, XXV) and elsewhere. Through these rites and rituals and in this manner through the sacrifices, man can participate in and be guided by the natural cycles of the universe.

Verse I, as mentioned above, is particularly interesting as it invokes Dhātr̥ who is a very ancient Vedic God. At the *garbhādhāna saṁskāra* or conception rite, Dhātr̥ as maker or creator is requested to place the embryo in the womb. This is part of the concept of universal fertilisation of women who are biologically similar to other female living beings. Dhātr̥ (*R̥V*, X; 190, 3) is also said to have placed Sūrya, the sun, who is giver of life on earth, in his place in the sky. All these expressions and rituals are interrelated and strengthen the concept discussed above and expressed in *R̥V*, VII; 103 that specific sacrifices, like frogs, are time-setters and markers for the correct observance of *r̥ta*. Frogs also play an important role in the performance of the last rites, because a new and different cycle, no longer controlled by the seasons, begins after death of the body. In *AV*, XVIII; 3, 60, it is said that after the fire has consumed the corpse, water plants and a frog are placed where the fire has burned, with the words: '. . . bless us in waters, female frog, soothe down here this Agni'.

YV, XVII; 6, is scientifically and poetically beautiful in its description of frogs, specially the female frog seen as an auspicious animal; more than just a good omen, the female frog is invoked also as a means to ensure the success of the sacrifice. The female frog is requested to accompany Lord Agni who as heat is *apām-napāt* or the energy in water and in everything else; in accompanying Lord Agni on many occasions, it is the frog, the female frog that makes the sacrifice successful by showing the rebirth of nature and its bright colours after the dormancy and dreary dull colours of the dry season.

There are other references to frogs in the *YV*, in the sense that they bring coolness and the female frog is again taken as a symbol of fertility and as an auspicious symbol. *YV*, XVII; 4, 6 says: 'with them come hither, female frog, and render this sacrifice of ours bright-hued, successful'.

Seen in this context the concepts expressed in the hymn to the *maṇḍūka* are absolutely correct, bio-ecologically valid and a sensible guide for a good life where seasons dictate the activities appropriate for the correct and rational observance and use of *ṛta* and all nature. These activities include animal husbandry, agricultural practices, travels, shiftings, building house, tools and chariots, in brief all life activities of settled and nomadic people. It is the basic knowledge acquired by the *ṛṣis* that underlines a single holistic philosophy, whether frogs, the seasons or astronomical fixes are discussed and correlated.

The Atirātra Sacrifice

A few commentaries on why the Atirātra is seen to be so important in this context as to be mentioned explicitly in *ṚV*, VII; 103. In fact, it is the only place in the *ṚV* where the Atirātra is mentioned explicitly, though it is given a prominent place in the Ṛgvedic *Brāhmaṇa*s.

It is particularly significant that the ritual is mentioned and details are given in the *Aitareya* and *Kauṣītaki Brāhmaṇa*s and it is mentioned elsewhere in the *śāstra*s, specially among the *saṁsthā*s of the *Agniṣṭoma* and the *Soma-yajña*, that are among the major and most ancient sacrifices.

The Atirātra is accompanied by libations and is followed by a recitation to the Aśvins made by the Hotṛ. All details of the rituals indicate the intention to link man to the date, the month, the solar year and as written: 'through the year the Atirātra is resolved in the Agniṣṭoma' and 'the sacrificial rites previous and subsequent to the Agniṣṭoma are resolved into the Agniṣṭoma'. *AitBrā Pañcikā* III; P. IV, A.1; P VI; A III. —*Kauṣītaki Brāhmaṇa Adhyāya* XVII, XXV. The Atirātra relieves man from fear just as the coming of the rains that was heralded by the frogs relieves man from the fearful hardships of the dry season and of the fear that the monsoon could fail. The myth related to the Atirātra describes how the *asura* took refuge in the night and Lord Indra asked who would accompany him to drive them away. The Gods, however, were afraid of night, darkness and cold, meaning: insecurity, ignorance and death: night resembles death. Only the *mantras* or metres followed Indra to help him drive away the *asuras*. The *mantras* alone can conquer the night by going round and round and thus they rescued Indra who when alone was afraid of night, darkness and death. In *Pañcikā* IV, I, a description is given of the Atirātra ritual in all details and instructions are given on how to equilibrate the number of chants and recitations of the night with those of the day so that night becomes similar in every way to the day, specially in the length or duration of day and night: '. . . thereby the night has *pavamānas*, thereby they become of equal portions'. Since the Atirātra marks the solstices, when day and night have different lengths, it is necessary to promote the equalisation and equilibrium between night and day to make them of like duration, a process that will be completed only at the following equinox, after which the imbalance grows again in the opposite sense, to become maximum at the following solstice. Hence the need for a year long rite to compensate accurately the length of day and night to define precisely solstices and equinoxes.

Man is also always looking to the future for betterment, thus it is said: 'what has been is limited, what is to be is unlimited, so win what is unlimited'. Consequently, to win what is unlimited, rituals are necessary and in this case only *mantras* were willing to accompany the Gods and man; therefore to participate in the cosmic drama, man must perform sacrifices. Thus: 'in that he recitates beyond the *stotra*, verily he wins whatever in him there is beyond the self'. Evidently the sacrifice is also a means for man to surpass himself and approach the Infinite Self, and immortality (*P*, IV; *Ad*, I).

In conclusion, the Atirātra ritual is a typical example of the practice of 'sympathetic magic' to promote the participation of man in the functioning and dynamics of the universe and of nature, and thus to extend human power 'beyond the self' in an 'unlimited way', in this case, to conquer the fear of darkness, night, death, ignorance, cold and death of the mind, body and spirit, as well as to determine the calendar with precision, the science of astrology or astronomy.

In *Pañcikā* VI, *Adhyāya* III the linkage with cosmic phenomena is emphasized by Indra who says to the *asura* after defeating them: 'so much as Viṣṇu three times traverses, so much be ours; let the rest be yours.... He traversed three worlds, then the Vedas, then speech'. This again recalls the Vāmana *avatāra*'s three steps that beyond the obvious meaning is also a symbol of the conquest of physical phenomena, of knowledge and of speech for the transmission of knowledge. It is also a reminder of the two solstices, one during the *uttarāyaṇa* (northern journey) and the other, the *dakṣiṇāyaṇa* (southern journey) of the Sun God: Sūrya. The two equinoxes are alike and are the middle point between the two passages. The summer solstice roughly coincides with the arrival of the monsoon in northern India and that is when the frogs sing their song of rejoicing.

The Atirātra is a nocturnal rite similar to the night long chant of the frogs and it has as its parallel the day long rite, the Viśvajit (*Kauṣītaki Brāhmaṇa*, XXV) that is also part of the *Soma-yajña*, and of the diurnal activities of the frogs. Though the Viśvajit is not mentioned in the hymn to the *maṇḍūka*, it clearly indicates, in the *R̥V Brāhmaṇas*, the only two times in a year long cycle when night and day have the same length or duration. This is why the two equinoxes are counted as one, and there are only three steps.

By reciting the same *mantras* as had assisted Indra to conquer the powers of night, darkness and cold, man assists and gives power to the Gods and thereby participates in the functioning of *r̥ta*. Man obtains spiritual immortality by reciting the *mantras* that celebrate the invincibility of natural phenomena, in a manner similar to what was called the 'mysteries' in Mediterranean cultures, specially the Greek mysteries of Eleusis. These are expressions of sympathetic magic at its best, based on the principle that, similar to the *mantras*, I help the Gods so that they may help me: a participatory strategy.

The recitation of the same *mantras* that helped Indra defeat the *asura*, now restores the equilibrium between the length of the day and the length of the night, by gradually shortening the night and lengthening the day after the winter solstice until when equality between the duration of the day and of the night is restored at the spring equinox. Thus the rite proves and celebrates the conquest over the powers of darkness. At the spring equinox the process is reversed, inequality again starts building up, days gradually become longer and nights shorter and the equilibrium is broken up and becomes maximum at the summer solstice when days have greatest length and nights are shorter. At the two equinoxes, the spring and autumn equinoxes, the balance between night and day is perfect but does not last long, and the symmetry is broken again in one sense or other, depending on whether the sun is going south or north. Because the two equinoxes are alike they are counted as one, but the two solstices are not only different, but opposed to one another and are therefore counted as two.

Rhythms, recitations, day and night cycles, solar and lunar years, are different aspects of time and of the measurement of time. One of the fundamental preoccupations of Vedic man was to determine his position in time, for which he had to determine his position in space, hence the early determination of latitude. Time and place had to be determined exactly to ensure the efficiency and successful performance of the sacrifices; errors in determining the correct time for the beginning and end of the *yajña* would have to be corrected by performing difficult expiatory rites.

To achieve its stated purpose, the Atirātra nocturnal sacrifice must be balanced by a corresponding diurnal sacrifice which is the Viśvajit, which is described in detail in the *Kauṣītaki Brāhmaṇa* of the *ṚV* (*KB*, XXV; 11-15) and is mentioned also at several places in the *Aitareya Brāhmaṇa*. The stated intention of the Viśvajit rite is to 'obtain the thirteenth month, which is as great as the year' and 'makes the year'. Evidently the rite is for the purpose of establishing the coincidence of the lunar year with the solar year; the Viśvajit is a one day rite that has validity for one year; it is a support rite. At *Kauṣītaki Brāhmaṇa* XXV, 14, it is said that if the Viśvajit is a one day rite or the middle of a night session, it should be an Atirātra: 'the Atirātra is complete Viśvajit; half of the Viśvajit performed by day and half by night'.

In conclusion it is evident that the purpose of associating the Atirātra with the Viśvajit is to complement one with the other with the purpose of balancing day and night and thus mark calendar fixes correctly as well as the coincidence of the solar and lunar calendars.

The Atirātra and the Viśvajit cannot be otherwise than year long sacrifices, even if only symbolically and performed mainly at the solstices and equinoxes, because they are meant to restore the order or symmetry that is incessantly broken by the travel of the sun. On the other hand movement is life, no life is possible without movement, the seasons are brought about by the movements of the sun, the seasons are the continuous renewal of life and with the changing of the seasons different aspects of life become manifest. The cyclic changes of seasons bring about different manifestations of life in a repetitive way, therefore Viṣṇu becomes the Preserver and Sustainer of Life.

Viṣṇu is not a solar deity as he has often been described; he is not a solar deity as such, but he is the one that marks the timing and therefore causes and sustains the seasons or rather, the cyclic changes of the seasons, therefore Lord Viṣṇu is the one who brings forth the beauty and periodical renewal and bounty of nature. From all sectors of the Vedas it can be seen that Viṣṇu is the preserver of *ṛta*, of the law that controls and regulates the seasons. In a way, however, he is Preserver only in a secondary manner, since he preserves physical life that is otherwise given by the Sun God. He is well represented by the Vāmana *avatāra* who regulates the course of life in just three strides that may be interpreted in many ways, including, as done here, that the strides mark the two solstices and the two equinoxes counted as one.

In conclusion, I believe that these are the main reasons why the Atirātra ritual is given such a prominent place in two of the most significant and important sacrifices, the Soma sacrifice and the Agniṣṭoma. At the Atirātra ritual the balancing of the duration of the day and night is brought about by *pavamāna*s, that means 'self-purifying'. It is significant that *mantra*s called '*pavamāna*s', that are self-regulating, are those in-charge of adjusting the length of day and night. The system is in fact a self-regulating or automatic process; it is a feedback input-output system regulated by astronomical phenomena beyond the reach or rule of man. It is therefore quite appropriate that the *pavamāna*s, self-purifying, are those called upon to regulate the day/night length that is inevitably disrupted by the passage of time; 'the *soma* juice has been pressed . . . with might' and 'by adding other *stotra*s . . . sing the *sandhi* (*sāman*). . . thereby the night has fifteen *stotra*s. . . thereby both have fifteen *stotra*s . . . they become equal. . . .' Then the *Aśvina Śāstra* follows the *sandhi stotra* at the Atirātra ceremony and is characterized by recitations to Agni, Uṣas, and the Aśvina. These evidently symbolize and invoke: life energy, daily awakening of life and good health respectively.

Frogs in the Avesta

In general in all cultures frogs are symbols of fecundity, happiness and joy. In the Avesta, however, frogs are seen as pernicious animals because they defile the water in which they live (*Vendidad*). Maybe the negative aspect of frogs is seen also in the fact that they chant their songs at night, a symbol of death. Much of the Avesta, as we have it, is concerned with the fear and repulsion of Death, of the *drug* or curse and pollution that accompanies death of the body. The repulsion and fear of death runs throughout most of the Avesta; while in the Veda efforts are made to conquer this natural fear, man appears to have succumbed to it in the Avesta.

It is interesting to note that in spite of common roots and unmistakable similarities in the religion of Ahura Mazda or Mazdeism, as reflected in the Avesta on one side, and the Veda as we have them on the other, the concepts and ideas expressed in them are often enantiomorphic to one another. The relationships among the concepts of the two are minor images of one another, with few exceptions that I can think of. A pair of enantiomorphic things are specular images of each other; enantiomorphic pairs, such as for instance lactic acid molecules or sugar crystals have identical chemical properties, but as identical hands of the same body, they are alike only when seen in a mirror and in whatever manner they are rotated they cannot cover each other as symmetrical objects do; they are not parallel to one another.

It can only be a matter of speculation why so many concepts of the Avesta, as we have it, are mirror image of Vedic concepts and ideas, which include the treatment given to earth, water, air and fire. Because these basic elements should not be polluted by the *drug* of death, Zoroastrians cannot bury, burn, release in water or air the dead bodies; these have to be consumed by vultures to avoid polluting the basic life-sustaining elements.

Unfortunately what has come down to us of the ancient religion of Persia is only a fraction of what appears to have been an extensive collection of sacred texts. The *gāthā*s by and large correspond to the Ṛgvedic **hymns** or songs of the seers and are part of the *Yasna* of the Avesta; they are written in a special dialect older than the general language of the main body of the

Avesta, and in this sense they are comparable to the ancient Sanskrit *gāthā* or songs that are not included in the Vedas probably because they are popular songs, perhaps profane. The sacred texts suffered many irreparable losses, beginning with Alexander the Great who burned the old sacred books when he traversed Persia on his travels of conquest towards India. The texts as we have them now are only fragments of the sacred literature of ancient Persia under the rule of the last Achemenian Kings (559-330 BC); they were originally the sacred books of the *Magi* and it was king Cyrus who introduced Mazdeism into Persia.

In the Avesta, time and space are called the 'first principles of the World' and the two basic concepts of Mazdeism are: first, there is a law in nature which is called *Asha* or *Asha Vahista* or the 'excellent *Asha*'; second, there is a constant struggle (the word used was war) in nature. The similarities and common origin of Vedism and Mazdeism have been discussed exhaustively by many scholars. What has also been discussed, interpreted and explained in different ways is the curious phenomenon of the dichotomy between the philosophies and religions that were developed over the course of time in Persia and in India. Almost everything in the two became the opposite of each other except for the central importance given to the worship of Fire. In some cases the divergence appears to have taken place in the Vedic-Brāhmaṇical-Hindu line of thought; in others it appears to have taken place in Mazdeism-Zoroastrianism. For instance the word *asura*; originally it means one possessed of great knowledge and magical power, as Agni, Varuṇa and Ahura Mazda: the 'maker of material worlds'. Varuṇa is the Supreme God of the Vedic age and Ahura Mazda of Mazdeism. Later, however, *asura* acquired in India the meaning of great power and embodiment of the forces of evil, while it retained the original meaning in Persia. On the other hand the *deva* retained their godly attributes and connotations in India, while the *Daeva* became the personification of all evils in the Avesta. The profession of faith that is given at the beginning of many texts and rituals of the Avesta is: 'I confess myself... one who hates the *Daevas* and obeys the laws of *Ahura* . . . I confess myself a worshipper of *Mazda*'. It is interesting to note that the *Śatapatha Brāhmaṇa* (K.l, *Adh*. 9, 3; 10-12) says: 'On the earth Viṣṇu strode by means of the *gāyatrī mantra*: excluded therefrom is he who hates us and whom we hate', also *YV*, 2, 15. It is also stated that in the sky Viṣṇu strode by the *jagatī* metre; in the air, by the triṣṭupa metre and on the earth by the *gāyatrī* metre—thereafter the sacrificer is liberated from his vow saying: 'Now I am he whom I really am' (*YV*, 2, 28).

It is still an open question whether the frequent inversion of the meaning and significance was purposeful or if it just happened because of changes in lifestyles, habits, needs and activities of people living under different environmental conditions. Would this be so, it would be a good example of how ecological constraints, laws and rules of nature influence man's beliefs and religion. Natural philosophy, or the science of nature is indeed different in different places. Frogs are seen as good or bad omen, as good or bad animals depending on whether water is abundant, scarce or oscillates between inundations and droughts.

The reason of bringing this up in this brief commentary of *R̥V*, VII; 103, is that in a monsoon regulated sun-year cycle, frogs appear as the heralds of good fortune, while in areas where the hydrological and climatological regimes are not primarily ruled by monsoons and where there are large arid and semi-arid areas, frogs would be found living in small bodies of water and would naturally be regarded as polluting the scarce resource. Nobody would like to find egg-masses or living frogs in one's backyard pond or water pot!

Indra however, as Indra Vr̥trahan in the Avesta and Indra Vr̥traha in the *R̥V*, is the killer of danger, of night and of darkness and therefore is the God who conquers light; this could well be a reminiscence of the very old myths detailed in the R̥gvedic *Brāhmaṇas* and the frequent mention of the slaying of

Vṛtra in the *ṚV* itself. Incidentally *Asha Vahista* of the Avesta is the holy order of the world, maintained chiefly by the sacrificial fire because of the *genius* of fire (p. LXXIV, 2, notes), a concept identical to the expression in the *ṚV* (Vannucci, 1994) where Lord Agni is the sustainer *ṛta*, as the 'fireness' in fire, as the personification of the concept of Fire.

The whole question of the similarities, ideas and concepts between Mazdeism-Zoroastrianism on one side and Vedism-Brāhmaṇism-Hinduism on the other is extremely interesting, but it would be out of place to discuss it here. Suffice to bring out the example of the perspective under which frogs are seen in the *ṚV* and in the Avesta. In the Avesta it is said that the frog is bad because it gnaws at the tree of everlasting life: *Vouru-Kasha*. It is considered bad because of the constant worry with keeping water pure and clean; where water is scarce it evidently needs to be taken care of with the utmost circumspection. The oath by Water and Fire in front of the God of Truth: Mitra, was the strongest that could be made under Mazdeism-Zoroastrianism. Early travellers justified the horror that people had of frogs and toads because it is they 'who cause the death of man since they continuously spoil the water where they live, the more frogs and toads are in the country so much more waters cause diseases and death' *(Ardvi Sura* in the *Vendidad*). It may be recalled here that though the so-called 'Persian wheel' used to elevate water is not a Persian invention, the ancient Iranians had developed a highly sophisticated system to draw pure drinking ground water that in that part of the world is found at great depths in the ground, and is retrieved only at the cost of much labour and through elaborate engineering works. Surface water is of easy access but is correctly pointed out as being frequently polluted and unfit for drinking.

Frogs and toads are obviously taken as elements of pollution; it is therefore logical that 'he shall kill a thousand land frogs (toads) and two thousand water frogs' to make atonement of sins committed.

Frogs in other Cultures

According to tradition, the ancestors of the Kalash people of Chitral, now in north Pakistan, wandered without knowing where to stay until when they finally settled in the valleys that they still occupy at present. Their main God is *Mahandeo* (Mahādeva) and the most important festival takes place on the occasion of the winter solstice when God Balumain/Indra comes to spend some time with his people. He then participates in their activities and listens to their prayers; his presence among the people is extended throughout the stay of the sun in his winter abode and departs only to return the following year, about a month after arriving on horseback. Only the shaman, however, is able to see either the God or his horse. We may recall incidentally, that in the *R̥V* it is mentioned that the tribe of Kaṇva wandered away and was lost forever.

Details of the Atirātra sacrifice remind one of the rites of the Kalash people and are remarkably similar to them; one is tempted to hypothesize that the descendants of the lost Kāṇva tribe may be the present-day people of those valleys of the Hindukush, quite isolated until recently. The rites that mark the celebration of the winter solstice period have many similarities with the Agniṣṭoma and Soma sacrifices in general and with the Atirātra ritual in particular. Among the Kalash the Supreme Being is called Dezau, which corresponds to the ancient Āryan God Dyaus; some rites involve offerings of wheat to Balumain and his horse; all the rites begin with lighting and worshipping Fire and pouring *ghī* on the sacrificial fire; other offerings are mainly *panīr* and *malāī* that had been wrapped in oak bark containers and kept for many months cool under irrigation ditches; wheat *capātī* are offered to the gods and abundant libations are made with recently pressed and fermented grapes juice. The ritual preparation of this wine reminds one of the ritual preparation of *soma* as repeated at several places in the Vedas. Early stages of celebration of the winter solstice involve night long vigorous dances by the women and it is believed that the more vigorous, the greater will be the efficiency of the celebrations made to propitiate the gods; the declared intention is to communicate with the Gods. The last day festival resembles closely the happy festivities of the *lohḍī* which is still now one of the important festivals of Punjab and other places in north India.

Day long ceremonies balance the night ceremonies and are a similar series of joyful festivals with the intention of restoring the balance between day and night and the declared intention of opposing day to night, light to darkness and life to death. Balumain/Indra is requested to eat, drink (grapes wine) and return satisfied to his abode only to come back one year later. The winter solstice festivals reveal a semi-ritualistic and semi-social revival of Indra's victory over the *asura*'s powers of darkness coupled to the completion of one more year cycle and the beginning of a new one. Of all calendar fixes the winter solstice is in practice the easiest to determine accurately at places north of the tropic of Cancer.

In China frogs are used or imitated to invoke rains and they were shown on bronze drums because they remind thunders and call for rains. At the equinoxes the firebird, *yang*, is transformed into a frog, *yin*, and is a symbol of water, then he later becomes again the firebird according to nature's cycles. The ancient Chinese instrument to predict earthquakes was a wide mouth bowl with spouts at four or eight equidistant points corresponding to the cardinal directions. Often these spouts were represented as frogs.

In Vietnam the frog is compared to a spider and the symbolism involved is that it is a soul travelling while the body sleeps, therefore it should not be harmed. Toads prognosticate rains and are a symbol of success.

In Japan the frog is in general considered to be a good omen and is regarded as the protector of travellers. The Kappa is usually represented somewhat like a frog and is endowed with an uncanny type of wisdom peculiar to himself, a figure widely loved throughout the country. It may be born aged and gradually as time passes he becomes younger and when he naturally dies he is very very young. The frog is considered to return always to its starting point, even if deranged. Again a recognition of cycles.

In ancient Egypt it was believed that four couples represented the elementary forces that preceded the organised creation of the world; frogs and serpents were among these couples. Toads and frogs were associated with the dead and mummified toads have been found in ancient tombs.

In the Americas in general, specially central and northern South America, frogs are a symbol of fertility and harbingers of good times; among the Maya-Quiché it is said that toads like men, pray to the God of rains for his favours. Among some, toads are considered to be deities.

Amphibians in general have figured prominently in witchcraft everywhere and they are supposed to have a 'magical' ability to heal wounds (Carmon, 1987); in fact the secretion of their skin contains antibiotic peptides. The venom of the parotid gland of many species of toads is a mild poison and has been used for different magical practices and for noxious preparations.

Among the South Siberian Turks there are special invocations to the spirit of the frog because it is the spirit that helps the shaman and travels with him while his body is in trance. The frog is eulogized together with the snake and she is invoked with the following words: 'can you and will you reach the land of Ulgan?' Ulgan among the South Siberian Turks is the Supreme Being, the one 'who brings good fortune and who distributes all that is good'. The frog is also the one who transports the home-made beer in a container made of bark to the Spirit Protector of the clan. Stylized figures of frogs and other figures are drawn on the lower half of the drum that is like an alter-ego of the shaman; all the figures have symbolic magical significance. The frog is also said to close with her feet the mouth of the vessel that contains the beer for the sacrifice. The frog's name is '*paya*', she keeps company with the shaman's spirit during the travels and again we see here the frog associated with concepts of the passage of time and the conquest of space.

In Christianity, communion is not sought to be achieved with all nature; there never is question of being one with, or being fused with nature; even the pantheism of Giordano Bruno would not have this fusion as its goal. Communion in Christianity is exclusively for union with the Godhead; the resurrection of Jesus Christ and the promise of resurrection from the dead are the means to attain immortality rather than the merger with the Godhead.

The Sūfis and the famous mathematician-astronomer Omar Khayyam approach the ideal identification and perfect union of all nature to the point of admitting the total loss of identity of the self and its fusion with the universe of creation. Omar Khayyam expresses this beautifully: 'respect this earthen water pot, it was once the hips of a lovely maiden'. This is not just an expression of cheap epicurism as sometimes misinterpreted; it is rather the poetic representation of the cycling of matter and energy in nature and the wholeness and sanctity of all creation, living and non-living.

The definition of Time and Space was a matter of primary importance for many people of most cultures. Among the Hebrews some rabbis said that the Sabbath, that begins on Friday night, is a time to 'sit back and relax'; the Sabbath 'is a day of magic'; it is a 'ceremony to be aware of the flow of time and how to measure it'; it is a 'ritual to sanctify time'. Special food is prepared and candles are lit by elder women who are the preservers of time; therefore, tradition. The Sabbath of the new moon that marks the beginning of a new month, is specially sacred. The climate in Palestine is not a monsoonal system and it is dry; a hymn to the frogs evidently could not have been developed there, but other markers were devised to mark the passage of time.

Most men have had the agonizing desire of eternal life; Vedic man was perhaps not the only one. He was, however, most probably the one who was nearest to achieve this goal by recognizing, not the dependence of man on nature, but the oneness and **identity in essence** of man with nature. This concept first expressed by the Vedic *r̥ṣi* evolved to its best formulation in Advaita Vedānta.

It is not the scope of this book to go into details of the rites and rituals of different cultures, but it is interesting to note that all cultures were concerned with time and the passage of time. The way by which this was done, was greatly influenced by local ecological characteristics. We may confidently say that one of the first preoccupations of thinking, cultured man, was with his position in time and space. This preoccupation he resolved with the discipline of rites and rituals; Vedic man thus 'resolved' this problem with, for instance, the Atirātra *yajña*.

Conclusion

In conclusion, the hymn about the frogs, *maṇḍūka*, far from being a joke, a pun, a song written in a lighter vein or satirisation of the brāhmaṇa, as variedly described by earlier and contemporary commentators, is an important hymn that gives some of the fundamentals of Vedic philosophy for what concerns the cause and effect links between the movements of the sun and life on Earth. Evidence of this is given in the hymn itself by referring to the Atirātra ceremony. This rite is detailed in the *Aitareya* and *Kauṣītaki Brāhmaṇas* of the *R̥gveda*, where the three strides of Viṣṇu are also referred to in the same context; as the measure of Time and Space. The *R̥V*, VII; 103 hymn explains how and why the Lord Viṣṇu is the deification of the abstract concept of the measure of Time in relation to Space and of Space in relation to Time. Viṣṇu preserves the interrelation between space and time that in turn ensures the maintenance of nature's rhythms and sustains the production of all the goods provided by each season.

All these ideas taken together are evidently the fruit of the endeavour to acquire knowledge that moved the Vedic man 'to unveil *ṛta*', as the *ṛṣi* said, aiming at understanding the Law and Order that rules the Universe. This is how Viṣṇu already in the *ṚV* and later more openly so in the Brāhmaṇical religion, is declared, invoked and worshipped as the Preserver of Life on Earth. He is the Preserver of Life on Earth **because** he is regulator of the seasons and the seasons vary as a function of space and time. The seasons in turn bring with them the constant renewal and increase of life on earth.

This is how the frogs: 'bring us cows in plenty'.

The officiating brāhmaṇa draws a frog, a lotus flower and a bamboo shoot across the central part of the fire altar during the *Śatarudriya* lustration when the seventh layer of the fire altar has been completed. This is one of the very last rituals for building the fire altar at the *Soma-yajña* which is one of the most imposing of the *Śrauta* rites. Agni is now fully installed, he has become Rudra, hence:

> When like a snorting stead that longeth for the pasture
> he started forth from the great enclosure
> then the wind fanned his flame and black was thy path
> *ṚV*, VII; 3, 2

Water dripped off Agni when in the beginning of time the vital airs made fire. The drops that dripped off the fire became frogs, lotus flowers and bamboo shoots; in other words, the animals, the water plants and trees, or plants in general that are the main three sources of food for man: 'Upon the earth, into the seed, into the rivers, descend thou, O Agni, thou art the energy of waters. With them come thou, O she-frog, and make the sacrifice bright coloured and propitious for us (*Śat Brā Kand.* 9, *Adh.* I, *Brhm.* 2).

Maybe this is why when offering the *sūrya namaskāram* to the rising Sun, the sunrays should be seen through the water offered out of joined palms: this is the relation between the energy of the sun and that of water for the creation and maintenance of life. Both are indispensable and if one of them is lacking, there can be no life. This is a basic biological fact clearly expressed several times in the Veda; the excess or absence of either one of them destroys all life (*R̥V*, IX; 3, 2), and this is the lesson that sage Vasiṣṭha tells us he learned from humble frogs.

O full of coolness, thou cool plant, full of fresh moisture freshening herb,
Come hither with the female frog: fill with delight this Agni here.

R̥V, X; 16, 14

2

The Wedding of Sūryā

ṚV. X; 85

ṛṣi* Manyu. Metres: *Anuṣṭup*; *Triṣṭup*; *Jagatī*; *Urobṛhatī

Introduction

> *May Agni the first of all gods liberate her children from the noose of death. May king Varuṇa accept this, so that this woman never weeps on account of grief relating to her children.*
>
> Seventh *mantra* of contemporary Marriage ritual

The hymn is objectively dedicated to the wedding of Sūryā, the daughter of Sūrya, the Sun God. It is first and foremost dedicated to the splendour and joy of living, what in French is expressed as 'joie de vivre'. It is however, a very serious joy, a happiness to be obtained after dutiful preparation and responsible behaviour. It is dedicated to the true, healthy happiness of married life and is more a guide towards the celebration of marriage than a hymn to the 'ideal bride', as often repeated. It is a promise of the fulfilment of the normal aspirations of human beings, the rewards and enjoyments of companionship, love, dedication, sexual intimacy, maternity, paternity and enduring friendship. How best to express the joy, the happiness, the pleasure of being alive than by describing the main steps in the life of **Woman** that culminate with the preparation and celebration of the wedding of the daughter of the Sun God, the giver of life on Earth? Logically Sūryā is the ideal bride, capable of perpetuating human life. Who else but Soma personified could prepare the scene for such an important event when all nature, all Gods and all men rejoice together? What the purpose of the preparations, ceremonies and festivities, if not to give to the human husband a godly wife, well born, well trained and knowledgeable in the art of living a good life and educating good progeny? What else than **woman** as the central pivot of the family?

Earlier commentators considered this hymn to be a patchwork or composite of various intentions, the first five stanzas being a panegyric of Soma personified. It was also said that the hymn is a justification of polyandry because three 'husbands' of Sūryā are mentioned before she is handed over to her life-partner, the human husband.

In my opinion, however, since the first stanzas do not mention only Soma but other gods as well, they are indeed a laudation of nature with the purpose of setting up a marvellous stage for this most important of events, which is a wedding. The wedding is the central happening in the life of woman, second only to motherhood, which in turn would not take place if there had not been a good wedding. As Marañon, the Spanish human physiologist, said a woman does not realize her full potential until when she becomes a mother.

Far from being patch-work, *Ṛ̥V*, X; 85 is the description and celebration of one of the most important aspects of human life, the consummation of marriage. The hymn is also an apotheosis of the close interaction between the human and the divine, between Man and God; it is an apotheosis of the oneness of the universe where everything is related to everything else, from Sūrya, through Sūryā, to the minutest details of the ceremony and of first days after the wedding ceremonies are concluded and married life begins. Once again it is the participation of man in nature that is emphasized; man is seen as just one of the infinitely large number of elements that constitute nature.

The personification of the ideal bride serves the purpose of giving a model, an example; it is the embodiment of a wish, but one that is effective only if the model, the ideal bride in this case, is a character of distinction, an impeccable example worth imitating, an example with no reproach, the realization of a desire, an urge brought within reach.

Instrument and tool-making are materializations of knowledge that in turn generate information used for the acquisition of more knowledge. On the other hand, the deification of abstract ideas and concepts, as for instance Lord Agni as the all-pervading energy of the universe (Vannucci, 1994), is the crystallization of the mental representation or understanding of natural phenomena. The deification of the abstract idea of Life as Savitṛ, is the personalization of the mystery of the concept formulated by the question: what is life? For these reasons I do not agree with Griffith and others who consider that the deity of *ṚV*, VII; 103, the hymn about the frogs, are the frogs themselves, or that Sūryā is the deity of this hymn. The intended meaning of this song goes much deeper into factual knowledge and understanding, and Sūryā is not a deity at all but a very human, human being.

On the other hand *vāk*, Word or Speech as Sound or the rhythm and music of recitation and chanting, are instruments for the tuning of man to his material and non-material environment, because rhythm underlies all natural cycles and most natural processes and events. For the same reason *ṛta* is the law that governs the universe, but *ṛta*, like *vāk*, is not a God. Man however must, as stated, be One with *ṛta* to participate, live and survive in Nature. In other words, if man recognizes and understands nature, or, as said: 'unveils *ṛta*', he will become competent and capable of living happily. *Vāk* helps to understand and explain *ṛta*.

Sūryā's wedding represents that aspect of *ṛta* that guides women and men towards a happy married life. This is a song of great joy.

According to some commentators this is a later hymn;

however some of its features suggest that it must have had its origins in olden days, as for instance the mention of the very ancient *gāthā* (St. 6.), but this does not preclude possible later interpolations.

Though joyful and gay, it is a most serious song to advise on and celebrate the institution of marriage. It is the glorification of married life in which the bride, the wife and future mother plays a central role. It is an example of the Vedic religious practices for a happy, healthy, generous and optimistic way of life for men and women who actively and jointly participate, each playing his role, in the governing of the family and in the clan's life. The participation expresses itself in singing, dancing and worshipping gods actively, by doing the same things that gods do, in obeisance to *ṛta*.

Finally this song also indicates that rites and rituals were already well developed in Vedic times, though undoubtedly more and more ritualistic details were added with time. With time all religious practices evolve and tend to become more punctilious and complex.

The roots of the hymn being undoubtedly very old, it seems appropriate to include a brief commentary on the evolution of the word and concept of *deva*.

In studying the Vedas it must be born in mind that the *Saṁhitās* as we have them now, are not a religious or philosophical treatise formulated purposefully as a single, coherent piece of work. What we are left with now are the remains of a probably much larger body of songs created and probably modified over a period of many centuries or perhaps a few millennia. The hymns themselves are not arranged in chronological order and interpolations in single hymns appear to have occurred at undefinable points in time.

The evolution of man from a purely bio-ecological being into the rational man who used his power of observation to try to understand the relations of cause and effect in nature, led to the building of a body of knowledge on which the Vedic man based his philosophy and religion. In the Indian traditional culture, however, knowledge was not an aim in itself; what was sought for was wisdom. Wisdom to be applied to all aspects of human life, to the day-to-day struggle for survival, to the relationship among humans and the relationship between man, his environment and the super-human. The word super-human is here used in the physical, intellectual and spiritual meanings of the word.

As the understanding of natural phenomena evolved, for instance the understanding that the sun's energy is at the root of life processes and therefore is the giver of all life on Earth, rites evolved from pure worship of the sun as an astral body, into a series of rites and rituals that were developed when further observations showed that the sun is more than just a giver of life as it is also the regulator of the cycles that govern the seasons and most of the biological and ecological processes and also that the sun is only one of the many heavenly bodies that influence earthly phenomena, such as tides, plant growth, reproduction of plants and animals and others.

The increasing complexity of details and sequences of rituals and rites over time is a result of the awareness of the complexity of natural phenomena. In practical terms, rituals themselves become longer and more complex with increasing faith, and faith necessarily grows as man perceives that the more he knows, the more there is to be known and that there is much more that he has not yet understood. On the other hand, length and complexity of rituals contribute to keep the mind focused on the deity, on the *ātman* and the *Brahman*. To perform the *sūrya namaskaram* is not an act of the body alone, but even more of the mind and spirit. Correct performance of any rite implies integration of the entire personality of the worshipper with the worshipped. Faith is needed to appease the unsatisfied urge to understand and the feeling that man will never be able to understand anything to its ultimate causation.

The evolution of the Gods in the mind of Vedic man, as Dandekar has conclusively demonstrated, is clearly indicated in the Vedas themselves. I would however like to point out that the Gods themselves are what they are and do not evolve; the changes and evolution take place in the minds of men as the understanding progresses. As human understanding of causes and effects of the phenomena of the Universe grow in depth, also ideas/concepts evolve and accordingly the personalities of the Gods **appear** to evolve since most Gods are personifications of ideas/concepts; this is how man represents mentally his understanding of the facts of nature. What evolves is human understanding.

As an example we may take the Sun-God Sūrya. Sūrya is the sun itself to begin with, the giver of light and warmth; Sūrya is the solar disc. Later sunlight acquires all the colours of the rainbow then, by inference, also all the colours that man cannot see. Finally the Sun is seen as the **measure**, then the **measurer** of Time and Space, and each one of these in relation to the other. Thus, Sūrya acquires more facets, one of them is of such importance that it develops a new personality, one more series of meanings and implications, a universe of new functions. A new God is added to the pantheon: this is Lord Viṣṇu, a minor deity in early times. He acquired the significance and meaning of measure and **measurer** of Space in relation to Time and **regulator** of the solar year and thereby becomes the **Great Preserver**. Sūrya is seen as the giver of light and life on Earth, this is how and why his daughter Sūryā is given in marriage to man; but he, Sūrya, is not regarded as the Preserver. To be the **The Preserver**, more is required than just to be the giver of life. The Preserver must ensure the availability everywhere and at all times, of the means for the preservation and maintenance of Life; hence the association between Viṣṇu and Savitr̥, who is the essence of the concept of Life.

Sūrya, independently of its cycles and periodicity, retains in the Veda his initial specific attributes, explained at length in *R̥V*, X; 85, but Viṣṇu, having acquired the value of Grand Preserver in Space and Time, because he is the Regulator of seasonal phenomena, eventually becomes one of the most important Gods of the Hindu Trinity. Viṣṇu is not mentioned in *R̥V*, X; 85, which is one more suggestion of the great antiquity of this hymn that celebrates the most ancient institution of social man: marriage. An institution specially important among the patriarchal Vedic Āryans who lived as well organised clans.

Interestingly enough, in the evolution of the Vedic Gods, as Viṣṇu takes over as the Grand Preserver, Sūrya recedes somewhat in the background and acquires many human characteristics while he does not acquire more specific godly ones. However Sūrya retains for everafter his natural character, position and function of giver of light and warmth, giver of plant-life on Earth, in obeisance to *r̥ta*. To perform correctly the *sūrya namaskāram*, water should be offered and the rays of the rising sun should be seen through it. Sūrya's daughter Sūryā brings with her as endowment the light of education, of health and of correct, methodical living, but above all she brings the power of giving birth. Lord Agni retains his attribute of being the energy of light, of heat, of life processes; he is the energy of mental and spiritual power (Vannucci 1994); while Sūrya retains his attributes of being an expression Lord Agni; Lord Savitr̥, the Great Vivifier, is the personification of the abstract concept or idea of **Life** and **Hope**, he is the Impeller who gives away the bride, that she may, in turn, become a vivifier in the world of the family.

सत्येनोत्तभिता भूमिः सूर्येणोत्तभिता द्यौः ।
ऋतेनादित्यास्तिष्ठन्ति दिवि सोमो अधि श्रितः ।। १ ।।

सोमेनादित्या बलिनः सोमेन पृथिवी मही ।
अथो नक्षत्राणामेषामुपस्थे सोम आहितः ।। २ ।।

satyenottabhitā bhūmiḥ sūryeṇottabhitā dyauḥ ।
ṛitenādityās tiṣṭhanti divi somo adhi śritaḥ ॥ 1 ॥

somenādityā balinaḥ somena pṛthivī mahī ।
ātho nakṣatrāṇām eṣām upasthe soma āhitaḥ ॥ 2 ॥

सोमं मन्यते पपिवान्यत्संपिंषन्त्योषधिम् ।
सोमं यं ब्रह्माणो विदुर्न तस्याश्नाति कश्चन ॥ ३ ॥

आच्छद्विधानैर्गुपितो बार्हतैः सोम रक्षितः ।
ग्राव्णामिच्छृण्वन्तिष्ठसि न ते अश्नाति पार्थिवः ॥ ४ ॥

यत्त्वा देव प्रपिबन्ति तत आ प्यायसे पुनः ।
वायुः सोमस्य रक्षिता समानां मास आकृतिः ॥ ५ ॥

रैभ्यासीदनुदेयी नाराशंसी न्योचनी ।
सूर्याया भद्रमिद्वासो गाथयैति परिष्कृतम् ॥ ६ ॥

चित्तिरा उपबर्हणं चक्षुरा अभ्यञ्जनम् ।
द्यौर्भूमिः कोश आसीद्यदयात्सूर्या पतिम् ॥ ७ ॥

स्तोमा आसन्प्रतिधयः कुरीरं छन्द ओपशः ।
सूर्याया अश्विना वराग्निरासीत्पुरोगवः ॥ ८ ॥

सोमो वधूयुरभवदश्विनास्तामुभा वरा ।
सूर्यां यत्पत्ये शंसन्तीं मनसा सवितादात् ॥ ९ ॥

somaṁ manyate papivān yat sampiṁṣanty oṣadhiṃ ।
somaṁ yaṁ brahmāṇo vidūr na tasyāśnāti kaścana ॥ 3 ॥

ācchadvidhānair guptio bārhataiḥ soma rakṣitaḥ ।
grāvṇām īcchṛṇvān tiṣṭhasi na te aśnāti pārthivaḥ ॥ 4 ॥

yat tvā deva prapībanti tata ā pyāyase pūnaḥ ।
vāyūḥ somasya rakṣitā samānāṁ māsa ākṛtiḥ ॥ 5 ॥

raibhy āsīd anudeyī nārāśaṁsī nyocanī ।
sūryāya bhadram id vāso gāthayaiti pariṣkṛtam ॥ 6 ॥

cittir ā upabarhaṇaṁ cakṣur ā abhyañjanam ।
dyaur bhūmiḥ koṣa āsīd yad ayāt sūryā patim ॥ 7 ॥

stomā āsan pratidhayaḥ kurīraṃ chanda opaśaḥ ।
sūryāyā aśvinā varāgnīr āsīt purogavaḥ ।। 8 ।।

somo vadhūyur abhavad aśvināstām ubhā varā ।
sūryāṁ yat patye śaṁsantīm manasā savitādadāt ।। 9 ।।

मनो अस्या अन आसीद्द्यौरासीदुत च्छदिः ।
शुक्रावनड्वाहावास्तां यदयात्सूर्या गृहम् ।। १० ।।

ऋक्सामाभ्यामभिहितौ गावौ ते सामनावितः ।
श्रोत्रं ते चक्रे आस्तां दिवि पन्थाश्चराचरः ।। ११ ।।

शुची ते चक्रे यात्या व्यानो अक्ष आहतः ।
अनो मनस्मयं सूर्यारोहत्प्रयती पतिम् ।। १२ ।।

सूर्याया वहतुः प्रागात्सविता यमवासृजत् ।
अघासु हन्यन्ते गावोऽर्जुन्योः पर्युह्यते ।। १३ ।।

यदश्विना पृच्छमानावयातं त्रिचक्रेण वहतुं सूर्यायाः ।
विश्वे देवा अनु तद्वामजानन्पुत्रः पितराववृणीत पूषा ।। १४ ।।

यदयातं शुभस्पती वरेयं सूर्यामुप ।
कैकं चक्रं वामासीत्क्व देष्ट्राय तस्थथुः ।। १५ ।।

mano asyā ana āsīd dyaur āsīd uta cchadīḥ ।
śukrāv anaḍvāhāv astāṁ yad ayāt sūryā gṛham ।। 10 ।।

ṛksāmābhyām abhibitau gāvau te sāmanāv itaḥ ।
śrotraṁ te cakre āstāṃ divi panthāś carācaraḥ ।। 11 ।।

śucī te cakre yātyā vyāno akṣa āhataḥ ।
ano manasmayaṁ sūryārohat prayatī patim ।। 12 ।।

suryāyā vahatuḥ prāgāt savitā yam avāsṛjat ।
aghāsu hanyante gāvo'rjunyoḥ pary uhyate ।। 13 ।।

yad aśvinā pṛcchamānāv ayātaṁ tricakreṇa vahatūṁ sūryāyāḥ ।
viśve devā anu tad vām ajānan putraḥ pitarāv avṛṇīta pūṣā ।। 14 ।।

yad ayātaṁ śubhas patī vareyaṁ sūryām ūpa ।
kvaikaṁ cakraṁ vām āsīt kva deṣṭrāya tasthathuḥ ।। 15 ।।

द्वे ते चक्रे सूर्ये ब्रह्माण ऋतुथा विदुः ।
अथैकं चक्रं यद्गुहा तदद्धातय इद्विदुः ।। १६ ।।

सूर्यायौ देवेभ्यो मित्राय वरुणाय च ।
ये भूतस्य प्रचेतस इदं तेभ्योऽकरं नमः ।। १७ ।।

पूर्वापरं चरतो माययैतौ शिशू क्रीळन्तौ परि यातो अध्वरम् ।
विश्वान्यन्यो भुवनाभिचष्ट ऋतूँरन्यो विदधज्जायते पुनः ।। १८ ।।

नवोनवो भवति जायमानोऽह्नां केतुरुषसामेत्यग्रम् ।
भागं देवेभ्यो वि दधात्यायन्प्र चन्द्रमास्तिरते दीर्घमायुः ।। १९ ।।

सकिंशुकं शल्मलिं विश्वरूपं हिरण्यवर्णं सुवृतं सुचक्रम् ।
आ रोह सूर्ये अमृतस्य लोकं स्योनं पत्ये वहतुं कृणुष्व ।। २० ।।

उदीर्ष्वातः पतिवती ह्येषा विश्वावसुं नमसा गीर्भिरीळे ।
अन्यामिच्छ पितृषदं व्यक्तां स ते भागो जनुषा तस्य विद्धि ।। २१ ।।

dve te cakre surye brahmāṇa r̥tuthā viduḥ ।
athaikaṁ cakraṁ yad guhā tad addhātaya id viduḥ ।। 16 ।।

sūryāyai devebhyo mitrāya varuṇāya ca ।
ye bhūtasya pracetasa idaṃ tebhyo'karaṁ namaḥ ।। 17 ।।

pūrvāparaṁ carato māyayaitau śiśū krīḷantau pari yāto adhvaram ।
viśvāny anyo bhuvanābhicaṣṭa r̥tūm̐ranyo vidadhaj jāyate punaḥ ।। 18 ।।

navonavo bhavati jāyamano'hnāṁ ketur uṣasām ety agram ।
bhāgaṁ devebhyo vi dadhāty āyan pra candramās tirate dīrgham āyuḥ ।। 19 ।।

sukiṁśukaṁ śalmaliṁ viśvarūpaṁ hiraṇyavarṇaṁ suvr̥taṁ sucakram ।
ā roha sūrye amr̥tasya lokaṁ syonaṁ patye vahatūṁ kr̥ṇuṣva ।। 20 ।।
ud īrṣvātaḥ pativatī hy éṣā viśvāvasuṁ namasā gīrbhir īḷe ।
anyām iccha pitr̥ṣadaṁ vyaktāṁ sa te bhāgo januṣā tasya viddhi ।। 21 ।।

उदीर्ष्वातो विश्वावसो नमसेळामहे त्वा ।
अन्यामिच्छ प्रफर्व्यं सं जायां पत्या सृज ।। २२ ।।

अनृक्षरा ऋजवः सन्तु पन्था येभिः सखायो यन्ति नो वरेयम् ।
समर्यमा सं भगो नो निनीयात्सं जास्पत्यं सुयममस्तु देवाः ।। २३ ।।

प्र त्वा मुञ्चामि वरुणस्य पाशाद्येन त्वाबध्नात्सविता सुशेवः ।
ऋतस्य योनौ सुकृतस्य लोकेऽरिष्टां त्वा सह पत्या दधामि ।। २४ ।।

प्रेतो मुञ्चामि नामुतः सुबद्धाममुतस्करम् ।
यथेयमिन्द्र मीढ्वः सुपुत्रा सुभगासति ।। २५ ।।

पूषा त्वेतो नयतु हस्तगृह्याश्विना त्वा प्र वहतां रथेन ।
गृहान्गच्छ गृहपत्नी यथासो वशिनी त्वं विदथमा वदासि ।। २६ ।।

इह प्रियं प्रजया ते समृध्यतामस्मिन्गृहे गार्हपत्याय जागृहि ।
एना पत्या तन्वं सं सृजस्वाधा जिव्री विदथमा वदाथ : ।। २७ ।।

ud īrṣvāto viśvāvaso nāmaseḷāmahe tvā ।
anyām iccha prapharvyaṁ saṁ jāyāṁ patyā sṛja ।। 22 ।।

anṛkṣarā ṛjavaḥ santu panthā yebhiḥ sakhāyo yanti no vareyam ।
sam aryamā saṁ bhago no ninīyāt saṁ jāspatyaṁ suyamam astu devāḥ ।। 23 ।।

pra tvā muñcāmi varuṇasya pāśād yena tvābadhnāt savitā suśévaḥ ।
ṛtasya yonau sukṛtasya loke'riṣṭāṃ tvā saha patyā dadhāmi ।। 24 ।।

preto muñcāmi nāmutaḥ subaddhām amūtas karam ।
yatheyam indra mīḍhvaḥ suputrā subhagāsati ।। 25 ।।

pūṣā tveto nayatu hastagṛhyāśvinā tvā pra vahatāṁ, rathena ।
gṛhān gaccha gṛhapatnī yathāso vaśinī tvaṁ vidathamā vadāsi ।। 26 ।।

iha priyaṁ prajayā te sam ṛdhyatām asmin gṛhé gārhapatyāya jāgṛhi ।
enā patyā tanvaṁ saṁ sṛjasvādhā jivrī vidatham ā vadāthaḥ ।। 27 ।।

नीललोहितं भवति कृत्यासक्तिर्व्यज्यते ।
एधन्ते अस्या ज्ञातयः पतिर्बन्धेषु बध्यते ।। २८ ।।

परा देहि शामुल्यं ब्रह्मभ्यो वि भजा वसु ।
कृत्यैषा पद्वती भूत्व्या जाया विशते पतिम् ।। २९ ।।

अश्रीरा तनूर्भवति रुशती पापयामुया ।
पतिर्यद्वध्वो३ वाससा स्वमङ्गमभिधित्सते ।। ३० ।।

ये वध्वश्चन्द्रं वहतुं यक्ष्मा यन्ति जनादनु ।
पुनस्तान्यज्ञिया देवा नयन्तु यत आगताः ।। ३१ ।।

मा विदन्परिपन्थिनो य आसीदन्ति दंपती ।
सुगेभिर्दुर्गमतीतामप द्रान्त्वरातयः ।। ३२ ।।

सुमङ्गलीरियं वधूरिमां समेत पश्यत ।
सौभाग्यमस्यै दत्वायाथास्तं वि परेतन ।। ३३ ।।

nīlalohitaṁ bhavati kṛtyāsaktir vy ajyate ।
edhante asyā jñātayaḥ pātir bandheṣu badhyate ।। 28 ।।

parā dehi śāmulyaṁ brahmabhyo vi bhajā vasu ।
kṛtyaiṣā padvatī bhūtvy ā jāyā viśate patim ।। 29 ।।

aśrīrā tanūr bhavati ruśatī pāpayāmuyā ।
patir yad vadhvo vāsasā svam aṅgam abhidhitsate ।। 30 ।।

ye vadhvaś candraṁ vahatuṁ yakṣmā yanti janād anu ।
punas tān yajñiyā devā nayantu yata āgatāḥ ।। 31 ।।

mā vidan paripanthino ya āsīdanti daṁpatī ।
sugebhir durgam atītām apa drāntv arātayaḥ ।। 32 ।।

sumaṅgalīr iyaṁ vadhūr imāṁ sameta paśyata ।
saubhāgyam asyai dattvāyātthāstaṁ vi paretana ।। 33 ।।

तृष्टमेतत्कटुकमेतदपाष्ठवद्विषवन्नैतदत्तवे ।
सूर्यां यो ब्रह्मा विद्यात्स इद्वाधूयमर्हति ।। ३४ ।।

आशसनं विशसनमथो अधिविकर्तनम् ।
सूर्यायाः पश्य रूपाणि तानि ब्रह्मा तु शुन्धति ।। ३५ ।।

गृभ्णामि ते सौभगत्वाय हस्तं मया पत्या जरदष्टिर्यथासः ।
भगो अर्यमा सविता पुरंधिर्मह्यं त्वादुर्गार्हपत्याय देवाः ।। ३६ ।।

तां पूषञ्छिवतमामेरयस्व यस्यां बीजं मनुष्या३ वपन्ति ।
या न ऊरू उशती विश्रयाते यस्यामुशन्तः प्रहराम शेपम् ।। ३७ ।।

तुभ्यमग्रे पर्यवहन्तसूर्यां वहतुना सह ।
पुनः पतिभ्यो जायां दा अग्ने प्रजया सह ।। ३८ ।।

पुनः पत्नीमग्निरदादायुषा सह वर्चसा ।
दीर्घायुरस्या यः पतिर्जीवाति शरदः शतम् ।। ३९ ।।

सोमः प्रथमो विविदे गन्धर्वो विविद उत्तरः ।
तृतीयो अग्निष्टे पतिस्तुरीयस्ते मनुष्यजाः ।। ४० ।।

tr̥ṣṭaṁ etat kaṭukam etad apāṣṭhavad viṣavan naitad attave ।
sūryāṁ yo brahmā vidyāt sa id vādhūyam arhati ।। 34 ।।

āśasanaṃ viśasanam atho adhivikartanam ।
sūryāyāḥ paśya rūpāṇi tāni brahmā tu śundhati ।। 35 ।।

gr̥bhṇāmi te saubhagatvāya hastaṁ mayā patyā jaradaṣṭir yathāsaḥ ।
bhago aryamā savitā puraṁdhir mahyaṁ tvādur gārhapatyāya devāḥ ।। 36 ।।
tāṁ pūṣañ chivatamām erayasva yasyāṁ bījaṁ manuṣyā vapanti ।
yā na urū uśatī viśrayāte yasyām uśantaḥ praharāma śepam ।। 37 ।।

tubhyam agre pary avahant sūryāṁ vahatunā saha ।
punaḥ patibhyo jāyām dā agne prajayā saha ।। 38 ।।

punaḥ patnīm agnir adād āyuṣā saha varcasā ।
dīrghāyur asyā yaḥ patir jīvāti śaradaḥ śatam ।। 39 ।।

somaḥ prathamo vivide gandharvo vivida uttaraḥ ।
tr̥tīyo agniṣ ṭe patis turīyas te manuṣyajāḥ ।। 40 ।।

सोमो ददद्गन्धर्वाय गन्धर्वो ददद‌ग्नये ।
रयिं च पुत्राँश्चादादग्निर्मह्यमथो इमाम् ।। ४१ ।।

इहैव स्तं मा वि यौष्टं विश्वमायुर्व्यश्नुतम् ।
क्रीळन्तौ पुत्रैर्नप्तृभिर्मोदमानौ स्वे गृहे ।। ४२ ।।

आ नः प्रजां जनयतु प्रजापतिराजरसाय समनक्त्वर्यमा ।
अदुर्मङ्गलीः पतिलोकमा विश शं नो भव द्विपदे शं चतुष्पदे।। ४३ ।।

अघोरचक्षुरपतिघ्न्येधि शिवा पशुभ्यः सुमनाः सुवर्चाः ।
वीरसूर्देवकामा स्योना शं नो भव द्विपदे शं चतुष्पदे ।। ४४ ।।

इमां त्वमिन्द्र मीढ्वः सुपुत्रां सुभगां कृणु ।
दशास्यां पुत्राना धेहि पतिमेकादशं कृधि ।। ४५ ।।

सम्राज्ञी श्वशुरे भव सम्राज्ञी श्वश्र्वां भव ।
ननान्दरि सम्राज्ञी भव सम्राज्ञी अधि देवृषु ।। ४६ ।।

समञ्जन्तु विश्वे देवाः समापो हृदयानि नौ ।
सं मातरिश्वा सं धाता समु देष्ट्री दधातु नौ ।। ४७ ।।

somo dadad gandharvāya gandharvo dadad agnaye ।
rayiṁ ca putrāṁś cādād agnir mahyam atho imām ।। 41 ।।

ihaiva staṁ mā vi yauṣṭaṃ viśvam āyur vy aśnutam ।
krīḷantau putrair naptṛbhir modamānau sve gṛhe ।। 42 ।।

ā naḥ prajāṁ janayatu prajāpatir ājarasāya sam anaktv aryamā ।
adurmaṅgalīḥ patilokamā viśa śaṁ no bhava dvipade śaṁ catuṣpade ।। 43 ।।

aghoracakṣur apatighny edhi śivā paśubhyaḥ sumanāḥ suvarcāḥ ।
vīrasūr devakāmā syonā śaṁ no bhava dvipade śaṁ catuṣpade ।। 44 ।।

imāṁ tvam indra mīḍhvaḥ suputrāṁ subhagāṁ kṛṇu ।
daśāsyāṁ putrān ā dhehi patim ekādaśaṁ kṛdhi ।। 45 ।।

samrājñī śvaśure bhava samrājñī śvaśrvāṁ bhava ।

nanāndari samrājñī bhava samrajñī adhi devṛṣu ॥ 46 ॥

sam añjantu viśve devāḥ sam āpo hṛdayāni nau ।
saṁ mātariśvā saṁ dhātā sam u deṣṭrī dadhātu nau ॥ 47 ॥

Translation

1. Truth is the base that bears the earth; by Sūrya are the heavens sustained.

   By Law the Ādityas stand secure, and Soma holds his place in Heaven.

2. By Soma are the Ādityas strong, by Soma mighty is the earth.

   Thus Soma in the midst of all these constellations hath his place.

3. One thinks, when they have brayed the plant, that he hath drunk the *soma*'s juice;

   Of him whom brāhmaṇas truly know as *soma* no one ever tastes.

4. Soma, secured by sheltering rules, guarded by hymns in Bṛhati,

   Thou standest listening to the stones: none tastes of thee who dwells on earth.

5. When they begin to drink thee then, O God, thou swellest out again.

   Vāyu is Soma's guardian God. The Moon is that which shapes the years.

6. Raibhi was her dear bridal friend, and Nārāśaṁśi led her home.

   Lovely was Sūryā's robe: she came to that which *gāthā* had adorned.

7. Thought was the pillow of her couch, sight was the

unguent for her eyes;

Her treasury was earth and heaven when Sūryā went unto her Lord.

8. Hymns were the cross-bars of the pole, *kurīra*-metre decked the car;

   The bridesmen were the Aśvin pair: Agni was leader of the train.

9. Soma was he who wooed the maid: the groomsmen were both Aśvins, when

   The sun-God Savitṛ bestowed his willing Sūryā on her Lord.

10. Her spirit was the bridal car; the covering thereof was heaven:

    Bright were both steers that drew it, when Sūryā approached her husband's home.

11. The steers were steady, kept in place by holy verse and *Sāma*-hymn:

    All ear were thy two chariot wheels: thy path was tremulous in the sky,

12. Clean, as thou wentest, were thy wheels: wind was the axle fastened there.

    Sūryā, proceeding to her Lord, mounted a spirit-fashioned car.

13. The bridal pomp of Sūryā, which Savitṛ started, moved along.

    In Māgha days are oxen slain, in Arjunis they wed the bride.

14. When on your three-wheeled chariot, O Aśvins, ye came

as wooers unto Sūryā's bridal,

Then all the Gods agreed to your proposal: Pūṣan as son elected you as Fathers.

15. O ye Two Lords of lustre, then when ye to Sūryā's wooing came,

    Where was one chariot wheel of yours? Where stood ye for the Sire's command?

16. The brāhmaṇas, by their seasons, know, O Sūryā, those two wheels of thine:

    One kept concealed, those only who are skilled in highest truths have learned.

17. To Sūryā and the deities, to Mitra and to Varuṇa.

    Who know aright the thing that is, this adoration have I paid.

18. By their own power these Twain in close succession move;

    They go as playing children round the sacrifice.

    One of the Pair beholdeth all existing things; the other ordereth seasons and is born again.

19. He, born afresh, is new and new for ever: ensign of days he goes before the mornings.

    Coming, the orders for the Gods their portion. The moon prolongs the days of our existence.

20. Mount this, all-shaped, gold-hued, with strong wheels, fashioned of Kiṁśuka and Śālmali, light-rolling,

    Bound for the world of life immortal, Sūryā: make for thy lord a happy bridal journey.

21. Rise up from hence: this maiden hath a husband. I laud

Viśvavasu with hymns and homage.

Seek in her fathers' home another fair one, and find the portion from of old assigned thee.

22. Rise up from hence, Viśvavasu: with reverence we worship thee.

 Seek thou another willing maid, and with her husband leave the bride.

23. Straight in direction be the paths, and thornless, whereon our fellows travel to the wooing.

 Let Aryaman and Bhaga lead us: perfect, O Gods, the union of the wife and husband.

24. Now from the noose of Varuṇa I free thee, wherewith most blessed Savitṛ hath bound thee.

 In Law's seat, to the world of virtuous action, I give thee up uninjured with thy consort.

25. Hence, and not thence, I send thee free. I make thee softly fettered there.

 That, Bounteous Indra, she may live blest in her fortune and her sons.

26. Let Pūṣan take thy hand and hence conduct thee; may the two Aśvins on their car transport thee.

 Go to the house to be the household's mistress and speak as lady to thy gathered people.

27. Happy be thou and prosper with thy children here: be vigilant to rule thy household in this home.

 Closely unite thy body with this man, thy lord. So shall ye, full of years, address your company.

28. Her hue is blue red: the fiend who clingeth close is driven

off.

Well thrive the kinsmen of this bride: the husband is bound fast in bonds.

29. Give thou the woollen robe away: deal treasure to the brāhmaṇa priests.

This female fiend hath got her feet, and as a wife attends her lord.

30. Unlovely is his body when it glistens with this wicked fiend,

What time the husband wraps about his limbs the garment of his wife.

31. Consumptions, from her people, which follow the bride's resplendent train,

These let the Holy Gods again bear to the place from which they came.

32. Let not the highway thieves who lie in ambush find the wedded pair.

By pleasent ways let them escape the danger, and let foes depart.

33. Sings of good fortune mark the bride: come all of you and look at her.

Wish her prosperity, and then return unto your homes again.

34. Pungent is this, and bitter this, filled, as it were with arrow-barbs, empoisoned and not fit for use.

The brāhmaṇa who knows Sūryā well deserves the garment of the bride.

35. The fringe, the cloth that decks her head, and then the triply parted robe,

Behold the hues which Sūryā wears: these doth the brāhmaṇa purify.

36. I take thy hand in mine for happy fortune that thou mayst reach old age with me thy husband.

    Gods, Aryaman, Bhaga, Savitṛ, Purandhi, have given thee to be my household's mistress.

37. O Pūṣan, send her on as most auspicious, her who shall be the sharer of my pleasures;

    Her who shall twine her loving arms about me, and welcome all my love and mine embraces.

38. For thee, with bridal train, they, first, escorted Sūryā to her home.

    Give to the husband in return, Agni, the wife with progeny.

39. Agni hath given the bride again with splendour and with ample life.

    Long lived be he who is her lord; a hundred autumns let him live.

40. Soma obtained her first of all; next the Gandharva was her lord.

    Agni was thy third husband: now one born of woman is thy fourth.

41. Soma to the Gandharva, and to Agni the Gandharva gave:

    And Agni hath bestowed on me riches and sons and this my spouse.

42. Be ye not parted; dwell ye here; reach the full time of human life.

With sons and grandsons sport and play, rejoicing in your own abode.

43. So may Prajāpati bring children forth to us; may Aryaman adorn us till old age come nigh.

Not unauspicious enter thou thy husband's house: bring blessing to our bipeds and our quadrupeds.

44. Not evil-eyed, no slayer of thy husband, bring weal to cattle, radiant, gentle-hearted;

Loving the Gods, delightful, bearing heroes, bring blessing to our quadrupeds and bipeds.

45. O Bounteous Indra, make this bride blest in her sons and fortunate.

Vouchsafe to her ten sons, and make her husband the eleventh man.

46. Over thy husband's father and thy husband's mother bear full away.

Over the sister of thy lord, over his brothers rule supreme.

47. So may the Universal Gods, so may the Waters join our hearts.

May Mātariśvan, Dhātṛ, and Deṣṭṛ together bind us close.

(transl. Griffith, 1889)

Commentaries

Stanza 1 — The hymn begins with an invocation to *satyam*, Truth, here equivalent to *ṛtam*; to Sūrya who is an expression and manifestation of Agni in the sky and is giver of life on earth; to the Ādityas, the most ancient Gods, sons of Aditi or Infinity, the bondless universal mother. These: Truth, Law, the Sun are respectively supporters of Earth, of Heaven (or sky) and of natural order. Soma is hailed as the supreme in Heaven (Griffith) or as Divine Love (SS and SV) and the personification of joy. *Soma* is in this hymn identified by name with the moon, *Candramas*. Moon is the regulator of many physiological processes, most obvious and important in the context of the bride, wife and mother, is the regulation of the menstrual cycle and pregnancy. Soma represents the joy that comes from grasping the idea and meaning of Truth, of the perfection of the universal law of nature and of the beauty and importance of the sun as giver of light. Of all the principles quoted, Soma is mentioned last, because he epitomizes the great joy to be had form Truth, Order, Life and the joy derived from the wisdom accrued from such knowledge.

Stanza 2 — The Ādityas, the most ancient deities, sons of Aditi, are here said to be strong by the power of Soma, which is the power obtained from the joy of living or, as SS and SV put it, the solar regions are strong by the elixir of divine love. A joyful and happy life is indeed a divine gift, 'by Soma Earth is great'. Soma is the embodiment of all the principles that make the universe real: Soma is the embodiment of *ṛta*.

Stanza 3 — Here a distinction is made between the *soma* drunk by the common man and the real Soma, which is the one prepared for the libation offered by the brāhmaṇas at the new and full moon rites of the Soma sacrifice, which propitiates the embodiment of knowledge. Full knowledge and wisdom are the fruits of study and understanding, of meditation, of chanting and performing rituals. Studying will bring the knowledge of the real Soma which brings true, unblemished spiritual happiness, as opposed to mere drinking for physical satisfaction and exhilaration.

Stanza 4 — The **real Soma** is the one covered by rules and laws and enlivened by chants and rules. Soma stands firm, aloof listening to the stones; these, presumably, are the pressing stones, a symbol of firmness, stability, eternity, as *Sanātana*

Dharma is. There will be eternal joy in a dhārmic way of life.

Stanza 5—Vāyu, the healthy, auspicious air or wind originated from the breath of *puruṣa*, is Soma's guardian while it fermentates during the process of preparation. This is the only place in the *R̥V* where Soma is identified with *Candramas*, the Moon, and it is here credited as a measure of the year. In fact, embryonic life is measured in lunar months and the menstrual cycle of women, including fertile and infertile days, is also attuned to the lunar month and year, rather than to the solar year. This is evidently important knowledge to impart to the bride and it is important when celebrating and preparing a young woman for her married life.

Stanza 6—Now the grand scenario where the bridal procession will take place is described and how it has come into existence. The hymn describes the central figure, the bride herself. She is here introduced by name: Sūryā, daughter of the sun; but she is not Dawn, as some authors have not convincingly interpreted. Dawn has its proper name in the Veda, namely Uṣā, while Sūryā definitely has a personality of her own as the offspring of the Sun, as her name indicates, and she is different from Uṣā.

Sūryā is adorned physically with special robes and she is supported by her friends Raibhi (ritual verses), and Nārāśaṁśī (eulogistic hymns), who guide her towards her new home. Interestingly *gāthā*s are also mentioned as her ornaments, which is a beautiful way of saying that those ancient secular and perhaps profane popular songs are indeed part of the personality of the bride: all knowledge is important: the intellectual and spiritual knowledge expressed as Raibhi and Nārāśaṁsī, as well as the physical, practical, daily experience and knowledge of everyday married life. *Gāthā*s are part of the dowry of the girl who will become the young woman conscious of the new life that is before her, with its joys, trials and rewards. *Gāthā*s are very ancient songs not included in the Vedas; they are here personified and this is the only place in the *R̥V* where they are mentioned by name. This again indicates the great antiquity of this hymn, the antiquity of the wedding ceremony and the all important role played by the bride. In most cultures of the world, and the Vedic culture is no exception, weddings are amongst the most ancient socio-religious ceremonies and *gāthā* is also the name given to the most ancient songs of the Avesta where the language is archaic and sometimes difficult to interpret because, as it has been stated, the grammar is still in a primitive form; therefore the meaning is not easily or readily understood precisely and sometimes cannot be understood at all.

The stanza indicates that the bride is to be led to her new home duly enriched and provided with ritualistic and religious traditional education and training, and also with the knowledge of everyday matters of daily living. A girl can only become a good bride when her education has been completed and she has learned how to run the household, the home, the family and how to bring up children. This aspect is further emphasized in the next stanza.

Stanza 7 — It is said that thought and foresight are her mental wealth; as much as earth and heaven are her treasury. The future wife and mother is the depository of the family's wealth, the material and spiritual culture. This is the great treasure she takes with her to her husband's home. Her qualities and riches are not only material, but above all religious, behavioural, practical and the excellence of character required of the future wife, the lady of the new household.

Stanza 8 — The cross bar of the chariot that carries the bride to her new destination is symbolically described as the stomas or hymns whose teachings will be the steady support and guidance of the bride, while the *kurira* metre will be the handle of the whip with which to stimulate forward the oxen that pull the cart. The Aśvina twins are the bridesmen, since the future lady of the house will have to know how to treat injuries and sickness of the family, their dependants and their bipeds and quadrupeds. Lord Agni, Fire and Energy, the God that pervades the universe and who is present at all sacrifices, rites, rituals and all life processes, leads the bridal procession.

Stanza 9 — All this is a consequence of Soma having initially wooed and educated the young maid who has, of course, to be approached with signs of rejoicing, here personified by the Aśvina, givers of good health. But the mastermind behind all the pomp is Savitṛ, the Divine Impeller, the Great Vivifier who gives away the bride 'ripe with mature intelligence' and who is **prepared** and **willing** to be wedded.

Stanza 10 — Having distributed all the roles as appropriate, the hymn steps back to give more details about the bride's journey. This journey symbolizes exogamy, the need to avoid endogamy, as also recommended in the *śāstras*. Emphasis is again put on the Mind being the real carrier, the chariot; and the Sun and the Moon who measure nature's rhythms, are the two driving oxen for Sūryā's journey through the sky or heaven, towards her husband's home. The pair of driving oxen must be well trained to trot together at the same pace, to ensure regular and safe progress of the car; only thus can Sūryā be delivered safely at her husband's home.

Stanza 11 — Here emphasis is on the Vedic verses; specially mentioned are the *Ṛk* and the *Sāman* who are the drivers of the oxen and who are responsible for their correct performance. The *Ṛk* embody tradition and ancient lore and wisdom; the *Sāman*s put them in rhythm and chant. We must remember here that it was the Metres who saved Indra from the *asura*s and from the fear of night, darkness or ignorance, and death (see *ṚV*, VII; 103, Vannucci 1995). Now the metres are those that ensure that the steers of the bride's chariot perform in perfect unison and are 'walking at the same pace', obviously in respect to nature's own rhythms. The two wheels of Sūryā's chariot are called 'ears' and they too are Metres; we are here reminded that it was the Metres who helped Indra conquer the fear of night, darkness and death, by '**going round and round**'; they also represent the receptiveness of the bride to all learning. Thus the bride will arrive at her husband's home not only well instructed and educated, but also well protected, including, protected against fear: the natural shyness of a girl about to become woman. Sāyaṇa interprets the two wheels as the ears; the ears that hear and learn the metres.

Stanza 12 — It is further stated that the 'wheels became pure': *śuci cakra*, as they revolve when the chariot is under way as *vyāna*, which is one of the vital airs along with *apāna*, *udāna*, *prāṇa*, *samāna*; this is the fastened axle. The vital breaths are indispensable to ensure the maintenance of life and regular breathing is important for good health, as practised in *yoga* exercises and in the *sūrya namaskāram*. Thus, Sūryā is carried by the chariot that represents the Mind, having steady, life-giving vital airs and pure, firm consciousness needed for an unpolluted, healthy, well regulated wedded life.

Stanza 13 — The bridal procession was put on its way by the Great Vivifier, the One who puts Life in motion, the Great Impeller, Savitṛ, personification of the principle and concept of Life. Now the procession starts moving. The pulling oxen are whipped at an auspicious time under the constellation of Māghas while the auspicious time of the wedding will be under Arjunī (Phālgunī: February-March). It is clearly stated, repeated amongst other places also in the *Gṛhyasūtra* of *Āpastamba* of the Taittirīya School of the Black *Yajurveda*, *Paṭala* 1, section 3, that under Māghas cows are provided and under Phālgunī the marriage is celebrated. Griffith translates: 'In Māgha days oxen are slain', which cannot be correct since what is said is that oxen, *gavo*, are whipped along, which could not be if they were dead. Traditionally it is trotting oxen that pull the bride's chariot. In the *Gṛhyasūtra* it is recommended, amongst other advices for the selection of the bride, to avoid a girl 'who's skin is like a frog's', which probably refers to smallpox marked, disfigured faces.

Weddings are the occasion to celebrate joyfully and gladly the happiness of being alive and of generating new life; the revolving of the wheels of seasons impelled by the Life principle who is Savitṛ are kept in the due course of *ṛta* by the Mind, i.e., by Reason, Knowledge and Wisdom. Since everything is in order, merry-making, singing and dancing come naturally. There is a reminder to avoid pollution, to maintain purity of thought and of action during the course of life and there is the recommendation to live 'in pace' with natural laws.

Stanza 14 — The Aśvina come to woo the bride. Appropriately it is the twin Health-Gods who select the girl fit to be a future wife and mother. They come in a three-wheeled chariot while all the Gods, all Nature applaud and give support and protection. Pūṣan, the guide and path-finder who selected the Aśvina as his fathers, is present to ensure that the bride will proceed on a physically and spiritually healthy path. Commentators have variously interpreted the meaning of the three-wheeled chariot. On the basis of the following verses that clearly indicate that astronomical observations should be made to determine the auspicious time for the wedding, I follow Sāyaṇa in considering the three wheels as the day, month and year — or perhaps the *muhūrta*, the day and the hour of the month for fixing the departure of the bride and the correct time of the various functions of the wedding itself.

Stanza 15 — Soma is here the Lord of lustre, of splendour, of happiness; Soma is the auspicious entity, the Sire, who approaches the father of the girl to seek permission, as it were, to train her in women's duties and wisdom. Soma is given symbolically the importance of a 'husband', because since childhood the girl must be wedded to her crucial role and duties of mistress of some future household. It is asked from Soma; 'where do you stand to make the gift?'. What is meant here is obviously the 'gift of knowledge' and the importance of 'where Soma stands' indicates the relevance of determining the correct time to impart the formal, practical, daily and long term training of the future bride. This includes the knowledge of traditional lore and understanding the wisdom derived from that knowledge. The meaning of this verse evidently is: when and in what astral position will the wedding be caused to be successful? When and at what time should the wooing Aśvina come? When will the bride be ready, physically and mentally?

Stanza 16 — This verse is a further confirmation of the two preceding ones. It reconfirms the need and obligation to hold the commemoration of the important events in the course of human life on earth, at accurately calculated times deemed to be auspicious. An auspicious time is when that particular human activity matches or is in tune with the events in nature and with the astronomical position of celestial bodies who move according to the rules of their own life. For this reason, Lord Savitṛ, the Impeller, equally Vivifies living beings on Earth and celestial bodies in the sky. The seasons: *ṛtutha*, are bound to *ṛta* and the brāhmaṇas know the two wheels of Sūrya who causes the revolving change of the seasons. But there is more and other knowledge than what is readily obtained from the observation of nature. There is knowledge that is 'concealed', which is a good expression to identify esoteric knowledge which is the wisdom that 'is known only to those skilled in the Highest Truth'. In Vedic times there was no distinction between astronomy and astrology, but it was important already at that time to decide on the auspicious time for weddings and all important acts of life, including animal husbandry and agriculture.

Stanza 17 — The bride is then blessed and the *ṛṣi* as everyone else, gives respect to *ṛtutha*, to Sūrya, to the *deva*, to Mitra (the one who prepares contracts and oversees to their implementation) and Varuṇa, the Great God of Vedic man, the God empowered with great magic power, ruler of the marvellous phenomena of this world and holder of the fetters that control nature in general and human life in particular, according to *ṛta*.

Stanza 18 — The two most spectacular celestial beings, the Sun and the Moon are invoked as the happy pair that goes round the sacrifices of living. They regulate the seasons, the monthly and daily cycles of living beings, they rule 'all existing things'. One, the Moon, quietly watches and secretly regulates the inner rhythms of living beings; the other, the Sun, is the main regulator of the outside world, he regulates day and night, the seasons, and is yearly born again. The importance given to the resonance of astronomical events on worldly affairs is clearly stated in stanzas 15 to 19.

Stanza 19 — The daily duties of the wife to be, the mistress of the household, are specifically emphasized here by reminding the bride that the Sun God — it is not necessary to remind Sūryā that he is her father — is born anew everyday. Each dawn brings with it the daily sacrifice to the Gods, the duties of both husband and wife. The girl and the boy must be well trained in homely duties and privileges to ensure a happy and successful family life. The Moon is specifically mentioned as 'prolonging the day of our existence'. This same expression is used in the *Brāhmaṇa*s (ex: *Śat Brā*) when describing and giving instructions for the great New Moon and Full Moon Soma sacrifice. The *yajamāna* and the *yajamānī* form an inseparable pair at the *śrauta* rites of which the *Soma-yajña* is one of the most important. A physically, ritualistically and religiously healthy way of life will ensure life-long happiness.

Stanzas 15 to 19 indicate the concern with the correct astrological setting and timing of the various ceremonies, beginning with the training and education of the young girl, poetically described as her wedding to Soma, the splendour of life. 'Wedding', in this case, also means total education. The first stage of the girl's life will be followed by her apprenticeship with the *gandharva*. It represents the stage of learning traditional lore, the songs, legends and mythology that she learns from her second guide, or 'husband', the *gandharva* Viśvavasu, the protector or tutor of virgins.

Stanza 20 — The transition from one stage to another, from one 'husband' to another is marked by this stanza that again refers to the allegorical chariot that takes the young girl, the bride to be, the ideal bride, on her journey; the happy and successful journey through life. The qualities of this chariot are emphasized; it is solid, reliable, made of good wood, *kiṁśuka* = *Butea frondosa* and *śālmali* = *Bombax heptaphyllum*(?) or *Bombax malabaricum*(?) it has the colour of gold and rolls along smoothly and rapidly on strong and steady wheels. The maiden needs not fear the future, she is and will be well taken care of and protected: the chariot is gold-hued, meaning rich in all goods; it is all-shaped, meaning that it is adapted and adaptable to all possible vicissitudes that life may bring. The maiden must be confident that such will be her married life, happily laborious and she will also be successful in making her husband happy. The couple's life will be as fortunate and happy as that of the immortals and through their dutiful and responsible existence they may reach immortality. Though the word is not used, what is in fact recommended is to lead a dhārmic existence to reach eternal bliss. More details are given in the *Ait Brā*, IV, and *Kauṣītaki Brā*, XVIII; 1.

Stanzas 21-22 — The maiden has thus been handed over to her second 'husband', the *gandharva* chief Viśvavasu, the kind, good 'Lord of everybody' (chief of the *gandharvas*, acc. to Griffith). This verse follows logically the preceding, which is the request to the *gandharva*, the great musician and singer, to take the young one into his care, that she may learn all aspects of tradition as well as the common songs, the lullabies, the myths, the legends, the family and clan's history, the common daily recitations, games and stories that the *gandharvas* know. Having done his duty, the *gandharva* is thanked thus: 'Viśvavasu seek another willing maid, this one does not need your protection any more. This maiden can be taken to her husband who will take care of her from now on'.

Stanza 23 — Two Ādityas, Aryaman who is the personification of the ideal noble Āryan man, and Bhaga or Good Fortune, often associated to Lord Savitṛ, are requested to oversee that the physical, mental and spiritual union of the husband and wife be perfect and therefore perennial.

The specific meaning of the two Ādityas, sons of Aditi: Aryaman and Bhaga, in the description and invocation of the perfect wedding of the ideal bride again indicate the great antiquity of this hymn that celebrates the institution of marriage. To marriage and wedded life the ancient Āryans gave a key importance in their culture, an importance that lives on to present days; marriage and the wedding ceremony are still the central events of people's lives. *Mantras* 20-23 are to be repeated when the bride mounts her chariot.

Stanza 24 — The young girl is now prepared to be wedded at the seat of law: ṛta. The wedding is conducted at the Fire altar and is presided over by Lord Agni. Hence Agni is called the third 'husband' of the bride, he is the one who sanctifies the wedding and, at the 'place of *ṛta*', gives the final instructions, recommendations and blessings to the young bride and, therefore, to the married couple. It is Lord Agni, and he only could do it, that frees the bride from her childhood obligations and fetters and hands her over, unfettered and knowledgeable of her new duties and responsibilities to her fourth and physically real husband in human form. The bride is now released from her duties to her own parents, before stepping into the new family where her new duties will reside. Agni as messenger between men and gods is here also the messenger between husband and wife, since the wedding is a godly ceremony with perennial importance that leads deserving couples to immortal life. The point is stressed that : 'on the seat of law, in a virtuous place, I give you unpolluted, untouched and uninjured to your husband'. Evidently only Agni can purify and sanctify the future wife to this extent. This verse implies the very important concept of the key role of the daughter, the sister, the mother, in brief, of womanhood in Vedic society. For the sake of health, education, good habits and permanence of the family, the mother is the one who organizes and maintains the stability of the family, guards its wholesome habits, trains her daughters, transmits the tradition to her children and aptly and in a disguised manner, corrects and guides both husband and sons along the path of a good and righteous life.

In fact, this stanza illustrates, not polyandry as commentators wrote, but the importance given to women in Vedic society. Agni, the concept of energy itself, purity and action personified, the messenger between men and Gods, the one who sublimates the material into spiritual, is the one who accepts the maiden for her new important role, that of wife and mother, and daughter of new parents. Only Agni can release the bride from her maiden filial duties and assign to her those of her future role which is central in the culture of Vedic man for the stability and cohesion of the community. Savitṛ, as Life, had bound the girl to her parents who had given life to her body; he now releases her from past bonds because she acquires new ones and new obligations in relation to her new family. The husband, who is not physically the bearer of a new life, will never be released of his bonds and duties to his own parents; it is the patriarchal way of life typical of Indo-Europeans.

Stanza 25 — Agni frees the bride from her obligations towards her father, mother, brothers, sisters, elders. He alone having removed these fetters can lead her on to other duties, for they are 'soft fetters'. Indra, the great chief, is invoked for valiant sons and Bhaga too is invoked that the sons may be fortunate. Bhaga, Hope, is *subhaga satī* and so full is he, that he can spill over some, or even much of good fortune on the bride to make her overwhelmingly fortunate. Living is not easy, there are material difficulties, social handicaps, psychological restraints, physical adjustments between husband and wife to be overcome.

Adaptation of two persons to one another is never spontaneous and perhaps never complete. Adaptation to one another is an act of will, of friendship, physical, emotional, psychological and spiritual understanding that rarely comes easily. The blessings of Agni are indispensable, the concurrence of the Gods is necessary, happiness and joy begin with friendship and forebearance that require Hope and staunch belief in the blessings of the gods for a happy future. The wedding ceremonies are to a large extent a psychological preparation of the young couple to their new and changed day-to-day life-style.

Stanza 26 — The *ṛṣi* continues his exhortation to the young bride, he encourages her to become the household mistress, the *gṛhapatnī* who will command respect and obedience from servants and all dependents and will promote friendship and unity among family members, old and young. Appropriately the ancient deities are invoked, again Pūṣan the excellent guide who is here requested to take Sūryā by hand and lead her on the path of right conduct. The other ancient divinities, the Aśvins, givers of good health and woers of the bride, will now transport her on their car to her new home. It is logical that the health givers and knowers of medicine are those who select, then woo and finally escort the wife to her husband's home.

Stanzas 27-37 — From this verse onwards the bride and bridegroom are instructed on how to proceed during the day of the wedding and the first days after the ceremonies have been concluded. In fact, the *Gṛhya-sūtra* of Āpastamba as well as some passages of the *Brāhmaṇa*s give many more practical details of do's and dont's of married life. Advices are also given for the *śrauta* rites, the *upanayana* and major sacrifices such as the Soma sacrifice and the daily care of the domestic fire. In the *Gṛhya-sūtra* there is also reference in the context to the *aśvameda yajña*.

In 27 the most important domestic duties and blessings, the *gārhapatya* of the future mistress of the household are spelled out: to prosper with your children; unite your body with your lord's body; grow in age both together; be watchful over the domestic fire. The *gārhapatya* is first to be lighted by the newly married husband, but thereafter it is the wife's duty to maintain the domestic fire and keep it going. As years add up, she will be fully apt to lead the family and relations.

Stanzas 28, 29, 30 — These appear to be secret instructions on how to avoid the pollution resulting from defloration of the bride and for the physical aspects of the first sexual intercourse. *Kṛtya* is a mysterious entity, perhaps magic personified, that has been variously understood as the 'uncertainty factor' (SS and SV), or 'magic personified' (Griffith) or a 'magic spirit, potent and dangerous though not necessarily evil' (O'Flaherty). This entity, a female fiend, is blue and red, it should be left behind and should not be allowed to take the place of the wife; she becomes active when the wife goes to her lord, she has her own feet and personalities, and her own wicked charm. Kṛttikā are also called the nine evil 'mothers', sometimes identified with the six Pleiades, or with child diseases; Kṛttikā is here most probably the mystery, the hazard, the uncertainty of reproduction, of which only women hold the secret; men will always be in awe of this crucial biological mystery, but the *ṛṣi* admonishes the bridegroom; do not let this fear overpower you. Kṛttikā is also black magic in contemporary marriage *mantras* and could be the jealousy of a rival. The bride's garments, soiled during the first marital act, should be given to the brāhmaṇas, probably to exorcise the evil spirit and purify the one who is to become the real wife, the *gṛhyapatnī*. It seems to me that Kṛtya or Kṛttikā is, as SS and SV have pointed out, the uncertainty factor that is always present at all acts of nature, human or otherwise. In other words, since no human being is perfect, since there may be hidden, mysterious tracts in the nature of the wife or of the husband, or in modern psychological terminology, there may be sub-conscious complexes or other factors that may turn out to be evil, they may be overcome only by 'binding thy husband fast in the bonds of love' and by exorcisms performed by expert brāhmaṇas, who, we are told in the *Gṛhyasūtra*, tear apart the blood stained garment of the bride and in so doing purify her and save the husband from the evil *alter ego* of the bride. In stanza 30, the husband is severely cautioned: 'if the husband wishes to cover his own body with the wife's garments, his body looks very ugly under the wicked charm'. In a literal sense this verse sets clear hygienic rules, better detailed in the *Gṛhyasūtra*; in a figurative manner it enjoins both husband and wife to adhere to their own specific roles faithfully. The *Gṛhyasūtra* spell very clearly the behaviour that the couple should follow not only during the first three or four days after the marriage ceremony, but for all the days of the menstrual cycle, to avoid pollution by the menstrual blood. Though marriage and married life are extremely auspicious, they are not immune to the dangers of pollution; these must be avoided to conserve the purity of the institution, of the family, of the couple. Auspiciousness and pollution are different aspects of the same natural acts, they do not exclude each other, they may be present at the same time and must be dealt with separately. The words *kṛtya* and *kṛttikā* come from the same ancient root as the Greek *Kritikos* which literally means 'able to discuss or judge'. Hence st. 28-30 could be interpreted thus: 'both husband and wife must learn to appreciate each other critically, so that you may adapt easily to one another through understanding of each other, including each other's wishes, likings, weaknesses and qualities'.

Stanzas 31, 32 — Invocations for the health, safety and well-being of the couple continue, hoping that diseases of 'others', those who have come with the bridal procession, and thieves, highway robbers and enemies at large, may all be removed from the new life of husband and wife. A streak of parochialism is present in Stanza 31, where it is said that *yakṣmā*, or malignant diseases, consumption (probably tuberculosis), should not be brought by the bride's retinue. This in fact implies that 'we' are healthier than 'they', though it is true that focusing on such matters is necessary for the education of the couple.

Stanza 33 — All these dangers however, are offset by the auspicious signs of good fortune that adorn the bride. Her party may return home safely after wishing her prosperity.

Stanzas 34, 35 — The soiled garment is again focused, as an afterthought that not enough has been said on the basically important question of the physical, mental and spiritual purity of the couple. The lady of the house is the centre of the family life, and on her purity of heart and mind, on her cleanliness physical and otherwise, on her practical knowledge of the facts of life depends the well-being and happiness of the family; the bride's garments are to be entrusted to 'the brāhmaṇa who knows Sūryā well', because only they can rid the bride and bridegroom of the impurities that may have existed before marriage. The sentence: 'the brāhmaṇa who knows Sūryā well deserves the garment of the bride' could perhaps refer to the oxen? Or perhaps to the chariot that plays a role in the *Soma-yajña*? Perhaps what is meant here is not to forget to give the *gurudakṣiṇā* to the deserving brāhmaṇa? Perhaps 'garment' means the clothes, utensils and gifts that the bride brings with her and that must be purified before entering into the new home. Also, the oxen could be given to the brāhmaṇas and should be offered in sacrifice in the *ārsa* form of marriage. In olden times, in this form of marriage, a pair of cows was given away with the bride herself; this form of marriage was current mostly in priestly families. However, already in the *Manu Smṛti*, the *ārsa vivāha* was considered to be improper because opposed to the concept of *kanyādāna*, or gift of the girl (Pandey, 1982). May the couple enter into a healthy, happy, joyful long-wedded life. The 'impurities before marriage' clearly are the *kṛtya* referred to in 30. It is clearly stated in the text that the past 'garments' must be purified away.

Stanza 36 — Here begins a return to the ceremony itself. How the bridegroom is to take the hand of the bride and which gods to invoke. The *Gṛhyasūtra* give the details of the acts and gestures and recitations. Many of these are in prose and reflect very ancient practices of pre-Vedic times kept alive by tradition to the very present (Oldenberg, introduction to the *Gṛhyasūtra*). The deities mentioned here are again āryaman, the prototype of noble behaviour, Bhaga the prototype of good fortune and success and Savitṛ, the personification of the abstract concept of Life. What is new in this verse that is otherwise almost a repetition of earlier verses, is that Savitṛ is eulogized with the epithet of Purandhir, the Intelligent, the Spirited. May then the new life of the couple be noble, intelligent and bold!

Stanza 37 — Pūṣan is finally invoked again to bring the perfect wife to the husband's loving embrace, the wife who may be the best possible fertile soil to receive the seed that will bloom into noble, fortunate, healthy and active progeny. The refrain says: 'she shall twine her loving arms around me whom lovingly we embrace'.

Stanzas 38, 39 — Again these are recapitulations. The earlier 'husbands' and bridal train escorted Sūryā to her new home and Agni, the last 'husband' or instructor hands her over to her real and 'final' husband, the human husband. Similarly the Roman Catholic nuns are symbolically wedded to Jesus Christ at the ordination ceremony and thereby become the mystical brides of their God. Agni hands over the bride fully prepared for her married life, full of healthy desires, full of beauty and splendour, full of knowledge, in one word, she he is an auspicious bride ready to enjoy life with her husband for 'hundred autumns', in marital and maternal long lasting bliss.

Stanzas 40-47 — These contain mainly exhortations to the bride and advices to the couple. There are repetitions of previous verses as well as injunctions for a happy marriage, as seen from the human husband's point of view; the wish is expressed for wealth and children. The wish is also expressed that the couple may not be parted, that they may live together to play with sons and grandsons and reach a full measure of human life. Prajāpati and Aryaman are invoked and this ideal bride is again exhorted to enter her husband's home in an auspicious manner, that she may bring prosperity to bipeds and quadrupeds. She is exhorted to be amiable and cheerful, tender to animals, God abiding, not evil-eyed, always friendly and mother of heroes.

It is made clear in 40 that only her fourth husband is born of woman, the first three: Soma, the *gandharva* and Agni are not born of woman.

In stanza 45, Indra is invoked that '. . . she may bear ten sons and make her husband the eleventh'. This sentence shows the importance given to women and to the wife in particular to shape and steer the moral character of the family; she is expected to be wife, companion, friend, guide, counsellor, educator, consoler and animator, giver of life and of what is good in life, as a mother and only a mother can be and give, not only to her children, but above all to her husband and life-partner.

Stanzas 46, 47 — These are the final invocations to the Viśvadevāḥ, to waters, to Mātariśvan, Dhātṛ, Deṣṭṛ (generous educator) that they may bind the couple closely. Sāyaṇa interprets this as the bountiful Sarasvatī; all those mentioned are the most ancient deities and this brings the hymn to the end, indicating again great antiquity.

Conclusion

ṚV, X; 85, celebrates the institution of marriage and stresses the importance of performing all the rituals accurately and at the right time. The wedding rites are to a large extent a psychological preparation of the young couple for married life. The importance of the bride, the wife and mother as the central figure of the family is repeatedly emphasized, specially in the last 8 stanzas that contain the final exhortation to the bride and to the couple teaching them how to lead a fruitful and happy existence. The key role played by the wife and mother as centre of the family life could not be expressed better than by wishing that: 'may your husband be your eleventh son'. Woman is the centre around which revolves family life, the family is the basis on which the society of Vedic man was built. Accordingly it is the marriage of Mahādeva that later became the model for human marriages.

The wedding ceremonies have not changed much since ancient times and details are given in both ancient and modern texts; both in Sanskrit and all other languages.

Appropriately Sūryā is the model of the ideal bride, since she is Sūrya's daughter and will be called, like her father, to carry on life, to generate more life and produce offsprings. Vedic man was not an idolater of natural phenomena, he was a student and believer in nature's principles, see *R̥V*, VIII; 71, 1-2. As the Sun was seen to be at the root of life on Earth, his daughter, the continuation of himself, is the one who perpetuates the human family, and the institution of the family is the central brick on which society is build.

Some of the most important and significant references in this sense, other than in *R̥V*, X; 85, are : *R̥V*, VIII; 70, 11; — *R̥V*, VIII, 71, 1-2 — *R̥V*, IX; 5 (where the important attributes of woman are described); *R̥V*, IX; 96, 18, 14 (where Soma is shown as ruler of the plants); *R̥V*, IX; 5; 23-5, 46 (where Soma is shown as giver of the sap of life and is mentioned in the plural form); *AV*, XII; 17, (where further details of the wedding ceremony are given); *AV*, XIV; 1 gives biological and physiological details. This list could be extended, but it is not necessary to do so here.

Another important aspect of this hymn is the well expressed sacred awe instilled into men by the power and reproductive capacity of women. Kr̥ttikā, the alter ego of the bride, is fearful, she continues to be a mystery, she is not understood by men, she is female and feminine, attuned to the bride, she may be dangerous but she may be conquered by love and kindness, though kindness should be extended with due precautions. She is an auspicious power but always in danger of becoming and causing pollution by the phenomena inherent to sexual intercourse, child-bearing and delivery; these are aspects of the reproductive cycle related to menstruation and lactation, though the latter is never polluting. Such is Kṛttikā's nature.

There have been long discussions among scholars on how far would ritualistic practices have evolved during Vedic times along the line leading to the complexity described in the *Brāhmaṇa*s. The *Śrauta* sacrifices are very complex and grandiose, they are lengthy and demand specialized training for correct performance. It has been repeated often that by this means the priest would perpetuate himself, would make himself indispensable in the highly structured Indian society. While there may be some truth in this, the fact remains that rites and rituals of pre-Vedic and Vedic times followed closely the observation of natural phenomena. Even if not exclusively motivated by the urge to understand and participate in the functioning of the universe, as time passed and more and more knowledge accrued to man and more understanding of the relations of cause and effect enriched his mind, man would have incorporated new actions in the rituals as a means to express the newly acquired understanding and to have always more intimate contact and participation in the phenomena of the universe.

This is very clear when reading the *Brāhmaṇa*s where the symbolism of each and every step, object, word and gesture of the *yajña* is related and shown to correspond to the natural events or things to which man belongs or wishes to belong. Many conclusions, however, were unfounded, mainly due to insufficient scientific knowledge. For instance the instructions given in the *Gobhila Gṛhyasūtra* and others, on what to do to ensure conception and to sire a male or female foetus at will, are totally irrelevant. It is only during this century and thanks to powerful scientific instruments that it has been possible to understand sex-determination in plants, animals and man. However, the few incorrect conclusions made by the *ācārya*s of the past do not invalidate the many correct observations and conclusions of the beautiful song of Sūryā's wedding.

The hymn to Sūryā indicates that in the Vedic period the celebration of marriage was already one of the building blocks around which the Vedic society was structured. The key role played by women is repeatedly described as being of primary importance in the life of the family and of the clan. While the husband's role was more of a physical and material nature, the wife's role was cultural, including care of the educational and spiritual aspects of the family as re-consecrated daily by the care of the home fire. It may be recalled that the home fire is first installed by the husband upon entering the home after the marriage ceremonies are over, but from that day on, it is the wife that nurtures it daily. The young bride also has direct access to the brāhmaṇas and to the *Brāhmaṇas* and her presence as *yajamānī* at *Śrauta* and *Gṛhya* rites is indispensable. The *Yajur* and the *Atharvaveda* give practical details for the wedding ceremony and for the consummation of the marriage that are further elaborated in all the *Gṛhyasūtra*.

Nothing else should be added here about wedding rites and habits. This subject has been treated extensively and is known in all its forms and varieties. In India itself, ceremonial details of betrothal and wedding, pre-marital and marital relationships vary according to caste, *gotra* and place. Several different types of marriage are described in the *Āśvalāyana Gṛhyasūtra*. Each has its own recognised validity as related to castes, sub-castes and groups among which it is the norm. For instance in the old Panjab before Partition, matrimonial habits were a hybrid of Hindu and Muslim customs with predominance of one or the other, depending on the religion of the bride and bridegroom. The poem of Waris Shah (1766): 'Hir and Ranjha', clearly reflects the interesting fusion of various customs in that area. Among the Indo-European communities of Asia and Europe and of the derived hybrid cultures of the Americas and Australia, traditional marriage ceremonies reflect closely the ancestral habits, which are in turn influenced by ecological constraints, as for instance Muslim marriages in Indonesia and Hindu marriages in Bali.

Basically all people of humankind among which the institution of marriage is practised, underline the principle to be observed or hoped for: good health of bride and bridegroom, compatible educational and moral principles, mutual respect, respect for the parental generation and, most important, rearing healthy offsprings. These principles have the common goal of establishing a closely knit, powerful extended family, for the stability of society, for strengthening the feeling of belonging to a major entity, the society of each and all, for good and for worse. The sense of belonging is psychologically extremely important to ensure individual fortitude to face the difficulties that life gifts freely to all social living beings and to ensure giving and receiving succour, when needed.

The wife and mother, the feminine element is the great protector of the husband and his parent's family, for this reason at a certain point of the ceremony the bridegroom recites: 'be devoted to me, be my companion': this is the magic charm of concord. Solidarity among members of a family and among families of the same clan is an important ecological factor for survival of the individual and of the group. The wisdom of the *r̥ṣi* is again apparent here.

All cultural aspects of the education of the bride, thereby also the education of the children and dependents in general, are well knit together to improve the quality of life of all by means of shared habits and beliefs. Thus, at the marriage ceremony, the bridegroom repeats to the bride the words of *R̥V*, X; 85, 40-41: 'first Soma had thee for his bride, the *gandharva* obtained thee next, Agni was thy third husband, thy fourth husband am I, born of man. Soma gave thee to the *gandharva*, the *gandharva* gave thee to Agni, and Agni has given thee to me for wealth and sons'.

Pūṣan, an ancient Vedic deity, the unfailing guide, the reliable path-finder, is invoked to 'lead her (the bride) to us, she in whom men pour their semen' and Pūṣan is also asked to 'guide the *sepam*' (penis). Different *mantras* must be recited at different steps of the ceremony, for instance when embarking in a boat or boarding the chariot, instructions are given on what sacrificial food is to be consumed; with time never-ending details were added which vary from place to place. These invocations and recommendations serve the purpose of giving confidence to the young couple who may henceforth embark with a sure footing in a new environment: different aspects of culture are influenced by ecological factors.

The Brāhmaṇical marriage ritual has remained to a great extent unchanged. What differences there are, they are mainly a change in the order of performing ritualistic details and adaptations that must inevitably be introduced because of changed lifestyles and environments. The shortening of the original very lengthy ritual is the ecologically most significant change; it is due to the gradual changes imposed by the evolution from pastoral life to settled agriculture and later urban socio-economic conditions. The quickening tempo of modern lifestyles has also had its impact on the duration of the ceremonies and of the rite in its totality. For instance the chariot, though still in use in rural areas, is not always drawn by trotting bullocks; though the bridegroom may arrive on horse back, the couple usually drives away after the ceremony in a car decorated with flowers. If the car is of the imported variety, so much the better. Several sections previously performed *de facto* are now often performed only symbolically. The daughter-in-law, however, specially in north India, is still called *bahūrānī* and she usually receives the household keys and duties from her mother-in-law. The rituals also vary with caste and geographic area, however the essential steps, ceremonies, rituals, intentions and meanings of all actions and acts from the preparation for the betrothal to the consummation of the marriage, still remain unchanged and follow the instructions contained in *R̥V*, X; 85, the corresponding *Brāhmaṇas* and the *Gr̥hyasūtras*.

Those parts of the *Gr̥hyasūtra* that refer to marriage rituals are repetitions with additions to instructions already given in *R̥V*, X; 85. More details are also given in other hymns of the four Vedas and in the *Brāhmaṇas*, but this is not the place to redescribe them. The point to be focused in the present context is the importance given to the institution of marriage, of family life and cohesion of the clan. The details of the ceremony and the habits themselves became, with time, adapted to the environmental realities of the place, but the central purpose of marriage, as a means to achieve a strong, well structured and well knit social structure, is well expressed in the *Khadira Gr̥hyasūtra*, where one of the instructions given to the bridegroom reads: 'when the menses are over, the husband should cohabit with the wife, with the invocation: give conception'. This and many other comparable details are to be found throughout the *śruti* and the *smr̥ti*.

May Heaven protect your back.
May Vāyu shield your thighs.
May the Aśvini devas protect your breasts.
May Savitar protect your sucking child.
May Br̥haspati protect you until you wear the vastra and thereafter
May the Viśvedevas protect you.

Mantra recited at contemporary
Hindu marriage rite

3

Araṇyāni, The Lady of the Forest

R̥V. X; 146

r̥ṣi Devamuni. Metre: *Anuṣṭup*

May rich mountains and flowing liberal waters and herbs growing on land, and Heaven and Earth consential with the Forest Lords and both world halves, preserve for us those riches.

R̥V, VII; 34, 23

Introduction

THIS is a hymn of only six *śloka*s, one of the shortest of the whole *R̥gveda* and one apparently of minor importance. It is about the 'Lady of the Forest', Araṇyāni, the 'one who tills not yet has stores of food'. This is the only place in the *R̥V* where she is mentioned by name.

The importance of this hymn lies not in the fact that she is mentioned by name, but in the fact that she is the focus of attention. In a similar way the considerate manner is to refer to one's wife as 'the lady of the house', 'the mistress of the home', 'my children's mother' or 'she', meaning **the important one**. Araṇyāni is not, as has been represented by some, a goddess, though she is sacred in the sense that everything is sacred in the universe, being part, as it is, of the Absolute, the Self without a Second, the Truth and Essence. Araṇyāni the deity is the forest personified, the Existence of the elusive Being that seems to vanish from sight. Man is to the forest like a baby who sucks at mother's breast without destroying her.

Araṇyāni is sacred as part of *ṛta*, the Cosmic Law and order and because all Nature is sacred not because it was created, but because it is intrinsically sacred. She is sacred as a mother who gives all she has and in turn requests only respect and love; she is sacred because she must be well taken care of to enable her to carry on the work of her own generous self. She is a deity in the sense that she is an **abstract-form**, the summation and integration of a concept that cannot be seen physically as a separate self-contained body, she can only be sensed through her parts and works; she is a deity with her own attributes, forms and functions; she is elusive and beyond grasp; she is perhaps better represented mentally as the spirit of the jungle. As appropriate of the feminine nature and of all mothers, although selfless and generous, she may cause death if ill-treated, misused or insulted by the wayfarer, the villager or 'another' (verse 5) who does not know her manners and restrictions.

All sacred forests in India, and once upon a time all forests were sacred, have a presiding deity, a protectress, each with a different name proper to the place, but almost always it is a female deity whose general connotations are the same everywhere and who is to be worshipped to ensure protection before entering and using the forest. Everywhere there are endless stories of hunters or gatherers or woodcutters who entered the forest without having propitiated the deity or did not ask her permission to carry out their business or did not offer *pūjā*. They were severely punished to the point of losing their life under an elephant's foot or a tiger's teeth or a snake bite or a poisonous plant. On the other hand, rich rewards are given to those who have acquitted themselves of their duty towards the queen. The duties towards Araṇyāni vary from place to place and from person to person; they may refer to the season or time for particular activities, such as collecting fuel-wood or grasses and leaves and branches for worship or fodder or thatching; or honey and plants for medicines and food, or edible seeds and fruits, or wax, oils and essences, gums, eggs, bigger animals for food and hides and horns, fish and so on. Whatever the item collected or allowed to be grazed upon, must be harvested in a moderate manner, with gratitude and leaving enough in place for conservation and replacement. The laws of the jungle must be obeyed by all.

Whatever the item collected, it should not be taken in an exhaustive way. The concept of conservation of productive forest is inbuilt in the concept of sacred forest; indeed it is expressed and seriously commanded by the word 'sacred'.

These basic rules of behaviour are observed to this day, specially by tribals whose subsistence is, or was, often entirely dependent on the forest.

Sanskrit Text

अरण्यानि अरण्यानि असौ या प्रऽइव नश्यसि।
कथा ग्रामम् न पृच्छसि न त्वा भीःऽइव विन्दतीइँ ।। १ ।।

वृषऽरवाय वदते यत् उपऽअवति चिच्चिकः।
आघाटिभिःऽइव धावयन् अरण्यानिः महीयते ।। २ ।।

उत गावःऽइव अदन्ति उत वेश्मऽइव दृश्यते।
उतो इति अरण्यानिः सायम् शकटीःऽइव सर्जति ।। ३ ।।

गाम् अङ्ग एषः आ ह्वयति दारु अङ्ग एषः अप अवधीत् ।
वसन् अरण्यान्याम् सायम् अक्रुक्षत् इति मन्यते ।। ४ ।।

न वै अरण्यानिः हन्ति अन्यः च इत् न अभिऽगच्छति ।
स्वादोः फलस्य जग्ध्वाय यथाऽकामम् नि पद्यते ।। ५ ।।

आञ्जनऽगन्धिम् सुरभिम् बहुऽअन्नाम् अकृषिऽवलाम्।
प्र अहम् मृगाणाम् मातरम् अरण्यानिम् अशंसिषम् ।। ६ ।।

araṇyāni araṇyāni asau yā pra'iva naśyasi ।
kathā grāmam na pṛcchasi na tvā bhī'iva vindatīm̐ ।। 1 ।।

vṛṣa'ravāya vadate yat upa'avati ciccikaḥ ।
āghāṭibhiḥ'va dhāvayan araṇyāniḥ mahīyate ।। 2 ।।

uta gāvaḥ'iva adanti uta veśma'iva dṛśyate ।
uto iti araṇyāniḥ sāyam śakaṭīḥ'iva sarjati ॥3॥

gām aṅga eṣaḥ ā hvayati dāru aṅga eṣaḥ apa avadhīt ।
vasan araṇyānyām sāyam akrukṣat iti manyate ॥4॥

na vai araṇyāniḥ hantiḥ anyaḥ ca it na abhi'gacchati ।
svādoḥ phalasya jagdhvāya yathā' kāmam ni padyate ॥5॥

āñjana'gandhim surabhim bahu'annām akṛṣi' valām ।
pra aham mṛgāṇām mātaram aaṇyānim aśaṁsiṣam ॥6॥

Translation

1. Goddess of wild and forest who seemest to vanish from the sight.

   How is it that thou seekest not the village? Art thou not afraid?

2. What time the grasshopper replies and swells the shrill cicala's voice,

   Seeming to sound with tinkling bells, the Lady of the Wood exults.

3. And, yonder, cattle seem to graze, what seems a dwelling-place appears:

   Or else at eve the Lady of the Forest seems to free the wains.

4. Here one is calling to his cow, another there hath felled a tree:

   At eve the dweller in the wood fancies that somebody hath screamed.

5. The Goddess never slays, unless some murderous enemy approach.

   Man eats of savoury fruit and then takes, even as he wills, his rest.

6. Now have I praised the Forest Queen, sweet-scented, redolent of balm,

   The Mother of all sylvan things, who tills not but hath stores of food.

(transl. Griffith, 1889)

Commentaries

Stanza 1 — The Lady of the forest is the presiding deity who 'seems to vanish from sight'. She is not afraid of the forest that is her domain, that is indeed herself and she needs not go and would not feel at home constricted within the boundaries of the village. The description of the spirit, or deity of body and form of the forest that vanishes from sight is a poetically beautiful description of the feeling that one has when walking through a forest where there are no horizons and where the visual scene changes unendingly at every step and every moment, like that of a slowly rotated kaleidoscope that continuously vanishes from sight. And why would she, the presiding deity, be afraid of living in her own abode; why would she emprison herself inside a village when here is the vast expanse where she dwells unbound from all sides, at all times? In the physical sense, she is the counterpart of Aditi, the primeval mother, unfettered, who roamed in all the worlds and who had absolute free will, the *liber arbitrius* within the laws of *ṛta*.

Stanza 2 — The Lady of the forest is never alone, as insects stridulate away their monotonous *cīcī-cīcī* and all animals make their characteristic sounds and sing their songs; she is never alone because the sounds of life are ever-present. In fact, whoever has stood still for any length of time in any forest, knows that even the 'silence' of the forest has a peculiarity of its own, a special sound, an orchestration of different calls and expressions that are continuously changing with the time of day or night and with season and place.

Stanza 3 — Even in the evening after the cattle and other grazers have laid down to sleep or gone back to their distant villages outside the forest, she is ever present, attentive, throbbing with life and regenerating death: the intensive turnover of matter and energy in the living jungle.

Stanza 4 — Each one pursues his own activities, each finding his livelihood in the jungle, every living being, plant or animal, including man. The shepherd grazes his cattle in the clearings, the wood-cutter fells the trees and others collect the forest bounties; but to all, night will be fearful if they have transgressed the rules imposed by the mistress: the law and order of the jungle. There are, however, unruly spirits; many of them roam about specially during night-time, ready to frighten those who are not in tune with the law. Maybe we should remember that even Indra, the Great Leader, was once afraid of Darkness, Night and Death.

Stanza 5 — She, the Good Provider, never kills unless some ill-intentioned person misbehaves. Sāyaṇa interprets the 'bad one' to be a robber or a tiger. She shares the fruits or produce of the forest with those who respect her laws, the laws are part of the great law of nature, of *r̥ta*. The respectful, law-abiding ones can partake of the bounty offered by the jungle at will and without fear, they will thus be able of resting in peace.

Stanza 6 — Araṇyāni is a Queen, a mother of all natural beings, plants and animals, winds and rains and soil, all the beings of her domain and she is sweet scented as the balm of plenty because she 'tills not but has stores of food'.

Forest, Trees, Plants elsewhere in the Vedas

The Lady of the Forest, Araṇyāni, is mentioned only once in the *R̥V*, in this short hymn entirely dedicated to her; a beautiful hymn without a second. Araṇyāni is the personification of the forest, in contemporary ecological parlance we would say that Araṇyāni represents, or is the name given to, the ecosystem forest, to the idea-concept of forest. In a comparable manner, Agni is the name given to the abstract concept of matter-energy or the energy principle in general.

Araṇyāni is the forest personified for the sake of a more direct, more physical tangible representation of the complex entity that is the forest ecosystem; consequently the concise hymn dedicated to the spirit, or the essence of the forest, is as beautiful, suggestive and awe inspiring as the forest itself. For this reason it is a hymn without a second. The generous forest, giver of all, dangerous and protective, powerful and fragile, is to be cherished, respected, loved and revered in the same manner as the Lady of the House is cherished, respected, loved, revered and obeyed by husband, in-laws, sons, dependents, domestic animals and the whole clan, who all equally depend on her wisdom, experience and resilience. The Lady of the Forest and the Lady of the Household are the depositaries of strength, power and endurance of their respective ecosystems, the forest and the family.

The *SV*, and *YV* and the *AV* repeat and give further details about the matters mentioned or only briefly pointed out in the *R̥V*. Though Araṇyāni is mentioned only once in the *R̥V*, trees, plants and vegetation in general are mentioned and discussed from different angles and aspects innumerable times. The distinction is clear: Araṇyāni is the spirit, the idea/concept of the forest as a whole, as a system, while the parts of the ecosystem, trees, plants, animals, waters are discussed separately, in themselves and for their intrinsic merits alone as well as their interactions.

The forest (*R̥V*, I; 55, 4), is readily identified as the ideal place of retreat for worshipping sages who in return glorify the forest with their presence and chants. The forest is recalled with respect and care over and over again. It is mostly seen through its most striking component, the one that sets the basic character of a forest: the tree, the tall, imposing, powerful, gigantic tree.

Though other derivations have been proposed for the word *vanaspati*, the most immediate and direct meaning, in the context of its uses in the Vedas, appears to be literally: 'Lord of the Forest'. Undoubtedly the presiding giant, powerful sovereign of the forest, is the tree. It must be recalled that the trees of the Indian sub-continent were still of a proverbial gigantic size as late as the whole nineteenth century; it took the destructiveness of the nineteenth and twentieth centuries to finish off the giants.

Vanaspati is the Lord of the forest because of its stature, strength, usefulness and above all because he is wood. Wood burns, it is the food of Lord Agni and the *araṇis* are made of wood; the sacrificial post, the *yūpa*, is made of wood; the container for the pressed *soma* juice was made of wood and in a similar manner, the container for pressed grapes juice is traditionally still made of wood. Of 'good forest wood' is made the boat which will carry physically and symbolically the bride and bridegroom to the other margin of the river after the wedding is over (contemporary marriage *mantra*). To this day wine is kept in wooden casks, oak wood being the best; oak is one of the most imposing of the giant trees. Finally (*R̥V*, X; 101) the most important structures of nomadic and settled Vedic man, the chariot as well as the beams, doors and windows of the house were made of wood. Some utensils and tools, the hoe and the plough themselves were, and still are, made of wood. Logically, frequent invocations and requests for blessings are addressed to Vanaspati.

Vanaspati is also the Lord of all the plants and animals which live in the domain that he oversees from his roots in the soil up to the lofty, majestic height of the canopy. Alive and standing, the tree overrules the living forest and when recumbent over his mother's bosom (*R̥V*, III; 8, 1) after being felled by age or man, he becomes the material for the worship of all gods by nourishing Agni who sublimates the material into spirit and is the intermediate between man and the Supreme. *R̥V*, I; 142, 11, an Apri hymn, and many others chant: 'O Vanaspate, give forth thyself and call the gods to sacrifice'.

Vanaspati is more frequently and pointedly mentioned in hymns to Viśvedevas, in Apri hymns and others to Agni. He is often mentioned in association with plants. The Plant itself is personified in *R̥V*, X; 145 as *Sapatnībādhanam*, where a spell is cast against a rival wife with the words: 'as a cow hastens to her calf, so let thy spirit speed to me, hasten like water on its way'.

Again the tree is also a model for man, in *R̥V*, III; 8, 11 it is said: 'Lord of the forest, rise with a hundred branches, so that with thousand branches we may rise to greatness'.

Soma is called the Lord of medicinal plants and it is said that Soma's glories are in the plants (*R̥V*, I; 23, 20 — *R̥V*, X; 97). Plants are everywhere praised and they are said that they are descended from heaven and existed long before the gods. Poisonous and medicinal plants are treated briefly in the *R̥V*, but at great length in the other Vedas, specially the *AV*; on this is based the science of *Āyurveda*.

R̥V, VII; 34 and many other hymns close with the petition: *yūpa pāta svastibhi svā naḥ* 'may you ever cherish us with blessings'.

The admiration and worship of trees, of plants, of the forest, is not exclusive to the Indo-European group of Āryans who eventually settled in the sub-continent. The pre-Āryan people of India, whether Dravidian, Tibeto-Burmese or others, were keen observers of nature and also admired, respected and worshipped trees and forests. This tradition is alive to the present day: sacred trees and sacred forests are a living part of daily and seasonal worship. Flowers, fruits, and other parts of plants are offered daily to the gods.

Some species of trees or other plants are specially worshipped because of their intrinsic properties, like the *deodār* (*Cedrus deodara*), the *aśvattha*, the *pīpal*, the basil, hemp, poppy or

Rawvolfia serpentina, but in a general way all trees, grasses and medicinal or food plants are treated with special care. The cult of plants and forests is widespread among most people of the earth. After publishing a short paper on Sacred Groves (Vannucci, 1991) I continued my studies of the topic and found that wherever I looked in the present or past, in the tropical or temperate areas, I could discern tree and forest-worship, independent of creed, religion and climate. Personalized or even anthropomorphized trees and forests occur in most legends and mythologies. In India, traditionally trees are worshipped and are inhabited by deities or are deities themselves. Many trees have special meaning and special legends are attributed to them, thus they are worshipped only at special occasions or seasons. Mention should be made of the legendary fabulous *kalpavr̥kṣa*, the wish-granting tree that in ancient times grew on Earth and would grant whatever they desired to those sitting under it. The *kalpavr̥kṣa* was later taken away from Earth to Indra's paradise because of misuse by greedy and lusty man. It is interesting to note that the Vedic tribes, which were essentially shepherds, had the Kāmadhenu, the miraculous cow, granting all wishes. Kāmdhenu was the cow of plenty that had surfaced at the time of the churning of the Ocean and was given by the gods to *r̥ṣi* Vasiṣṭha. It was perhaps a symbol of the great knowledge and wisdom, capable of granting desires, of *r̥ṣi* Vasiṣṭha who could grant whatever man asked of him in good faith.

The Christian Tree of Life and the Christmas tree, the Sacred Groves of Mangrove trees in as widely apart areas as west Africa and east India, the sitting under the cherry tree in bloom in Japan or the agave species of Mexico and innumerable other examples are different forms of tree and forest-worship throughout the world and among different people.

Conclusion

This hymn has been variously interpreted, for instance Araṇyāni is called a goddess of the wood by Griffith. O'Flaherty interprets the hymn as the description of the hardships that a traveller has to undergo in the forest: 'a traveller lost in the forest becomes frightened and succumbs to twilight mirages. He begs the female spirit of the forest not to harm him'. Besides the fact that mirages do not occur in forests, at best there could be illusions; this interpretation of the hymn is fanciful, while the hymn is instead one very realistic and down to earth. It refers directly to the everyday life of forest dwellers of ancient India that was entirely or almost so covered by jungle, including the tall-tree forests.

The Spirit of the Forest, Araṇyāni, does not kill and to her, praises should be offered; she rests at night in contrast to the goblins, spirits and demons of the jungle who are set loose in the darkness of night.

I see this hymn dedicated to Araṇyāni as a laudation of the same deity that is to this day worshipped as Banodebi, Vanodevi or Banobibi and innumerable other specific names in many parts of South and South-East Asia. Together with Hindu and Muslim villagers I have myself paid respect to the presiding deity of that part of the mangrove forest of the Sunderbans of Bengal, where she is called Banobibi. The presiding deity of a forest, except for few exceptions, is always feminine. An interesting example of a masculine forest deity is from a former mangrove forest, now raised above high tide level and no longer a mangrove, on the Coromandel coast of south-east India. However it appears more logical to have a feminine forest deity, because she is giver of life and refuge, she is generous, fertile, prolific and as a mother she is worshipped by countless off-springs.

Forests are among the most important formations in nature and they are sacred in their own right because of their role in the functioning of nature. The worship of forests is not exclusive to India, or south and south-east Asia in general. Sacred trees and sacred groves are known from all cultures. Here, however, the forest stands not only for our present concept of a forest which is a natural or man-made formation with tall trees and undergrowth, but the word *araṇya* is used also for jungle in general, including savannahs; at present it can be used also for all sorts of un-tilled or uncultivated natural areas. In other words, Araṇyāni is the mistress of the wild vegetation and of all the animals associated with it. She is that particular aspect of *prakr̥ti* or Nature that is a high forest or is sparsely covered with trees, shrubs, creepers. She is the root concept of 'sacred forest' and is best designated with the contemporary use of the word *jungle*, which is feminine.

This hymn reaffirms a basic concept of the Vedic ethos: the respect for nature that gives us its all. The terrain where the energy of the Sun together with water generates Life, and the care that man must have with *prakr̥ti*, is the same care as each one of us has for mother.

Worship of the forces of nature that dominate the forest was particularly strong in pre-Vedic India and is still very strong among tribals who are the descendents of the autochthonous population. Trees, grasses and flowers later acquired particular importance and significance in religious practices of the Vedic and Brāhmaṇical classic periods (Agrawala, 1970); it has been argued that the non-Vedic word and practice of *pūjā* may be derived from the word *puchei*, an old Dravidian root-word for flower, still in use. Among the *ādivāsīs* of the Indian sub-continent, plants and animals were treated at par with man, hence the sacredness of the forest. Suffice to mention the lotus, the *pīpal*, the *deodāra*, cows, snakes and practically all plants and animals whose good and bad qualities were well known.

In the whole *R̥V* Araṇyāni is mentioned by name only in this hymn. Though revered and respected, neither *prakr̥ti* nor Araṇyāni are anywhere seen as goddesses, often not even as deities. They are manifestation and materialization of the

Godhead, they are their embodiment governed by *ṛta*. They are different aspects of *ṛta*, the structure and dynamics of the Universe that must be accepted and respected as such and of which we ourselves are part. *Ṛta* is what is and cannot be changed by man. Man must abide by natural laws or face dire consequences; a lesson that twentieth-century man should learn. If the traveller or the villager behave well, if they use wisely the produce of the jungle, of the wild, forest or savannah or pasture-land and do not squander it, Araṇyāni, the Queen, will reward the traveller with good food, peaceful rest and many other things for him, for his family, for his animals and his village. If not, he may die.

What a warning to today's man, the ruthless exploiter of nature!

Finally it must be pointed out that it is significant that the three hymns: Sūryā's wedding (*ṚV*, X; 85), the story of Naciketas (*ṚV*, X; 135) and the hymn to Araṇyānī (*ṚV*, 146) are all from the last *maṇḍala*. Though the Ṛgvedic hymns are not arranged chronologically, the last *maṇḍala* is usually considered to contain later hymns, even if on no other ground than linguistic and stylistic features. These three hymns appear to be a fullstop on the statement of three basic dhārmic principles: the sanctity and the duty to preserve the institution of marriage and of the extended family; the blind obedience and reasoned devotion to the father; and finally, the respect towards all nature and the imperative duty to abide by the laws of that particular aspect of *ṛta*, which is *prakṛti*.

The fire altar itself is made in the shape of a bird. It is sprinkled with water at the beginning of the *Śrauta* sacrifices. The *vedī* is sprung from good soil and the chief Vedic metres, the *gāyatrī*, the *triṣṭup* and the *jagatī* are represented by three lines drawn with the *sphya* on the sides of the *vedī*. They are: soil, water, air to produce the sound of the metres, fire as energy and Fire as the sublimation of matter into energy, that dissolves into *ākāśa*.

> *May the Gandharvas and Apsaras that reside in the big forest tree, be auspicious to this bride. Let them do her no harm for taking the dowry with her.*
>
> Comtemporary marriage *mantra*

4

Indra and Varuṇa, Material and Immaterial Reality*

THIS chapter focuses on a specific aspect of the logic and wisdom of the ancient ṛṣis. The ṛṣis we know by name and the sages who preceded them which are referred to as 'the ancients', or 'the ancestors', all had a clear vision of the fact that there are two categories of Reality; one is material, the other, immaterial. Reality is powerful, hence two powerful personalities represent material and immaterial reality: they are Indra, the Great King of humans and *deva*, and Varuṇa, the Great *devatā* imbued with infinite *māyā*, mysterious more often than not.

Even a short and concise analysis as this will show how the two aspects of reality are invoked, prayed to and represented in the *Ṛgveda* by two separate personalities. They are occasionally at odds with each other, as realities may be or become.

Material reality is more readily perceived by man; it is needed daily to satisfy man's immediate biological needs, such

---

* Paper read at the Xth World Sanskrit Conference, Bangalore, 1997. After writing this chapter I had the good fortune of meeting Dr. Uma Chakravarty and Dr. Jyotish Nath and I could have in hand R.N. Dandekar's latest book (1997). I am indebted to Dr. Uma Chakravarty for her critical reading of my first book and for many constructive discussions and clarifications, specially on the meaning of Sanskrit words. I am deeply grateful to all of them.

as food, shelter, clothing; it is also needed to satisfy man's aspirations for better living, such as lands, space, habitation, as well as intellectual and spiritual needs. Indra is a very human personality, more a King than a God, eulogized as divine, Great God, Resplendent and so on; a Great Leader and conqueror by wars, rather than by introspection and observation followed by logical deduction. Varuṇa on the other hand is the Great *asura* having infinite *māyā*, not easily understood or comprehended even by his great devotee, *r̥ṣi* Vasiṣṭha; his power is ever felt; though ever present he is unattainable; though existent, he cannot be visualized or mentally represented in the same way as Indra can; he operates through moral and spiritual fetters that bind man and all nature to *r̥ta*; he is the governor and overseer of *r̥ta*. Immaterial realities are difficult to realize mentally, more difficult to perceive and even more difficult to explain; Varuṇa would be invoked more rarely, more reverentially and in greater awe, few persons would dare approach him directly except in his tangible manifestations through *r̥ta*. Every human being wishes to satisfy material needs, thus Indra is frequently sought, but only the spiritually advanced perceive and pursue non-material, intellectual and spiritual drives.

The objective of this chapter is to show that the ancient *r̥ṣi* distinguished clearly material and immaterial reality, as they also made a clear distinction between conscious and unconscious time. In other words, the *r̥ṣi* recognised the existence of a form of reality that is not easily grasped by the sense-organs of the human body.

Material reality impinges constantly on man, hence the personalization of the concept of material reality, Indra, who is accessible to the mind of man through the same sense-organs that monitor sensuous material reality and the phenomenal world at large. Inevitably Indra is very human, with frailties and qualities of man, as for instance, when he pursued the *asura* who had takes refuge in night he had to ask for cover to the metres, that are an aspect of *ṛta*, because he feared night, darkness and cold, other names for Insecurity, Ignorance and Death. It is also mentioned often that he needs a drought of the exhilarating *soma* drink, before going to battle. The personality of Indra has been the object of countless studies, but I will refer here only to the two latest, by Dandekar (1997) and Chakravarty (1997) who summarize the extensive literature on the subject. Both authors conclude that Indra was a deified human being, a great Chief and Leader.

Words

In this contemporary world, when one mentions reality, the word evokes the idea of material existence, the reality of things that can be perceived by one or more sense-organs. Reality therefore, is usually considered to be something that can be touched, smelled, heard, seen or tasted. A so-called 'sixth-sense' is sometimes invoked when something that cannot be directly or immediately related to one or more of the five biological sense-organs is perceived by the mind, something which is immaterial at the level of human sense-organs.

The concept of 'sixth sense' however, is not taken very seriously and is usually dismissed by 'reasonable' persons, as for instance many scientists. In the Indian tradition the mind, *manas* or reason, is the *indriya*, or faculty, that controls the five senses and the five action faculties. Mind can apprehend Immaterial Reality, though its existence cannot be readily perceived by any of the five sense-organs.

The meaning of words evolves with time and may be different in different cultures. For the sake of precision, the meaning of a few words as used here, follows. Vocabularies and Dictionaries teach us that the word **'real'** comes from the Latin *res*, for thing or fact; it is akin to the Sanskrit *rai* for property. Incidentally it is significant to note that agricultural fields are still measured in *rai* in Thailand. The word **reality** is given as the quality, or state of being real. Existence, say the vocabularies, means to 'have real being, whether material or spiritual'. The word **Reality** is here used in the sense of **existence.**

Vocabularies thus explain one word with the other, therefore 'real' and 'existent' are here used interchangeably. If something is real, it exists and if it exists, it is real. The word **existence** comes from the Latin *ex-sistĕre* that derives from *stare*, therefore existĕre means to come into being. The dictionaries however tell us that 'existence is reality as opposed to appearance' and by this statement deny immaterial existence. The English language has further slant over the word *real* when it is used in sentences like: 'dreams become real', which implies that dreams are not real, or in other words, that there is no immaterial existence, or immaterial reality. Further the word *real* is explained as: 'not artificial, fraudulent, illusionary or apparent; real is something having objective, independent existence', thus immaterial existence or immaterial reality are totally disregarded; the definitions given are therefore not satisfactory.

Here I use the words **real** and **existent** to designate something that **IS** and therefore has independent reality, whether material or not.

The Verb **to know** I use here in the sense of being aware of, to perceive and recognise with certainty. The word **wisdom** I use in the sense of soundness in judgement in matters related to life, individual and collective conduct, logical thinking leading to correct behaviour.

Finally I would note that the word *asura* is remarkably similar to the Latin, neo-Latin and English words: to assure, assert, insure, assurance, insurance which are reminders of pledge, certainty. The prefix *ass* indicates enhancement as for instance in: assume, assistant, associated, assiduous, asset, asseveration, assessment. The most powerful ancient gods, like Agni and Varuṇa, were called *asura* Varuṇa and *asura* Agni as a recognition of their great power, a power beyond human understanding therefore deemed to be magic power; some gods more than others were imbued with great *asu*, great *māyā*, and Varuṇa more than any other. Another possible derivation of the word *asura* is from the ancient root *as*, meaning Lord, Chief, the Leader capable of incredible feats. According to Nath (1996) *asura* in both the Avesta and the older religion of the Vedas, means Lord, both human and godly. Dandekar explained exhaustively the origin of the term *asura* and its use in relation to the ancient gods such as Varuṇa and Agni. I would like to point out that the two derivations proposed by scholars, the roots *asu* and *as* do not contradict but rather reinforce each other.

Though the ancients perceived Reality in all its forms, there are no defined postulates, hypotheses, or theories expressed categorically in the Vedas. Often questions are formulated, they confirm the eagerness to acquire knowledge with the purpose of understanding the phenomena of nature and their mutual relationships, the being and becoming of everything in the universe, of the universe itself and of man's role in the functioning of the universe; many questions and answers are given in the form of myths, but theories were not expressed or stated mathematically; no fixed answers were sought perhaps because it was realised that everything is relative and impermanent and everything constantly evolves and changes. Even the character of the gods evolve with time and the gods themselves pass away at the end of a *kalpa*. The scientific attitude of the *ṛṣis* in the contemporary sense of the word science and scientific, is to acquire information, transform it into knowledge (science) with the stated purpose of generating understanding (philosophy). Philosophy is then translated into religion for the everyday use of human beings; philosophy is also translated into instructions for practical purpose, as for instance how to determine latitude at any point north or south of the Tropical line; or how to solve a square angle triangle (see Appendix I). For these reasons and for the purpose to be achieved, it was irrelevant to define whether information relates to material or immaterial reality.

Whatever leads to understanding is valid.

Material reality can be easily tested but immaterial reality is difficult to qualify by the unaided five sense-organs and even more difficult to quantify; it could not be readily tested by the means available to ancient man. At present, immaterial reality, as for instance the existence, the working, the effects and uses of electromagnetic waves, can be tested and proved to exist through their effects on the living and non-living material entities; they can be measured by machines and immaterial reality has been harnessed for material purposes.

The recognition of the existence of immaterial reality always was and still is considered to be **magic**. While much of the common street-'magics' are nothing more than tricks or illusionism, there is much real and efficient magic that uses the forces and energies of the non-tangible natural entities such as radiation, magnetism or gravity. The forces of immaterial reality that were perceived by ancient man before he learned how to harness them, have nowadays been used, and are intensively used by science and technology for very practical or material purposes.

The circle is now closed. In the West, after centuries of disbelief and after considering science as opposed to religion, science has re-discovered the existence of immaterial reality and technologies were and are being developed to make use of the forces and energy of immaterial reality to satisfy the needs and greeds of man.

This chapter is concerned with the Vedic man's perception of Reality and of how he expressed and represented his perception of the different types of Reality, both those he could sense materially and those whose existence he could not prove tangibly, but which he sensed with the mind and through logical deductions from observation, from mathematics, astronomy and his own spiritual perceptions: the 'sixth sense' of man. Reality in the Vedic context is the *Brahmaṇ*, the Absolute Reality, the Absolute

Truth, the Self-Existent, the All, *Ka* (*R̥V*, X; 121) which, as such, is both material and immaterial (Vannucci, 1994).

The R̥gvedic Figures Indra and Varuṇa

Human minds evolve in different directions; some went as far as denying material reality. Thus the Japanese Buddhist priest Sargyo (1118-90) said: 'Since I am convinced that reality is in no wayreal How am I to admit that dreams are dreams?' While this attitude may be laudable from a mystic or philosophical point of view, it was not the attitude of the ancient *r̥ṣis* who pursued knowledge and the wisdom derived therefrom in a philosophically practical manner, in turn followed by religious practices because of the belief and faith put into the philosophical truths translated into Vedic sacrifices. However this is not the place to discuss ancient philosophy or that of Ādi Śaṅkara.

To the ancients, all that exists, that can be grasped and visualised by the sense-organs and organized by the mind, or reason: **IS**, and therefore is **real**. Thus even dreams and the spirit are or may be real. Material reality can be 'grasped' by the five bodily sense-organs while the immaterial reality can only be 'grasped' by the mind, *manas*. *Manas* is the *indriya*, or rational faculty that co-ordinates all other faculties, which are the five faculties of sensation and five faculties of action. Western bio-philosophy recognizes five sense-organs, those that give the perception of material reality. Leonardo da Vinci most probably had mystic experiences in his childhood and youth, but engrossed in the assessment of physical phenomena and their fluctuations in space and time, apparently abandoned all concerns with immaterial reality when he said: 'Non c 'é veritã alcuna che non sia prima passata dai nostri sensi' (There is no Truth, or: we can know no truth whatesoever that has not been acquired by our senses). However the very rational Leonardo himself in his paintings succumbed to the human need of illustrating non-material reality, such as the saints' and angels' *aurea*. More often, however, Leonardo expressed the immaterial, which he decried as reality, by the bodily and eye expression of his figures. Leonardo and other great artists and artisans were able to express the *forma mentis* of the characters that they portrayed by using their own mind to capture the immaterial reality alive in another's mind. The serene expression of the Śiva-Naṭarāja of the Cola bronzes reflects the Lord's experience of the immaterial while at the same time his body is engaged in the furious *tāṇḍava* dance over Time, *kāla*, which is material reality in action. It is well-known that when Leonardo was rebuked because he delayed finishing the great painting of the Last Supper for the convent of Santa Maria delle Grazie in Milano, he excused himself by saying that he had not yet found the living model for Judas Iscariot. What the scientist in Leonardo really said was that his mind had not yet found a human being whose expression would betray the immaterial reality of the thoughts of the would-be traitor. Thoughts are real, though immaterial.

Indra in the *Ṛgveda* is often described and praised, Varuṇa is not described, but invoked. Indra satisfies his worldly needs and those of his followers, Varuṇa has no known material needs, though *soma* is occasionally offered to him at the celebration of certain sacrifices.

Greek culture, taken as a late evolutionary form of the Indo-European original cultures, has no counterpart for Varuṇa, except for the philosophical ideas of Plato. The gods of the Greek mythology of the classical period are akin to Indra and his associates. Once Lokesh Chandra (pers. comm.) pointed out the possible derivation of the Greek word for man: *andros*, from Indra. This appears to be correct, or, more probably, both words come from the same root. In fact, Indra could well have been taken as the prototype of man in the prehistoric Hellenistic period. Would there have been a derivate of Varuṇa in the pre-historic or historic Hellenistic period? I see Varuṇa's counterpart as *Fate*, certainly not Uranous, as has mistakingly been said and repeated. Fate was a powerful figure ever present in the historical

Greek classical period and was usually invoked when no other solution or explanation of any problem or event was in sight. Fate was not personalized but was above and ruled even over Kronos, Uranous and Zeus themselves, as the great Varuṇa rules over the Vedic Gods with his fetters, according to *ṛta*. Fate, like Varuṇa, is a determining cause. Fate, *fatum* in Latin, literally means: 'what has been spoken'. Some Greek mysteries were carried over into the classical historic period from the Mycenean or pre-historic period. The Greek myth and mysteries of Orpheus who was capable of conquering the forces of nature, shows that in actual fact he was able to put evil to rest, but not to destroy it: Orpheus himself succumbs to death of the body because he was unable to overcome his own insufficiency due to lack of inner immaterial fortitude. In a somewhat parallel, though older myth, Indra had to call the metres to his help to overcome the personalized powers of evil: the *asura* who had taken refuge in the darkness of night. Further, classical Hinduism recognizes the need of the creation of *avatāra*s to surmount the insufficiencies of man.

Although man has always attempted to control immaterial reality, he does not have the power to do so. He can use such forces to a point, but does not have total control over them. Follows the need of religious, shamanistic, magic or scientific practices to overcome or make use of immaterial forces, which in such cases were usually called 'forces of occult powers'. Shamanism is not a religion, but a practice to be found in all cultures and religions in one form or another. It is a practice by which persons endowed with special powers, use these powers to contact different sorts of forces, including psychologic forces, to obtain from them whatever items of help are desired by other human beings. Orpheus was too pragmatic, he succeeded in contacting the powers of the netherworld but failed in the last crucial and vital test to bring his beloved Eurydice back to the light-drenched world of the living: the failure was due to his spiritual weakness, he did not have enough power. Similarly

Indra vacillates in his determination to vanquish the powers of evil, the *asura*, but is successful in cajoling the metres to ensure their help. Help is given because the metres know the Law, *ṛta*, that governs the material and immaterial universe. This of course, could not be done without the approval of the administrator of the cosmic law and order, Varuṇa. Orpheus failed in his pursuit because he was imbued with a selfish desire to which he was committed by words rather than altruistic wisdom: Orpheus cannot be successful in the immaterial aspects of his quest; Indra, supported by the immaterial reality of the metres, is successful in his altruistic endeavour.

Indra — The personality of Indra evolves in the Vedas themselves (see Dandekar, 1997; Chakravarty, 1997). The personality, or personalities of Indra have been studied by many scholars, from many points of view. Indra is one of the best known ancient gods. The exploits and myths related to and attributed to Indra are numerous and wonderful; they cover an extensive geographic and temporal area: the migration of the Ārya and the occupation of Saptasindhu. Most probably the name Indra does not designate a single person; it probably covers a series of remarkable chiefs and conquerors. The migration from Balkh to Saptasindhu, the innumerable skermishes and wars for the conquest and occupation of the new land, the destruction of impediments, would have taken much longer than a single human life-span. If this is so, the name Indra could be seen more as a title, an honorific appellation or a patronymic rather than the personal name of a single hero. To support this opinion I quote from Chakravarty (1997) 'The word Indra was initially an adjective . . . later an epithet, following a very normal course was transformed into his name'. To this I would add that, given the many feats attributed to Indra that cover a very long span of time, probably centuries, a single person could not have done it all. Further, considering the changes in character of the Great King of humans and gods, the Great God who becomes bolder and bolder as time passes emerging as an invincible conqueror and later loses his lustre in the *Atharvaveda* and behaves in a more human and not so godly manner, we may conclude that Indra was in fact the supreme title given to the invading Āryan clans who fought both Āryan and Anāryan enemies during the progress into the new lands. The migration of the Āryan clans did not happen as a single mass migration and would certainly have taken a few generations before achieving a permanent settlement in the Indian subcontinent.

In *Ṛgveda*, IV; 20, 6 it is said that the 'terrible Indra is born since the beginning of time . . . ' and in *Ṛgveda*, VII; 20, 5, he is said to be born from a human father and mother; then again he is said to be the youngest of the gods (*TS*, VI; 6, 11, 2, and Chakravarty, *l.c.*). Indra is fully anthropomorphic and his personality, already in the *Ṛgveda*, appears to be a recapitulation of past history with several leaders telescoped into a single name. In a comparable manner, the name of the Roman Caesar became the honorific for Western kings. In the course of time the name Indra was divinized and more and more exploits and successes were attributed to him as the embodiment of the whole race, as amply documented by the profuse eulogies offered to him. By eulogizing the leader, the conquerors eulogized themselves. Indra is called the King of Kings, the King of Gods, but he never lost his human attributes: love of material pleasures, dexterity in the use of arms, wise leadership in war and peace and greatness in battle. As a king he is invoked to provide his followers with material wealth: lands and space, paths, shelter, habitation, protection, food, cattle, horses and other riches. As a king he accepts offerings and oblations and rewards accordingly his faithful Āryas.

Indra is eulogized for conquering and occupying Saptasindhu and for providing the Āryas with a permanent home; he is a king conscious of his duties and responsibilities as well as of his prerogatives as a human being, a king enjoying *soma*, women and the excitement of the battlefield. Indra, the yellow bearded and yellow haired, is associated with the sun and the dawn because Āryans acted and fought their battles only during daylight. As a human being he is afraid of night, darkness and cold and more than once he is in need of encouragement which he receives through songs and prayers from other Ādityas, from sages, priests, the *yajamāna* and all men who are in need of the material benefits that he can provide. He is later associated to life-giving Sūryā, to rain and rivers. As a ruler he provides for channelling and storing waters for irrigation, making and bursting impoundments; he is an intelligent chief in conquest and wise leader in peace, he does not order the impossible and knows how to select his helpers. He abides by *ṛta*. Pūṣan, the path-finder, helps him to recover the cattle and the ancient, divine and able Tvaṣṭṛ made his *vajra* from Dadhīca's bones: a gift that is above material, also a divine investiture. The deification of Indra by Vedic man is discussed and exemplified exhaustively by Chakravarty and Dandekar (*l.c.*).

Indra is indeed a glorious, divinized personification of material realities; this is the reason why the greatest number of hymns of the *Ṛgveda*, second only to Agni, are addressed to him. The greatest God of Vedic man was Varuṇa who, amongst other attributes, is also the essence, the concept of immaterial reality.

Follow a few quotations from the many that could be made, to substantiate the above:

Indra, King, giver of rewards: *ṚV*, I; 10,11 . . . 'cause the seer to win a thousand gifts';

Indra makes water works; he restrains the floods of rivers, builds dams, releases the waters: *ṚV*, IV; 30, 12, as the most important riches; in a *Vālakhilya* hymn: 3, 6, it is said: 'him when thou aidest . . . to give away again obtains great wealth to nourish him', thus enforcing human solidarity and mutual support among his people;

Indra is a King, a conqueror of quick action: 'Giver who pauses not to think', *R̥V*, IV; 31, 7;
He is wielder of punitive justice: *R̥V*, IV; 32, 5;
whose manly deeds are sung by the poet, *R̥V*, IV, 32, 11;
and has supreme wisdom, *R̥V*, V; 35, 2 as a King;

Indra as a good King and leader is also a good companion, *R̥V*, VIII; 86, 7-8: 'sit down with us, be the companion at our feast';

Indra, riches of the rich, Lord of treasures (*R̥V*, I; 5, 2); 'easy to drive away... is the spoil bestowed by Indra': *R̥V*, I; 10,7; gives succour in battles and ensures victory: throughout the *R̥V* and III; 41, 11; 'in him gods have stored manliness ... and wild joy of *soma* and conquest': *R̥V*, I; 52, 10 — 53, 3 — 80, 15 etc.

Indra, the Father made thee slayer: *R̥V*, I; 129, 11;

Indra Śatakratu, Lord of hundred acts: *R̥V*, I; 4,8; 'can fulfil all our wishes with horses and cattle': *R̥V*, 16, 9 and 'of wealth and men thou art the ruler': *R̥V*, IV; 20, 8, but even the King 'can aid man only from the seat of order': *R̥V*, IV; 21, 3, which is *r̥ta*.

Indra, prototype of the perfect King is well characterized in *R̥V*, I; 100. He bestows on men all material benefits, according to law; it is not astonishing that he is the most frequently invoked god;

Indra, throughout, represents very much the **power of the Present**;

Indra is an Āditya whom Aditi acknowledges as her son, hence he is said to have existed since always, he is 'the hero of our ancient home': *R̥V*, I; 30,9. Most frequently Indra is remembered as the slayer of Vr̥tra. Whoever was Vr̥tra, and the scholars have different opinions, he or it undoubtedly were the greatest impediments, the first enemies and difficulties to be conquered by the Āryans during their progress into Saptasindhu. The recurrent theme of all the laudations to Indra, are his feats of strength; it is this spectacular material strength that brings about his accomplishments. In fact, Indra's very name is the embodiment of all his power, as befits a Lord, a Master, a King, a Conqueror who subjugates a large amount of enemies and evil powers, human or not: Vr̥tra, *asuras*, *panis*, *dasyus*, *dāsas*, *rākṣasas*.

Of the Ādityas, Indra, Varuṇa, Mitra and Aryaman are repeatedly invoked together: material and immaterial reality, Indra and Varuṇa are both governed by the Law, as everything else: Varuṇa works through the advocacy of Mitra and Indra through the nobility of Aryaman.

Among the Kalash people of the Gilgit-Hunza area, Imra (Indra) is the Great God/warrior who comes riding his horse to visit his people at the celebrations of the winter solstice. Though he is seen only by the shaman who has invoked his presence and power, he 'participates' in the rituals and his presence is felt by all the people. Newly pressed and fermented grapes' wine is offered to Imra and is consumed ritually by everybody.

Indra and Varuṇa are both 'performers of sacrifice, winners in war and holy works': *R̥V*, VIII; 38, 1 and *r̥ṣi* Vasiṣṭha in *R̥V*, VII; 82 begins with a strong request to Indra and to Varuṇa, mighty and very rich, to grant us their strong protection, to subdue the enemy and to provide for man's well-being with blessings. The important lesson to be gained here is that material and immaterial elements of Reality are all needed for the well-being of man. This ties up with the ability of *r̥ṣi* Vasiṣṭha who was successful in harmonizing the rivalry between Indra and Varuṇa and thus avoid a possible schism in Hinduism. This aspect was analysed masterly by Dandekar (1979, 1997) and nothing more can be added. In *R̥V*, VII; 28, 3-4 Vasiṣṭha indicated clearly the discrimination between the King of the living world of man, who is Indra who 'rules over everything that is contained on Earth, that we may win cars and steed and cattle . . . and hostile men'. . . and concludes that 'our sin that sinless discovered, the wondrous one Varuṇa, hath long ago forgiven'. Thus *ṛṣi* Vasiṣṭha gives the final word of wisdom: both material and immaterial reality exist, both are needed and no dignified human life is possible without the concourse of both: *Ṛ̥V*, X; 99, 10 . . . 'Indra, the wonderful, giving like Varuṇa who works with magic'.

I would like to close by referring to Chakravarty (1997) who discusses how, with time, Indra becomes the *adhirāja*, or King of Kings, the supreme god of the Kṣatriyas and how later he evolves into an agriculture god and acquires more and more human characteristics. She finally concludes, like Dandekar, that Indra was a human hero.

Varuṇa — Dandekar (1979, 1997) studied in detail the personality of the great *asura* Varuṇa as he appears in the Vedas. Dandekar begins by saying that his 'essential personality remains enigmatic' (1979). In brief we could summarize: Varuṇa has unchallenged supremacy over all the gods; Varuṇa establishes cosmic order, he controls and regulates the functioning of the universe by binding it down with his *pāśas* that work through subtle, intangible ways; Varuṇa is closely linked to *ṛta,* the cosmic Law and Order that rules the Universe; Varuṇa is specially associated to the concepts of *māyā* and *ṛta*; his personality is more fully developed on the moral-spiritual rather than physiological side; he is the guardian of Law and Truth; Varuṇa is respected as a magician; Varuṇa, like the Avestan Mitra, is *ṛtāvṛdh* (*Ṛ̥V*, I; 23, 5) or promoter of *ṛta*; similarly the Avestan Mitra also represents an ethical-moral abstraction. The dual gods Mitra-Varuṇa (*Ṛ̥V*, VIII; 25, 9) are 'path-finders with closed eyes'.

Varuṇa is the greatest god of Vedic man and one of the ancientmost, one of spiritual and intellectual light, an abstract thought (Dandekar, *l.c.*) without any trace of 'naturalism'.

Dandekar also shows that the ancient believed in the existence of a fluid, a sort of magical power-substance called *asu*, quite different from physical strength: Varuṇa was imbued with *asu*. Though also other Vedic gods are called *asura*, none, not even Agni was as often thus invoked as Varuṇa. Macnicol (apud Dandekar, *l.c.*), says: 'As we discern his figure, Varuṇa seems to be in the act of passing from physical limitations to take his place as a moral Lord over the consciousness of man'.

Varuṇa always dwells in the abstract, ethical and spiritual realms and is never constrained by material limitations; he never belongs to the physical world and even Varuṇa's fetters are immaterial, they are ethical, spiritual and symbolic, or all of these together, but they nonetheless exist and are real.

Dandekar points out: 'the two currents of thought underlying the words: *asura* and *māyā*, make the essential personality of Varuṇa in the Veda quite clear, Varuṇa is the great *asura* who possesses the largest amount of the magic power substance *asu* and his *māyā* becomes manifest in the creation of the incromprehensible majestic miracle of the cosmos'.

Because of his magical immaterial nature, so much more complex and evolved than human nature, God Varuṇa is difficult to understand. The very ancient and omniscient Varuṇa obtains results that cannot be obtained otherwise, thanks to his magic power, as the very awe inspiring magician he is beyond man's power and intelligence. Though difficult to understand, the reality of the existence of immaterial Varuṇa was perceived by early pre-Vedic man even before the Āryan clans split and migrated to Saptasindhu and what is now Iran respectively, as is evident for instance from the existence of Varuṇa's counterpart is the Avesta: Ahura Mazda. Internal evidence in the *Ṛgveda* points in the same direction: the great antiquity of *asura* Varuṇa who, specially as invoked in the Vasiṣṭa hymns, has already become a religious entity in addition to having retained his primordial philosophical genius.

In the present context, namely the aspect of *asura* Varuṇa as the symbol of immaterial reality, there are two relevant features to be noted: (1) Āditya-Varuṇa is closely associated to other Ādityas, specially Mitra and Aryaman, but also Bhaga (Hope) and Indra; (2) only Varuṇa, however, holds the *pāśa* which are only his, they are the fetters or limitations with which he binds or frees for good or for bad human beings and everything else in the cosmos. Aditi, the mother of infinity is unbound, unfettered, while the first Āditya, Varuṇa, is the master of the *pāśa*s.The Ādityas closely associated to Varuṇa are limited by their own nature, though some may also be abstract thoughts, or concepts or symbols that represent immaterial reality.

Varuṇa is responsible for establishing *ṛta* and he controls the functioning of the universe and *ṛta*'s path itself is maintained by 'rays of light', literally: '. . . the path is spun by threads of light' (*ṚV*, I; 136, 2). The Āditya-Mitra is mentioned almost exclusively in association with Varuṇa; he is the one who oversees and applies the law and maintains the order of all human relations in the world. Mitra is the practical guardian of realities, specially the intellectual and spiritual realities of mankind and the relations between individuals and contracts. Mitra is indeed in many ways the means by which Varuṇa expresses himself; in a way we can see Mitra as the concrete element of the abstract entity: Varuṇa. The Mithra of the Avesta maintains very much the same characteristics.

Varuṇa is the controller of cosmic forces that regulate material reality: he established *ṛta*, he separated Sky, or Heaven, and Earth and he controls the forces that move waters, because he holds the *pāśa*s that bind the world; the fetters that keep the system working in good order and smoothly. In contemporary scientific terminology I would say that Varuṇa represents the forces that act on all ecological factors which in turn regulate the functioning and dynamics of worldly nature.

Aryaman, the third Āditya often mentioned in connection

with Varuṇa and Mitra, is the prototype of the noble character who abides by law, while Savitṛ and Bhaga are personifications of the abstract concepts of Life and Hope respectively; they are also often associated to Varuṇa (Vannucci, 1994). These are the essential prerequisites for the normal functioning of the world. The Ādityas represent the association of *dharma*, *māyā*, magic power, life and hope, an association necessary for the gods to become manifest and express their functions, some of them expressed mathematically. To these, another Āditya was added **later**: Indra, whom Aditi recognized as her son born from a **human father**. Indra represents the courage and valour of the conqueror, the winner of battles, he represents the subjection of others for the purpose of providing lands and riches for his own people.

The non-material reality of Varuṇa is specially important from the point-of-view of time fixing, of mathematics and astronomy (*ṚV*, I; 136). Numerology is of great importance, perhaps fundamental in the *Ṛgveda*, for instance: the seven metres each have three stations, three times seven makes 21 and there are 21 names of Vāk, the Voice, or Word, or Speech, Knowledge and wisdom are expressed through the metres, the *mantras*, because they are fully competent of expressing the Abstract Truth, mathematically. This understanding was the special grace that Varuṇa bestowed to Vasiṣṭha. (see Appendix I).

Varuṇa the mighty, mysterious, incredible, omnipotent by means of his magical, infinite potence and through his aids and spies, has control over everything in the cosmos, from specks of dust and gravel to the movement of the stars and all heavenly bodies including planets and constellations. By acquiring this knowledge, man achieves immortality.

The dual divinity Varuṇa-Mitra is a personification of the Reality, material and Immaterial that oversees the maintenance of Law and Order in the whole universe, including this world, by means of immaterial *pāśa*s. They cannot be dissociated or exist independently.

The 'complementarity' of Indra and Varuṇa, albeit seen from a slightly different point of view, is convincingly discussed by Dandekar (1997): 'In his Indravarunau hymns, Vasiṣṭha has taken special pain to reiterate that Indra, the war god, sponsored the Vedic Āryans exploits of conquest and colonization (*pr̥tanasu*), while Varuṇa, the moral governor, blessed their efforts in connection with the establishment of law and order (*kṣemasya prasave*), *R̥V*, VII; 82, 4ab, 5cd, 6'. Further Dandekar quotes from Vasiṣṭha (*R̥V*, VII; 83, 9) 'One of the two gods . . . vanquishes the enemies in battle, while the other ever sustains the socio-ethical laws' . . . In other words, says Dandekar, 'Indra **conquers** and Varuna **rules**'.

To this I would like to add that it seems to me that Vedic man recognized few Gods, as evidenced by the tendency to form dual divinities, as studied by Dandekar (1997), but deities, which are manifestations of Gods, rather than Gods themselves, are many, perhaps innumerable, though in **translations** they are also called gods and goddesses.

Though the studies on the personality of Varuṇa are by far less numerous and exhaustive than those that refer to Indra, I would like to refer here to the latest scholarly studies by Chakravarty (1997), Dandekar (1997) and Nath (1996). These authors discuss earlier studies in detail and focus on various aspects of King Indra as a human leader divinized as a God. These authors give an exhaustive bibliography, but nowhere have I seen references to Indra and Varuṇa respectively as personifications of material and immaterial reality.

Conclusion

In the context of the present approach, *R̥V*, X; 86 is particularly interesting. It can be interpreted in the sense that there is no distinction between material and immaterial reality; no dividing line, no schism, no abrupt discontinuity between the two. The material/immaterial reality is seen as one more pair of merging opposites like the energy/matter pair and the time/space continuum. Different readings can be made of *R̥V*, X; 86, the refrain of all its verses reaffirms: '*Indra uttaraḥ*', a simple direct interpretation could be as follows: Indra here represents the Soul complaining that it has been neglected by man; Vr̥ṣākapi, whom Indra calls son and friend, is the Mind, as flickering and inconstant as the 'strong ape' he is; Indrāṇī is Intellect at odds with the restless ape Vr̥ṣākapi, but Indra reigns supreme over all. Indra and Indrāṇī are immortal (verse 11), but nothing is said about the longevity of Vr̥ṣākapi. The restless ape is a good representation of Man and is as mortal as the human body is. The spirit survives bodily death, the intellect and its fruits survive and are eternal through the teachings given to others; the intellect is feminine, Indrāṇī, as Vāk, the word, also is. The spirit is of necessity vigorous, full of virility, even if at times it must be 'recharged', it is masculine (verse 17) and endowed with the power of begetting children. Indra, as ths soul of man, inspects the sacrificial area and calls the Mind to order; the Soul distinguishes between the Ārya and the Dāsa and cherishes those who perform the sacrifice in earnest and offer the 'simple votary's *soma* juice'. Vr̥ṣākapi pacifies Indrāṇī calling her mother (verse 7) though the animosity between the constant, orderly, methodical, regularly law abiding intellect steeped in *r̥ta*, here personified as Indrāṇī, will always be at odds with the mind of man which is always quivering, always restless, unruly and overactive. It takes Indra's overlordship to 'put the house in order'.

In this way, in *R̥V*, X; 86, the material reality personified almost exclusively as a Great Conqueror and a Great Chief, Leader and King, becomes a symbol of the human soul that rules over immaterial reality at the personal level: the Intellect and the Mind, represented by Indrāṇī and Vr̥ṣākapi respectively. Naturally Vr̥ṣākapi as Mind, is also the destroyer of dreams and needs to be purified by the water of the oblations before it can ascend to the gods. The mind is by its own nature self-centered and takes on the role of the self, an affront to the soul which has disturbed Indrāṇī, the Intellect: hence the need of the pacifying action of Indra, the King, the Lord, very human and understanding. The gap between material and immaterial reality is thus bridged. Indra is *svarāj*, Varuṇa is *samrāj* (*R̥V*, VII; 82, 2). Chakravarty essentially expresses the same idea when she writes: 'Varuṇa's responsibility is to maintain *r̥ta* . . . whereas Indra's duty is to protect earthly people from enemies', to which I would add: 'all sorts of enemies'.

It should further be recognised, in the context of Indra's personality, and whether he was one or many leaders telescoped into one single image, that it is well recognized at present that the Indo-Āryans came to Saptasindhu in more than one wave (see also Nath 1996). This is further attested by the fact that in the famous Dasarajña war, King Sudās fought against non-Āryans as well as against Āryans who had earlier made alliance with them.

Varuṇa continues to be the *virtual* image of the immaterial attributes of the Self. Indra is the *real* image of the material attributes of the Self, *Brahman*. Neither of them can exist or express itself in the world and in the mind of man without the other. This great Truth was sung by *r̥ṣi* Vasiṣṭha when he saw Varuṇa and Indra linked in a single continuum as a dual divinity: Indra-Varuṇau.

Maybe, unlike Descartes, the *r̥ṣis* lived in the persuasion that: SUM ERGO COGITO, rather than: COGITO ERGO SUM.

Appendix I

The Carpenter and Pythagoras Theorem

An International Conference on Sanskrit and Culture was held at Thrissur, Kerala, India, in 1997. At the end of the Session that I chaired on 11 January, there was a lively discussion on the relevance of Vedic studies for modern living. The last word was with Eng. T. B. Swaminathan who was kind enough to put in writing what he taught us on that day. His text follows:

When Smt. Rama Bai of the Department of Sanskrit of Madras University was reading her paper on 'Yajurveda and Mathematics' in which she has highlighted the achievements in Mathematics particularly in Geometry of the Vedic Indians, my mind went back about fifteen years: finding that the carpenter whom I had called in for some work at my residence was a knowledgeable person, I questioned him about the Theorem of Pythagoras on the Hypotenuse of a right-angled triangle with given perpendicular sides (or, what is the same, the diagonal of a rectangle of given length and width). No, he had not heard of Pythagoras, nor was he aware of *Baudhāyana's Sūtra* and other *Śulba Sūtras*, which our ancients had been using, long before Pythagoras, for construction of sacrificial altars. (These *sūtra*s state, like Pythagoras, that the square on the diagonal of a rectangle is equal to the sum of the squares on its length and width). But, all the same he could work out the length of the diagonal without finding the square-root of their sum. His method was based on a Malayalam verse, which he said had been granted down from father to son in his family for generations. To the best of my memory, the verse runs (. . . . . in Malayalam):

. . . (?) Deerghathintashta Bhagathe
Ezhukondu Gunikkuka
Vidkararadham Koottiyikku (?)
Kannam cheika Yathavidhi

Translation:
Multiply by seven the eighth part of the length (i.e determine 7/9 thus of the length) and add half of the width to get the length of the diagonal. Example: Suppose the rectangle is 4 units long and 3 units wide. Then, the length of the diagonal $4\times7/8+3\times\frac{1}{2} = 3\frac{1}{2}+1\frac{1}{2} = 5$ units.

(according to the *Śulba Sūtra*s and Pythagoras the diagonal is $\sqrt{4^2+3^2} = \sqrt{25} = 5$)

Again if the rectangle is 12 (units) long and 5 (units) wide, the length of the diagonal $7/8\times12+\frac{1}{2}\times5 = 10\frac{1}{2}+2\frac{1}{2} = 13$

(According to the *Sūtra*s, and Pythagoras, diagonal $\sqrt{12^2+5^2} = \sqrt{169} = 13$)

When I pointed out to the carpenter that the method fails when the sides of the rectangle are not in the proportion of 3 : 4, or 5 : 12, he said there are a few variations of the above verse, and these would cover other situations (i.e. where the proportions of the sides are different from the above) which usually arise in the course of the carpenter's work.

Sometime after my conversation with the carpenter, I participated in a conference on Vedic Mathematics in Thrissur. There were delegates from Tamil Nadu and Andhra Pradesh, and I found to my pleasant surprise that carpenters in their states had similar verses in the respective languages. It will be worthwhile to find out if there are similar verses in the other languages of our country and whether all these have a common source in the Vedas or writings of the ancient Indian mathematicians.

It is a long time now since I saw the carpenter last. I know that a son of his is (or was) working as carpenter in some Gulf country. Another son is now a Doctor. I wonder if the sons know the verse which their father was familiar with and which he quoted for my benefit.

T.B. Swaminathan
(Retd.) Asst. Commissioner of Income-tax
XXIV/388,
Thrissur - 680002

Appendix II

On the Identity of the Soma Plant

Kashikar (1990) and Dandekar (1997) have recently reviewed the most important studies dealing with the botanical identity of the *soma* plant. To begin with, both these authors refute the groundless hypothesis put forward by Wasson (1969, 1971, 1972, apud Kashikar, *l.c.*) that the *soma* juice was extracted by pressing a mushroom: *Amanita muscaria* L., widely known as a potent poison. In a detailed study based on scholarly analyses of the pertinent Vedic texts and based on the botanical studies by Stein (1932), Mahdihassan (1962) and Qazilbash (in Kashikar) both the above-mentioned authors conclude by endorsing the view that the *soma* drink could never have been extracted from a mushroom but was instead obtained from plants of the genus *Ephedra*. This genus comprises over 30 species found in Asia, Europe and the Americas, some of them extending into tropical regions. Many of these species have a significant pharmacological and commercial value because they are the source of the chemical *ephedrine*, which is a decongestant drug. Ephedrine is an alkaloid of the group of *epinephrines* that like adrenaline is released at the nerve endings. The most important producer of ephedrine is the species *Ephedra sinica*, though other species of the genus yield the same chemical compound and other related alkaloids.

The most common use of ephedrine in contemporary pharmacology and physiological research, as well as in medical practice, is that of a decongestant drug, effective for instance in the quick cure of common colds; ephedrine, however, has to be inhaled frequently to be effective. If used too frequently and too intensively, the drug is absorbed by the blood causing nervousness, insomnia, dizziness, palpitations, headache. Admittedly different species of the genus *Ephedra* could most probably have a somewhat different composition, hence the different value of *Ephedra* for making *soma* from plants from various different places, which is reflected in the texts. The genus *Ephedra* is the only one of the family Ephedraceae of the order Gnetales that comprises relatively few species some of which are 'creepers', climbers or vines. The word for creeper or vine used in *Āyurveda* is '*lata*' according to the *Vr̥kṣāyurveda* of Surapala, translated by Sadhale (1995).

On the other hand the sparse descriptions of the *soma* plant to be found in the *R̥gveda* and other texts, could well apply to species of the worldwide family *Vitaceae*, which comprises about 60 species of cultivated and wild grapes, the most important of which is *Vitis vinifera*, which is the species most commonly cultivated to make wine. The area south of the Caspian Sea is the place of origin of this species which has in the course of time occupied the whole region from Iran to India. Grape vines were already cultivated in Egypt about 2400 BC.

Finally, I would also recall that the word *soma* in Greek means body, corporal existence, material being, which is evidently reminiscent of the invigorating properties of the *soma* drink.

In brief, the arguments in favour of *Vitis vinifera* being either the original or the substitute of the *soma* plant can be summarized as follows:

1. Descriptions of the *soma* plant are few, scattered and repetitive, they are not sufficient to determine the species or even the genus of the plant with botanical accuracy. Dandekar (*l.c.*) says that . . . 'the *R̥gveda* refers only to that component

of *soma* which is most essential from the point of view of the Vedic ritual, namely *aṁśu* (shoot, stalk, filament)'. Kashikar (*l.c.*) adds to this description that the shoots and juice are tawny coloured and astringent, while Sanskrit authors refer to the *soma* plant as a creeper. The word '**creeper**' could include the current definition of '**vine**' and also of '**climber**'. In translation, the *soma* plant is usually described as a creeper, while most species of grapes are vines and climbers. Though there is a difference in the modality of growth between creepers and vines, the distinction would not be apparent from the Sanskrit text. The short descriptions given in the Vedic texts and in the *Brāhmaṇa*s and summarized by later commentators, could well apply to some of the many species of wild or cultivated grapes. Both *Vitis vinifera* and other species grow in the Himālayas and Karākorum ranges and extend well into Afghanistan and Iran, as well as southwards in the Western Ghāṭs of India (Kumbhojkar and Vartak, 1998). There is no doubt that the Haoma of the Avesta is the same as the *soma* of the Vedas. Finally I have personally found species of the genus *Vitis*, including *Vitis vinifera* in the Western Himālayas up to about 2000m altitude.

2. Parts of the grapes plant that were and are still consumed in one way or another, include the berries, raw or cooked, leaves, tendrils, shoots, young stalks, varying in different species. Grapes' leaves and tendrils are a regular ingredient of different dishes of Mediterranean cooking as they are reputed to be very healthy food. Incidentally, tendrils which are typical of most species of the family *Vitaceae*, are translated as 'filaments', from *aṁśu* by Dandekar, because this is what they look like. There are no tendrils in *Ephedra* which belongs to the order Gnetales, which are Gymnosperms like pines and related flowerless and naked-seed species of shrubs and trees. Kashikar (1990) quotes from Qazilbash saying: 'fresh or dried crushed green branches of this plant

are a popular remedy for coughs, colds, urticaria, itching and other skin troubles'... 'in Khyber and parts of Afghanistan'. The local uses of this remedy agree with the pharmacological well-known action of *ephedrine* as a decongestant.

Again quoting from Kashikar, the identity of *soma* with the *Avestan Haoma* is unquestionable and the local name for *Ephedra pachyclada* (the Latin name means: *Ephedra* with thick or stout branches or shoots) in the Chitral area is known by the local name *soma* and in Baluchistan and adjoining territories the same species is known as *uma* or *uman*. This word is very similar to *um*, *umbu*, derived from the Sanskrit *udumbara* which means berry in general, and in local dialects from Iran to India is applied to Afghan wild grapes. However, the Sanskrit word for grapes is, I believe, *drakṣa*.

4. Finally, as reported by Robertson (1887), Loude and Lièvre (1984), and Lièvre and Loude (1990) newly fermented grapes wine, a 'foul drink' according to Robertson, is prepared by the people of the Chitral area of northern Pakistan and is drunk ritualistically at the celebrations of the winter solstice when they are visited by god Imra (or Balumain, or Mahandeo) to mark the advent of the new year. The way in which the wine is made is very similar to that described by Kashikar according to the Vedic procedure for the preparation of the *soma* drink, which is also summarized and referred to by Dandekar (*l.c.*): '*soma* was crushed with a stone . . . or was pressed with stones, . . . to produce the *soma*-draught. The drops were poured upon . . . and made to pass over the drainer of sheep's wool. . . . After passing through, *soma* was then mixed with water (. . .). Soma is also described as having three kinds of admixture (. . .)'. It is repeatedly mentioned that the *soma* juice is mixed with water, milk, curds or gruel. In fact, the fermented juice of the *soma* plant would readily mix with other fermented liquids, including

fermented honey.

Kashikar also summarizes the procedure for making *soma* thus: 'at the morning pressing *soma* shoots were pounded and mixed with water on a lower stone placed on a bull hide which was spread out so to make a hollow on two wooden planks'... 'The juice was extracted out of nearly half the quantity with the addition of adequate quantity of water and was collected in a jar known as *adhavanīya*'.... 'a woollen filter was placed on the *Putabhṛt* jar... and milk was poured into the jar with filtered *soma* juice. The milk was then fermented and different things were added: hot milk to thc cup of Mitra-Varuṇa, flour of parched barley into the Manthi cup etc.' (from Kashikar, *l.c.*).

I shall not enter into further ritualistic details except to emphasize the fact that all the admixtures mentioned would quicken the fermentation process—a practice that could become necessary in the cold climate of mountain areas. To the present day, in many Mediterranean countries, as for instance Italy, a glass of wine is mixed half-half with water, and customarily drunk with food at the midday and evening meals. Wine is also mixed with a variety of substances to make selected choice beverages and medicines.

Grapes' wine rightfully can be said to have all the qualities attributed to *soma*. To this day alcoholic drinks, both fermented and distilled, are given to men of all ranks before they engage in field battles.

There is one property of ephedrine that is rightly pointed out by Kashikar as having special significance. This is that taken in large quantities, ephedrine can cause insomnia. This could be welcome by those brāhmaṇas engaged in night-long sacrifices, as for instance the Atirātra (see earlier in this volume), which is part of the *soma-yajña*.

Robert Graves in the 'Foreword' of the 1960 edition of his *Greek Myths*, obviously influenced by the numerous studies and experiments with the traditional but at that time newly discovered naturally occurring psychedelic drugs, many of them produced by hallucinogenic mushrooms, says that the evidence summarized in his 'What the Centaurs Ate' (Steps, Cassell and Co., 1958) suggests that 'satyrs . . . centaurs . . . and their maenad womenfolk, used these brews (wine or ivy ale) to wash down mouthfulls of a far stronger drug, namely a raw mushroom, *amanita* (sic) *muscaria*, which induces hallucinations, senseless rioting, prophetic sight, erotic energy and remarkable muscular strength' . . . Unfortunately by stating that mythological figures such as satyrs, centaurs and maenads consumed hallucinogenic mushrooms, Graves invalidates his own theory since the would-be consumers never existed in reality. Further, *Amanita muscaria* is downright poisonous, not just hallucinogenic. Graves also states, but does not give the source, that the use of mushrooms was current occurrence in the celebrations of the Dionysian and other Mysteries, but he fails to bring any convincing argument; he writes: 'it '*seems*' (italics mine) that ambrosia, nectar and the *cecyon* used at the Orphic, Eleusinian and mysteries associated with Dionysos were laced with such psychotropic substances'. Graves further finds parallelisms between the Aztec god Tlaloc, which he unwarrantedly calls the mushroom god, and the Greek Dionysos and wonders when the European and Central American cultures came in contact, in spite of the difference of centuries in real occurrence. Such far-fetched interpretations are more mythical and fanciful than the myths themselves. Myths however have a far greater power than drugs to over-emphasize the extraordinary feats and behaviour of its heroes and gods.

The tentative conclusion of this note is that, without excluding the possibility that *Ephedra* may have been a constituent of the *soma* drink, we must further consider the possibility that grapes' wine since ancient times, may have been the main ingredient of *soma*. Alcoholic fermented drinks give special vigour and endurance to the drinker, specially in winter, in cold weather and at high altitude. Such drinks are almost indispensable to conquer the harsh climate.

Edible species of wild grapes and mode of preparation are listed in Kumbhojkar and Vartak (*l.c.*).

Glossary

Āp — water, one of the *mahābhūtas*.

Abhaya — fear not; *abhaya mudrā*, a blessing posture of the right hand.

Ācārya — teacher, guide, preceptor of spiritual and practical knowledge including the martial arts; Droṇa was the famous *ācārya* of the Pāṇḍavas.

Ādhibhautika — literal, material or social interpretation of the texts.

Ādhidaivika — godly, universal or cosmic interpretation of the texts.

Adhvaryu — priests who perform definite functions and the physical acts of the sacrifice, specially knowledgeable of the *YV*.

Ādhyātmika — inner, spiritual, subjective reading of the texts.

Adhyāya — literally: hundred lectures.

Aditi — original human mother, mother of infinity, free from bonds, free from Varuṇa's fetters; mother of the Ādityas; universal mother.

Ādityas — sons of Aditi, the most ancient gods: Varuṇa, Mitra, Aryaman, Dakṣa, Aṁśa, Dhātṛ; later six gods were added to the original six, amongst them Bhaga.

Advaita Vedānta — the *śruti* texts posterior to the Veda.

Agnāyī — the consort of Agni.

Agni — God of Fire and all sorts of energy, including heat, light, life energy, reproductive energy of living beings.

Agniṣṭoma — special rites of devotion and offerings to Lord Agni.

Ahura Mazda — supreme God of Mazdeism.

Aitareya Brāhmaṇa — one of the major Brāhmaṇical texts.

Ājamayū — onomatopoetic rendering of animal voices.

Ākāśa — void, nothing, nothingness; the first of the five besic elements or *pañca mahābhūtāni*: *ākāśa*, *vāyu*, *tejas*, *āp*, *pṛthvī*, according to the Sāṁkhya system of philosophy.

Amṛta — the nectar of knowledge and wisdom.

Anārya — non-Āryan people; term also used to mean vile, untrustworthy, despicable, unreliable.

Aṅgiras — one of the seven *mahā-ṛṣi* to whom many hymns are attributed; related to Agni and fire rituals.

Aṅgirases — descendants of Aṅgiras; the Bharadvājas are also called Aṅgirases, as they are considered to be descendants of Aṅgiras.

Apām-napāt — offspring of waters, an epithet of *Agni.*

Apāna — one of the forms of breathing; the other vital airs are: *vyāna*, *udāna*, *prāna*, *samāna.*

Āpastamba — author of one of the *gṛhyasūtra.*

Apri — special hymns of the *ṚV* dedicated to Lord Agni.

Apsarās — feminine super-human beings comparable to nymphs.

Araṇi — the fire sticks used to produce sparks by attrition, the sparks are then collected on dry grass to ignite the fire; also called the two mothers of Agni.

Araṇya — forest, jungle.

Araṇyāni — the Lady of the Forest; the Forest.

Ardvi Sura — a subdivision of the Avesta.

Arjunī — one of the 12 months of the Hindu solar calendar, corresponds to present-day Phālgun, or February-March.

Ārṣa vivāha — one form of Hindu marriage; the bridegroom is bound to offer a gift to the bride's father.

Artha — all the practical arts and much of what is now known as science and technology.

Ārya — noble, self-appellation of the Āryans.

Aryaman — close friend, god of hospitality, together with Mitra and other Ādityas, sons of Aditi, sometimes regarded as other aspects of Varuṇa.

Āryan, Āryas — the branch of Indo-European speaking group of people who migrated into India; the meaning is faithful, loyal; the opposite is *an-ārya* or non-Āryan.

Asha Vahista — the Law of Nature in the Avesta, literally: the excellent Asha.

Āśrama — the four stages of the life of brāhmaṇas; the *brahmacarya*, the *gṛhasthya*, the *vānaprastha* and the *saṁnyāsa*: also the hermitage of a *ṛṣi* or sage where *saṁnyāsī* and brāhmaṇas in the fourth stage of life could retire; permanent camps for the education of the younger generation.

Āsu — magic power substance or magic power.

Asura — Lord God imbued with magic power, specially used for Gods who have *māyā*; *asurya*: highest lordship; *asurasya*: *asura* rule; later use: demon.

Āśvalāyana Gṛhyasūtra — the *Gṛhyasūtra* given by *ācārya* Āśvalāyana.

Aśvins — twins precursors of dawn, coming on horseback; knowledgeable of medicine and medicinal plants; Aśvinau, dual form.

Aśvamedayajña — the horse sacrifice, one of the most imposing Vedic ceremonials; also held by other Indo-European speaking people.

Aśvattha — *pīpal*, the sacred fig tree: *Ficus religiosa* from which the upper *araṇi* is made.

Aśvapati — Lord of horses; name of the father of Satyavān, the truthful.

Atharvan — the first man to make fire and to offer sacrifice; a Prajāpati, associated to Aṅgiras; his descendants, the Atharvana are closely associated to the descendants of Aṅgiras, hence the dual Atharvana Aṅgirasa.

Atharvaveda — the last and recentmost of the four Vedas; initially only three Veda were mentioned; Manu himself speaks of three Veda; partly prose, contains large number of incantations in addition to speculative hymns.

Atirātra — year long sacrifice; it also marks calendar fixes; is part of Soma sacrifice.

Ātman — individual soul.

Aurobindo Ghosh — 1872-1950, Calcutta; poet, philosopher, mystic; developed what he called a 'synthetic philosophy'.

Avatāra — incarnations of Lord Viṣṇu.

Avesta — the sacred book of the Āryans who migrated from Balkh to what is now Iran; sacred book of the Zoroastrians; the Avestan *gāthās* and the Vedic *mantras* have something in common and both have their origin in the Āryan language of the proto-Āryan people; the development of the Avesta must have proceeded in a similar way as that of the Veda. Most of the sacred books of the Avesta were destroyed by Alexander the Great and many of the surviving ones by Islamic conquerors.

Avidyā — lack of knowledge, ignorance.

Axis mundi — Latin expression: the axis that sustains the world and around which it revolves.

Āyurveda — the Veda of life, knowledge of life, later considered by some as an appendix of the *Atharvaveda*; medical and medicinal knowledge.

Bahūrānī — daughter-in-law, wife of the elder son; she becomes the *rānī* (queen) of the household after marriage.

Balkh — the region of Balkh; area where Indo-European tribes settled for some time when they migrated in a S- and then south-east and western directions after leaving their original home in the Ural-Altaï region; they settled in this area for a long time in parts of what is now Afghanistan; area inhabited by proto-Āryan people.

Balumain, Balumain-Indra — God of the winter solstice festivities of the Kalash people of north Pakistan, great intermediate between men and the great God Kodaï, symbolically visits the Kalash valleys once a year.

Banobibi, Banodevi — the goddess of the forest; Banodebi in Bengali language; the main deity of the Sunderbans.

Barhiṣ — sacred grass; several species are considered to be sacred, the most important are the *kuśa* whose scientific name is *Poa cynosuroides* and *dūrva*, whose scientific name is *Panicum dactylon*.

Bhaga — one of the Ādityas, brings hope and good fortune, closely associated to Lord Savitṛ.

Bhakti — unconditional devotion and surrender due to attachment to God; derived from the same root as Bhaga, one of the Ādityas and giver of good fortune, therefore adorable. According to the *Padma Purāṇa*, the *bhakti* movement stems from a Dravidian doctrine.

Bharadvāja — an Aṅgiras *maharṣi* who authored many hymns of the *ṚV*; one of the *saptaṛṣi*, the seven *ṛṣi* who are enshrined in the constellation of the Great Bear.

Bhṛgu — an ancient *ṛṣi*; in the *Vāyu Purāṇa* his name is added to the *saptaṛṣi*, making eight in all. Author of the *Bhṛgu Saṁhitā* that gives the genealogy of most *gotras* down to present; still kept in written form and consulted by people conscious of their lineage.

Bhūta — a being or creature; acquired later the meaning of ghosts, goblins, often malignant; attendants of Śiva.

Black *Yajurveda* — one of the branches of the *Yajurveda*, the other being the White *Yajurveda*.

Biology — the science of life and living beings.

Bombax malabaricus — one of the silk-cotton trees.

Brāhmaṇa — members of the sacerdotal caste, the priests; priests are brāhmaṇas but not all brāhmaṇas are priests.

Brahmā — the creator of the universe.

Brahman—the Supreme Being, the Ultimate Reality, Self-Existent, Absolute.

Brahmacārī—the first of the four *āśramas* in which is divided the life of a brāhmaṇa; the brāhmaṇa student, assistant of his preceptor to whom he owes undiscussed and unwavering obedience.

Bṛhaspati—also Brahmaṇaspati, the Lord of Prayer, the heavenly brāhmaṇa, the prototype priest, *guru* and counsellor of the Gods; prototype of the *purohita* or family priest and counsellor to kings; also called a *ṛṣi*.

Bṛhat—great, important Sāman; the Bṛhat-Sāman is one of the most important *Sāma* hymns; from the root *bṛh*: the 'stirring up of thoughts' and the fullness of feeling for God.

Cakra—wheel, circle, said to be innumerable in the human body, they represent centres of energy; the main *cakra*, the *padma*, corresponds to the solar plexus of the human body.

Candramas—the moon.

Capātī—unleavened whole-wheat bread made at the time of eating.

Capēre—Latin word from which is derived the English word capacity or volume of the internal space of a container, cubic content; also mental power, function and character.

Chalcopyrite—sulphide of copper and iron ore, $CuFeS_2$.

Chaos—total confusion, lack of order; the mathematical word designates a special type of order that can best be described as a 'deterministic randomness'.

Circadian rhythms—oscillation of behaviour and events that follow approximately or precisely a 24-hour pattern; events that take place every 24 hours or approximately so.

Conch—vernacular name of the shell of a gastropod mollusc whose scientific name is *Xanchus pyraeum*, it applies particularly to Kṛṣṇa's conch, the *pāñcajanya*; the oldest archaeological findings of the conch show that it was used for jewellery, the earliest artifacts are from the basal level of Mehragarh, at the foot of the Bholan Pass that links Baluchistan to the Iranian plateau. The fragments of *Xanchus* found there are from the pre-Harappan period III or proto-Harappan period, they are dated from the third millennium BC. Many other and later sites have yielded archaeological remains of the conch. It was gradually used as a war trumpet to produce a loud calling and warning sound.

Corpus — Latin noun; body, body of a doctrine, body of evidence, etc.

Cyrus — Achemenian King who waged wars with the Greeks.

Dadhīca, Dadhikrās — later form: Dadīca; a *ṛṣi* son of Atharvan who, according to myth, sacrificed himself to enable the Gods to make invincible weapons with his bones for the destruction of Vṛtra and the *asura*s.

Dadhikrāvan — see Dadhīca, the name appears to be interchangeable with Dadhikrās.

Daeva — Gods, in the Avesta.

*Daitya*s — a race of giant evil demons.

Dakṣiṇāyaṇa — southern travel of the sun.

Dante Alighieri — 1265-1321, Florence, foremost Italian poet and leading scholastic and political philosopher.

Dards — people of the Hindukush and Himālaya areas, nomads or frequently on the move, already known to Ptolemy, Strabo and mentioned in the *Viṣṇu Purāṇa*.

Dāsa — savages, enemies, foes, infidels; non-Āryan tribes and people hostile to the incoming Āryans; subjugated by the new-comers.

Dāśarājña, dāśarājña yuddha — the battle of the ten kings, differently dated about 1900, 2700-1800 or 2700 BC by different authors.

Dayānanda — 1824-83; Śaivite brāhmaṇa from Kaṭhiāwāḍ, philosopher and Vedic commentator, joined the Ārya Samāj movement.

Delphi — a small temple town, seat of the oracle of Phoebus (Apollo) in ancient Greece whose temple was on the shelf of Mount Parnassos, about 600m above sea level, facing south; the Delphic oracle figured prominently in Greek legends, the verdicts were pronounced by the Pythian oracle.

Deterministic randomness — a characteristic of chaotic state in mathematical terms. An uphazard distribution of elements determined by independent non pre-arranged forces. Chaos is a special type of order that appears to be the result of deterministic randomness caused by a multiplicity of impingent forces.

Dezau — the supreme Being of the Kalash people.

Dharma — duty, justice, virtue, law, righteousness. Duty personified in *R̥V*, VIII; 35, 13. The universal law of the cosmos; the law that upholds caste, group and individual law, duties and code of conduct.

Dhātr̥ — Creator, maker, very ancient God, one of the Ādityas, later preserver of health and identified with Prajāpati or Brahmā.

Droṇakalaśa — large container for *soma*, similar ones are still in use to collect grapes' juice for fermentation among the Kalash people.

Diogenes — fourth century BC, the first of the cynic philosophers who declared to be a citizen of the world.

Dīrghatamas — one of the sage-poets who composed the Vedic hymns.

Dundubhi — drum, ceremonial war drum.

Dvādaśasya — the 12-month solar year.

Dyaus — the sky as father.

Ecology — the science of the environment where all living beings find their home, the study of the exchange of matter and energy among living beings and between them and their living and non-living environment.

Eleusis — very ancient temple-city in Attika, not far from Athens, seat of the cult of Demeter, an agricultural goddess; the

Eleusis mysteries were imported into Greece and marked the introduction of hexaploid wheat cultivation; the Eleusis mysteries were held during about 2000 years and were considered to be 'excellent' by Cicero himself.

Enzyme — organic catalyst, a ferment, substances produced by living cells of plants, animals and microbes, capable of varying the rate of specific chemical reactions, usually speeding them; they promote the majority of chemical transformations, including bodily dissolution after death; most enzymes are proteins, ex: amylase acts upon and hydrolizes molecules of starch.

Equinox — Spring and autumn day when day and night are of equal length.

Evaya, Evayamarut — the one who performs his regular routine duty, orderly and speedily; encompassing all; one who runs on his course.

Fire — combustion; as God it is Agni, as common fire it is also called agni; Agni is object and means and aim of worship.

Forma mentis — a Latin expression to signify how the mind is shaped, how it reacts and how it behaves, how it operates and how it contributes to decision-making.

Foudre de Guerre — French expression applied to great war generals: Napoleon Bonaparte is described as a 'foudre de guerre'.

Furore — Italian noun, indicates irresistible and passionate urge to do something, bad or good, evil or right; same root as furia or fury in English.

Galileo Galilei — 1564-1642, Italian astronomer, defensor of Copernicus' heliocentric theory, laid the foundations of the rational scientific experimental method; condemned by the Inquisition.

Gandharva — celestial musicians.

Gaṇeśa — elephant-headed, son of Śiva and Pārvatī.

Garbhādhāna saṁskāra — the sacralization of conception.

Gārhapatya — the Law of the household, of the home; the Lord of the Law of the home.

Gāthā — the name applies to sacred hymns of the Avesta as well as to very ancient popular, perhaps profane songs not included in the Veda.

Gavām ayanam — God's appointed order.

Gavo — cattle, oxen.

Gāyatrī — the most important, luminous metre; a very powerful *mantra*, particularly sacred: *R̥V*, III; 62, 10, *r̥ṣi* Viśvāmitra.

Gestalt, Gestalt Psychology — briefly stated, gestaltism is the theory that ascertains that the outside world is first perceived and reacted to as a whole, before any analysis or breakdown of the situation is done by the mind.

Ghī — butter oil, butter clarified by boiling.

Gr̥ha-praveśa — the rite of instalment of the home fire.

Gr̥hya — home, domestic rites.

Gr̥hyapatnī — the lady, the mistress of the household.

Gr̥hyasūtra — the discourse, the rites and ceremonies of the inner circle of the home and family.

Gobhila — author of one of the *Gr̥hyasūtra*.

Gotra — lineage.

Guru — preceptor, spiritual leader; the disciple or *śiṣya* remained for years in the *guru's āśrama* for training.

Gurudakṣiṇā — reward, usually in kind, to be given to the *guru* or the officiating brāhmaṇa.

Hermeneutics — the science of the 'mysteries' or occult knowledge and of the art to decipher them, specially the ancient Egyptian mysteries that aimed at inspiring wisdom in man as a pathway to eternity.

Haoma — the Avestan/Persian counterpart of the Hindu *Homa* rites.

Hermes Trismegistus — thrice great Hermes; legendary individual, clan or God of ancient Egypt and keeper of traditional mysteries; the aspect of the Greek God Hermes, related to the ancient Egyptian God Thot, representative of Re, the Supreme God.

Hīr and Rāñjhā — the names of the heroin and hero of a classic very popular Punjabi novel.

Hominidae — the name of the family, in the zoological nomenclature, to which the single genus *Homo* belongs; the only species of the genus is now *Homo sapiens* that is the scientific name of the present-day human species.

Homo sapiens — scientific name of the human species; *Homo sapiens sapiens* is the scientific name of the sub-species to which we belong.

Hotṛ — chief priest who makes the invocations.

Ilā — food, libation of milk or refreshment, personified and sanctified; according to Sāyaṇa, she is the goddess presiding on the Earth; 'Ilā's sacred place' is the sacrificial fire.

Imra — partly identified with Indra by the Kalash people; God of creation; divider of the annual course of the sun, important personality of the winter solstice rites, though not materially present.

Indo-European — a varied assemblage of people whose languages have much in common, a similar syntax and probably common roots; the terms was first used in the modern sense by R.G. Latham in 1851, with no reference to racial or national characteristics.

Indra — king of the Gods; probably a deified historical chief and leader.

Inoculum — Latin noun indicates a small portion of a pure microbial or tissue culture that is transferred to another culture medium to replicate and multiply the cultures.

Intelligĕre — Latin verb: to understand, to conceptualize, to visualize the connection and interaction between different concepts. Litterally: to find together.

Jagatī — one of the Vedic metres.

Jātavedas — the all knowing, omniscient; an epithet of Lord Agni.

Jñānam — knowledge.

Kāfir — word used to designate non-muslim people, infidels.

Kalash — people of Kafiristan, now Nuristan, Gilgit, Hunza, most probably descendants of early migrant Āryan tribes.

Kalpa — a day and night of Brahmā, equal to 4,320,000,000 human years, also the ceremonial of the Vedas.

Kalpavṛkṣa — the tree that grants all desires. The tree granting many goods was alive in Italy as the 'albero della cuccagna', in Portugal and Brazil, as 'Pau de Sebo', etc. At specific times, all sorts of goods were tied at the top of a well greased pole, making climbing it very difficult; it was then a free for all men. Whoever reached the top and beat the goods down, took possession of them. The symbolism, translated into practice, is obvious.

Kāma — desire of good in general, power that satisfies desires, love.

Kāmadhenu — the all giving cow, mainly food.

Kanyādāna — the gift of the bride; the dowry.

Karma — principle of universal causality, cosmic law that is eternally recurrent and retributes the good and the bad of the doer; the sum total of man's thoughts, feelings, desires and actions, the right and evil consequences of it may be effected in the present or in future incarnations.

Kauṣītaki Brāhmaṇa — one of the most important *Brāhmaṇa*s.

Kawa — species of the genus *Hydnocarpus*, family Flacourtiaceae; oil extracted from the seeds has several medicinal properties; specific for leprosy; parasiticide. The *kawa* of the people of Fiji islands comes from a different plant, of the gemus Piper.

Khadira Gṛhyasūtra — *gṛhyasūtra* of Khadira.

Khorassan — a geographical area in present-day Afghanistan.

Kiṁśuka — *Butea frondosa*.

Kirāta — non-Āryan people, may designate one or more than one specific group of non-Āryan people, specially forest and mountain dwellers; in the *Rāmāyaṇa*, they are described as islanders and coastal fish-eaters.

Knowledge — spiritual and intellectual understanding, has several aspects: *vidyā*, learning, science; *prajña*, spiritual insight, wisdom; *saṁjñā*, comprehension, intellectual grasp, awareness; *jñāna*, contemplative knowledge. Opposite is *avidyā* or lack of knowledge and understanding.

Kuśika — the *ṛṣi* who founded the Kauśika family of Kānyakubja, from whom sage Viśvāmitra descended.

Kusira — a metre.

Lactase — enzyme present in intestinal juices, hydrolizes lactose into dextrose and galactose.

Ladakh — north-eastern part of Jammu and Kashmir state of India having Tibetan culture.

Lāmā — Tibetan monks followers of Mahāyāna Buddhism.

Lavoisier, Antoine Laurent — 1743-94. French chemist, established the law of conservation of matter, executed under the French Revolution.

Leonardo da Vinci — 1452-1519, Italian artist, scientist, engineer, inventor, an extraordinarily gifted man.

Liber arbitrius — the power of free will which empowers man to make his own decisions.

Limonite — iron ore, hydrated ferrous oxide with about 30-32 per cent iron.

Lohār — ironsmiths, traditionally nomadic.

Lohḍī — a Hindu, most particularly a Punjabi festival which includes merry-making, dancing and singing.

Lopāmudrā — the wife of *maharṣi* Agastya, a sage herself.

Māgha — the month of January-February of the Hindu calendar.

Maghavan — an epithet of Indra, Lord of Bounty.

Mahābhūta — the five basic elements: earth, water, air, fire and *ākāśa*, ether or void.

Mahandeo — important God of the Kalash people, the name corresponds to Mahādeva; protector of the people; he safeguards, promises and protects, is messenger between men and the Creator; presiding deity of an important open-air sacred area or temple that displays four prominent wooden sculptured horse heads, at Rumbur, just west of the Chitral area.

Malachite — copper ore, $CuCo_3Cu(OH)_2$, dark green with different coloured layers; called azurrite when bluish.

Malāī — milk cream.

Mantra — metrical poetic verses, sacred verses from the texts, mainly the *śruti*; main corpus of the Vedic *Saṁhitā*, most ancient and sacred part of the Vedic tradition.

Manu Smṛti — the writings of Manu; *smṛti* are the delivered sacred texts; *śruti* are the revealed texts.

Maruts — wind and storm deities, allied of Indra.

Mātariśvan — ancient Vedic God.

Mazdeism — the religion of Ahura Mazda, the supreme God of ancient Persian religion.

Menhir — prehistoric megaliths usually standing erect, often phallic, whose function may have been ceremonial and also as markers of astronomical phenomena.

Michelangelo Buonarroti — 1474-1563, Florence, Italian sculptor, architect, painter, poet, engineer.

Mitra — God of laws, contracts and correct behaviour, great enemy of falsehood, has a parallel in the Avestan God Mithra.

Mokṣa — salvation, final liberation.

Monism — negation of duality, essential identity of matter and spirit or mind.

Mudrā — seal, gesture; part of the position taken by the body to express particular ideas, words, emotions, sentiments.

Mythology — collection of myths and legends of all cultures; the science and study of myths.

Naciketas — the name of the boy whose dialogue with Yamarāja makes the central subject of the *Kaṭha Upaniṣad.*

Nāga — the cobra, the multiheaded cobra; the *nāga* people.

Nārāśaṁsa — the praise of men, an epithet of Lord Agni.

Nirukta — one of the Vedāṅgas, literal meaning is: glossary or etymology; the text intends to explain and clarify the meaning of Vedic words; the *Nirukta* of Yāska mentions seventeen earlier writings, parts of the *Nirukta* may have been lost to us; the first critical study and translation was done by Roth whom R.N. Dandekar defines as the 'grandsire of Vedic studies'.

Ovum — the egg-cell, ovule is the haploid mature female gamete or germ cell of plants and animals, the sperm cell or spermatozooid is the mature male gamete.

Pāda — a semi-hemistich or line; each stanza or verse contains three, four or more *pāda*s. Corresponds to the Latin poetic-metric-foot, or 'pes'.

Pañcagavya — the five gifts of the cow: dung, urine, milk, *ghī* and curd.

Pañcajanya — Kṛṣṇa's conch made from the shell of a sea demon called Pañcajāna.

Pāñcatantra — five books; famous Sanskrit story-book in five parts; contains the teachings of Viṣṇuśarmā to royal princes mainly through animal stories.

Panīr — coagulated milk casein, same as Italian ricotta.

Pāṇini — sixth-fifth centuries BC, Sanskrit grammarian whose masterpiece is the *Aṣṭādhyāyī* that fixed the rules of the Sanskrit language.

Paṇis — savage, niggards, false, senseless, non-worshipping, evil-speaking thieves of cattle.

Parī — fairies.

Pariṇāma — theory of evolution in the Sāṁkhya system; in *Āyurveda* the *pariṇāmana* aspects of Agni are those of conversion of matter, in the process of generation of heat of the food consumed and the achievement of the benefits of nutrition. *Parjanya* the rain cloud, rain personified, rain god; also one of the Ādityas.

Pavamāna — self-purifying, an epithet of Lord Agni, see also Soma-Pavamāna.

Phālguna — the month of February-March.

Pīpal — the sacred fig-tree or *aśvattha*; horse stand; the scientific name is *Ficus religiosa*; the Gods assemble under its shade and Viṣṇu was born under one, associated to healing powers of nature and spiritual understanding; the bodh tree under which the Buddha received enlightenment. Symbol of eternal life.

Pitṛ — ancestors, Latin patres, fathers, manes, ancestral spirits; the *yajñas* to the *pitṛ*s, the *pitṛ-yajña* is one of the most sacred sacrifices, to be performed at fixed periods and times.

pH — symbol to express the hydrogen-ion concentration (H^+) or hydroxyl-ion (OH^-) concentration of a solution; indicates acidity or alkalinity of a solution.

Pheromones — volatile substances secreted by animals, powerful attractants of the other sex; first described for insects.

Placenta — the temporary organ or structure that attaches the embryo or foetus of mammals to the mother's uterus, similar structures in other animals and the tissues that attach the ovule to the ovary of the fruits of plants.

Polyphemus — one of the giant Cyclops of Greek mythology having only one eye in the middle of the forehead; Polyphemus was outwitted by Odysseus (Ulysses) and his companions whom he kept emprisoned in his cave; he was intoxicated with newly fermented grapes wine, blinded with the tip of a fire-hardened tree-trunk and the prisoners escaped hidden under the belly of Polyphemus' sheep that were endowed with very long wool.

Prajāpati — Lord of creation, title of some of the earliest Gods; later elevated to the rank of Supreme Creator, God Lord of Gods and Men.

Prakṛti — Nature, natural languages; the vernacular languages and dialects that emerged from the fusion of the *ādi bhāṣā* or original language with the local ones; also provincial dialects of Sanskrit, some, like Pāli, retained root forms of ancient Vedic Sanskrit.

Pramantha — the drill or upper *araṇi* made with the wood of the *aśvattha* or sacred fig-tree: the *pīpal* or *Ficus religiosa*; Prometheus may have been conceptually the Greek counterpart of the *pramantha*.

Prāṇa — breath, breath of life, wind; one of the forms of breathing.

Primum mobile — Latin expression meaning 'the first cause'.

Pṛthvī — the broad Earth, mother of all beings; our earth is *bhūmi*; also called *urvī*, wide.

Prometheus — the legendary man of Greek mythology who stole fire from the Gods to give it to man; he was condemned to be chained to the Caucasus mountains while a vulture unendingly feeds on his liver; may be the Greek counterpart of the *pramantha*.

Puruṣa — original man; the principle that animates *prakṛti*; the *Puruṣasūkta* was the original *yajña* for the creation of the castes.

Purandhṛ — a surname of Savitṛ, means the intelligent, the spirited.

Pyrite — iron ore, FeS_2.

Raibhi — a feminine name.

Rana cyanophlyctes — *Rana tigrina* — scientific names of two species of frogs.

Rawvolfia serpentina — scientific name of a plant of the family Apocynaceae used in Āyurvedic and modern allopathic medicine. *Sarpa-gandha* in Sanskrit.

Ṛbhus — skillful, clever, industrious, three brothers divinized because of their wisdom; the eldest is Ṛbhukśan; descendants of Aṅgiras, expert artisans, specially of metal objects.

Ṛgveda — the first and ancientmost of the four Vedas, has affinities with the Avesta.

Ṛṣi — ancient sages and poets, authors of Vedic hymns, the seven-*ṛṣi* or *saptaṛṣi* are mind-born sons of Brahmā and are represented in the sky by the seven stars of the Great Bear; the *Śatapatha Brāhmaṇa* names them: Gautama, Bharadvāja, Viśvāmitra, Jamadagni, Vasiṣṭha, Kāśyapa, Atri; Bhṛgu is added to the seven in the *Vāyu Purāṇa*; *Viṣṇu Purāṇa* adds Dakṣa and makes the *Brahmaṛṣis* to be nine; more were later added to the original seven.

Ṛta — true, righteous, straight, order and law of the Universe, the Cosmic Law and Order; Cosmic Ethics.

Rudra — the one who roars and howls, who is terrible; God of storms, father of Rudras and Maruts, both destructive and beneficial as healer of men and cattle; first called Mahādeva in the *Yajurveda*; in the *Bṛhadāraṇyaka Upaniṣad*, Rudras are the ten vital *prāṇa*; later identified with Śiva.

Rūmī — Mawlana Jalal al-Din, 1207-73, born in Balkh, Khorassan; mystic, supreme Sūfī poet of the Persian language.

Sacred — from Latin *sacrum*, consecrated, holy, God esteemed, hallowed by specific rites, cannot be desecrated, dedicated to a God or deity.

Sacred forests — forests where a presiding deity resides; nothing can be removed from the sacred forests, they serve the purpose of nature reserves; the concept in varying forms can be found in most cultures where total or partial conservation of selected areas is enforced.

Sacrifacĕre — Latin verb: to make sacred, to sanctify; to deify by appropriate rites.

Sacrifice — rites and rituals, acts of giving offerings to Gods and Deities; sacrifices may involve ritual slaughtering of animals; first institutors of sacrifice were Aṅgiras, Atharvan, Bhṛgu and Manu.

Sacrum — Latin, meaning sacred, as *sanctum* means saint and *sanctum sanctorum* means the sacredmost place among all the sacred spaces of a temple; sacred enclosure or sacred area.

Sādhu — ascetic who has perhaps acquired supernatural powers, may have acquired such powers through the practice of *yoga*: a *yogī*.

Sage — wise man, used as a synonym of *ṛṣi*.

Sahasramuṣka — having a thousand testicles, an epithet of Lord Indra.

Śakti — energy, power, the consorts of Gods and Deities who are their manifest power; the God and his consort; specially the consort of Lord Śiva or Devī who is expressed in many forms.

Śālmali — *Bombax heptaphyllum* (?) and/or *Bombax malabaricus* (?), the silk-cotton group of trees.

Sāman — hymns of the *Sāmaveda*, songs.

Sāmaveda — the melodious Veda; the *Sāmaveda Saṁhitā* contains material mostly from the *ṚV*.

Saṁgha — monastic order; association of equally-minded persons; society.

Saṁhitā — collection of hymns, refers specially to Vedic hymns.

Śami — wood of the *śami* tree from which the lower *araṇi* is made, for this reason Agni is said to have the *śami* for its womb; the *araṇi*s also are objects or worship.

Saṁnyāsī — those who have renounced the world; fourth *āśrama* of the brāhmaṇa's religious life; religious mendicants and wanderers in general.

*Saṁskāra*s — Vedic rites, rituals, sacrifices.

Sanātana Dharma — sacred law, eternally valid.

Sandhi — particular hymns to be recited on special occasions.

Śaṅkara — 788-820, Kaladi, Kerala; also called Śaṅkarācārya; philosopher, greatest exponent of Advaita, a form of extreme monism.

Sapēre — Latin verb: to know, to taste.

Sapientia — Latin for wisdom, knowledge, the gist of knowing; derived forms in English are: sapience for wisdom and knowledge; sapid for savory or tasty, opposite of tasteless or insipid, meaning with no salt.

Saptaṛṣi — the seven original *ṛṣi*.

Saptasindhu — land of the seven rivers: Gaṅgā, Yamunā, Sarasvatī, Sutudrī, Paruṣnī (now Rāvī), Marudvṛhā, Ārjīkīya or Vipāśā (now Beās); also called *sapta-sindhava.*

Sarasvatī — flowing waters, a river and a Deity; the sacred river Sarasvatī marked the early boundary of Āryāvarta and the personified goddess was worshipped for bestowing fertility, wealth and health thanks to the cleansing power of its waters; the name later became that of the Goddess of learning, arts and sciences, but the river dried out in due course of time due to a curse, however remains of a 'fossil' river may be seen on remote sensing imagery.

Sasarparī — running swiftly everywhere, may be an epithet of Vāk as daughter of Sūrya, as such she is intelligence and thinks rapidly; Sasarparī was gifted by the Jamadagnis because being intelligence she could dispel famine.

Śāstra — treatises, books having great authority, sacred texts, includes *śruti* and *smṛti.*

Satyam — Truth.

Savitṛ — Vivifier, stimulator, generator; personification of Life and Hope, represented by the Sun as giver of life on Earth; a very ancient God and at times considered to be one of the Ādityas.

Sāyaṇa — prime minister of the king of Vijayanagar in the fourteenth century; the great scholiast who wrote a most important commentary of the Veda and who, according to H.H. Wilson, 'must have been in possession of all the interpretations which had been perpetuated by tradition'.

Science — English from the Latin *scientia*; word given to methodically formulated knowledge acquired systematically.

Scīre — Latin verb, to know.

Seers — sages, the *ṛṣis*, they received the *śruti* or revealed Truth through visions.

Seven rivers — *saptasindhava,* see Saptasindhu.

Shaman — medicine man, magician, possessed of supernatural abilities; the man or woman endowed with magical powers that enable him or her to establish contact with supernatural entities on behalf of and to obtain benefits for human beings who do not have such powers.

Singularité — French for peculiarity.

Śiṣya — the disciple of a *guru*, bound to give unremitting and unquestionable obedience and service to his *guru* from whom he receives the highest teachings, training, guidance and knowledge.

Sītā — furrow, symbol of femininity, generosity, purity and good agricultural practices to whom one owes loyalty and faithfulness; daughter of Mother Earth, brought up by king Janaka and returned to Mother Earth to attest to her purity; personification of agricultural and vegetation cycles and fertility, Rāma's consort, mother of twins, Lava and Kuśa.

Śiva — the auspicious one, gradually emerged as Mahādeva and Mahāyogī, though he is referred to only once and indirectly in the *R̥V*.

Śloka — stanza having a full meaning in itself.

Śatapatha Brāhmaṇa — *ŚatBrā*. One of the most important, lengthy and detailed *Brāhmaṇa*s of the *R̥V*.

Smṛti — what was being learned, remembered and transmitted by tradition; the Vedāṅgas, Sūtra, *Rāmāyaṇa*, *Mahābhārata*, Purāṇas etc.

Solstice — the time and point of the ecliptic at which the sun is farthest away north or south of the equator.

Soma-yajña — the Soma sacrifice, one of the most imposing and binding of the *Śrauta* rites.

Species — Latin noun, same in English, used in biological sciences to designate all the individuals who are morphologically similar, physiologically compatible, who can reproduce sexually and whose descendants are fertile; chemical species are the chemical elements.

Sperm cell — male gamete.

Sphya — pointed stick made of wood, with which a line is drawn.

Stotra — hymns of prayers and praise of Gods, liturgical poems; the Vedic hymns are the greatest *stotras* of all.

Subhaga satī — full of hope, overflowing with hope.

Śuci cakra — pure, immaculate, unpolluted wheels.

Sudās — leader of the Bharatas, most probably the second wave of Āryan immigrants; great warrior and great statesman, he won over to his side the powerful Tṛtsus of whom he became king to jointly overpower the Pañcajanāḥ and the neighbouring non-Āryan principalities. The *purohita* of the Bhārata was Bharadvāja who was later replaced by Viśvāmitra, while Vasiṣṭha was the *purohita* of the Tṛtsus. As a result of the alliance of the Bhāratas with the Tṛtsus, Vasiṣṭha replaced Viśvāmitra as the *purohita* of the Bhāratas and the latter in great anger passed over to the Pañcajanāḥ. This was the origin of the great war of the ten kings with the Bhāratas and Tṛtsus led by Sudās and Vasiṣṭha on one side and the 'Ten Kings' and Viśvāmitra on the other; described in the *ṚV* as the *Dāśarājña*.

Sūfi — word of doubtful origin, already in use about AD 900-1000, maybe derived from the Arabic word *soof* that means wool and refers to the robe of early Muslim mystics; the word *sufism* was first used in 1821 by German scholars; the term Sūfī is normally applied to enlightened saints whose spiritual experiences are much above the understanding of ordinary or learned men.

Summum bonum — Latin expression meaning the maximum good.

Śutudrī — former Śatadru, flowing in hundred channels, one of the seven rivers of Saptasindhu, present-day Sutlej, the Zaradrus of the Greek and Hesudrus of the Romans.

Śruti — revelation, what was heard, sub-tones of the Indian musical scale, revealed Truth, Veda, *Brāhmaṇa* and Upaniṣad.

Śūnya — zero, emptiness, nothingness, void.

Sūrya — sun, deified and personalized, giver of light, warmth, life; one of the most often referred to deities in the Veda, specially the *ṚV*; sun-worship is common to most ancient cultures.

Svastika — meaning it is well, derived from *su* and *asti* where *ka* is a case ending; the *svastika* may be derived from the *cakra*, wheel, or from the *araṇis* that are usually kept in a cross position; the right hand or clockwise *svastika* is considered to be masculine, auspicious; the left hand or counter clockwise, is considered to be feminine and unauspicious; a common very ancient symbol throughout the world.

Tantra — different derivations proposed, very ancient teachings, probably pre-Vedic and of obscure origin; many tantric texts are available but more have been kept secret although Tantrism contains some of the loftiest philosophies as well as unusual bodily practices.

Tanū-napāt — son of himself, an epithet of Lord Agni, fire can only be ignited or produced by fire.

Tapas — heat, ardour, active means for the acquisition of merit and spiritual power; improper translation: ascetism.

Thom, Alexander — 1894-1985, Scotland; professor of Engineering

Science, University of Oxford, 1945-61; active life-long interest in prehistoric megalithic structures and sites of Britain and Brittany.

Ṭhugs — secret fraternity of assassins, included both Hindus and Muslims.

Triṣṭup — one of the Vedic metres.

Trita — very old Vedic God whose character is not clear, Trita Āptya appears to be related to atmospheric waters, brings rains; the word *āptya* is etymologically connected with *āp* — water; has something to do with the preparation of *soma*; Thrita is known in the Avesta and is older than Indra, his function appears to have been that to overcome the cloud demon, an achievement later imitated by Indra 'in the manner of Trita' (*R̥V*, I; 52, 5). Trita Āptya and Agni Apām-napāt are both born in waters, a feature shared by no other deity.

Tvaṣṭr̥ — artisan *par excellence,* originally regarded as having fashioned the universe, in later mythology his functions were taken over by other Gods.

Udāna — one of the breathing phases.

Ulysses — Latin name of the ancient Greek hero Odysseus, wisest and most cunning of the Greek heroes of the Trojan war.

Upanayana — the rite of investitute of the Sacred Thread.

Uttarāyaṇa — the northern travel of the sun.

Ur-Gott — German word: original God.

Uṣas — Dawn, feminine.

Vāk, Vāc — speech, word. Speech personified.

Vaiśvānara — beloved of all, dear to all men, belonging to all men, an epithet of Lord Agni.

Vālakhilya — eleven hymns of *R̥V Maṇḍala* VIIIth, not included in Sāyaṇa's commentaries, usually interpolated after No. 48 and Numbered 49-59.

Vanaspati — Lord of the forest, tall tree, sovereign tree, forest, plants.

Vanodevi — Goddess of the forest.

Varadā — bestower of boons, an epithet of Sarasvatī.

Varuṇa — an Āditya, the only unfettered Āditya, unfound like Aditi his mother, one who encompasses everything, name derived from root *vṛ* meaning 'to bind'; Varuṇa bound and regulated the universe because he possessed *asu*, the universal magic potence; the *asura par excellence*, the Samrāṭ who enforced and upheld *ṛta*, the cosmic universal law.

Vasiṣṭha — most wealthy; one of the seven *ṛṣis*, seer of many hymns of the *ṚV*, belonged to the Tṛtsu tribe, celebrated in the *Rm*, the *MBh*, the *Ps*: all the hymns of *ṚV Maṇḍala* VIIth are by *ṛṣi* Vasiṣṭha; one of the most powerful thinkers among the *ṛṣis*.

Vāyu — air, wind; often associated with Indra, resides in the air; said to have been originated by the breath of *puruṣa*; king of *gandharvas*.

Vyāsa — Veda-Vyāsa, compiler, arranger, reputed to have arranged the Vedas and compiled the *Mahābhārata*.

Vidyā — knowledge, wisdom, discrimination, understanding.

Vipāśa — unbound, present-day river Beās, former Byas, Hyphasis of the Greek; one of the seven rivers; the Vipāśa refused to drown sage Vasiṣṭha who had thrown himself bound up into the river as he wished to die; the river returned him unbound: Vipāśā, on its banks.

Viśvacārṣaṇih — God of all men, an epithet of Lord Agni, Viṣṇu.

Viśvedevāḥ — all Gods, preservers of men and bestowers of rewards; many hymns are addressed to them; they later constitute a special class of ten Gods: Vasu, Satya, Kratu, Dakṣa, Kāla, Kāma, Dhṛti, Kuru, Purūravas and Mādravas.

Viśvāmitra — friend of all, one of the seven *ṛṣis*; born a kṣatriya he elevated himself to brāhmaṇhood through extraordinary *tapas*; author of most hymns of *Maṇḍala* IIIrd of the *ṚV*; mentioned both as Kuśika descendant of Kuśa or of Gādhi; has a prominent position in the *Rm* and the *MBh*, life-long enemy of sage Vasiṣṭha, the final reconciliation of the two arch-enemies is given in the *Rm*.

Vratapati — Lord of vows, an epithet of Lord Agni.

Yajamāna, *yajamānī* — the institutor of a *yajña* or other ceremonial ritual and his wife.

Yajurveda — the fourth Veda, borrows extensively from the *ṚV*, may be a later addition to the earlier three Vedas.

Yakṣa — meaning uncertain.

Yajur — The 'Wite *Yajurveda*', together with the 'Black *Yajurveda*' constitute the *Yajurveda*.

Yakṣmā — malignant disease; tuberculosis, consumption.

Yajña — Vedic sacrifice, personified in the Purāṇas as son of Rūci and husband of Dakṣiṇā, has the head of a deer and was killed at Dakṣa's sacrifice.

Yajus — sacrificial text and formula.

Yasna — the main sector of the Avesta.

Yoga — one of six schools of philosophy, founded by sage Yājñavalkya who is also the author of the White *YV*, the *SPBr*, the *BṛUp* and other *smṛti*.

Yūpa — sacrificial post, usually made of *daru* or *deodār* wood, with a knob at the top for fixing a wheel on which the priest or the *yajamāna* sat and were whirled around three times on the occasion of a very ancient rite, the *dūrcana* meaning distant, difficult climb, symbolizing the elevation from the profane to the sacred; the rite was also associated with mounting the chariot, hence the title of *cakravartin* given to the great ancient emperors; the *dhvaja* or flagstaff erected in front of temples may be a later development of the *yūpa*.

YV — *Yajurveda*.

Bibliography

Agrawala, V.S., 1970, *Ancient India Folk Cults*, 216 pp., Prithvi Prakashan, New Delhi.

Andrewartha, H.G. and L.C. Birch, 1954, *The Distribution and Abundance of Animals*, xv+782 pp., Univ. of Chicago Press, Chicago.

Anonymous, 1987, Iroquois, in: *National Geographic Magazine*, 172 (3), 370-473.

Arrianos, circa AD 95-175, *Storia di Alessandro*, ed. & comm. by L. Belloni, 1980, 471 pp., 1 map, Rusconi, Milano.

Brain, C.K. and A. Sillen, 1988, Evidence from the Swartkrans cave for the earliest use of fire, *Nature*, 336; 464-66.

Carson, R., 1962, *Silent Spring*, Houghton Mifflin, U.S.A.

Chakravarty, U., 1997, *Indra and Other Vedic Deities*. 232 pp., D.K. Printworld, New Delhi.

Dandekar, R.N., 1979a, *Vedic Mythological Tracts, Select Writings* I. 383pp., Ajanta Publ., Delhi at Bhandarkar Inst. Press, Poona.

———, 1979b, *Insights into Hinduism, Select Writings II*, 394pp. Ajanta Publ., Delhi at Bhandarkar Inst. Press, Poona.

———, 1979c, New light on the Vedic god Savitṛ, 1-27pp. in: R.N. Dandekar, *Select Writings* I, 383 pp. BORI, Pune, India.

———, 1981, *Exercises in Indology*, *Select Writings III*, 385pp. Ajanta Publ., Delhi at Bhandarkar Inst. Press, Poona.

———, New light on the Vedic god Savitṛ, 1-27, in: R.N. Dandekar, select writings 1, 383 pp., BORI, Pune, India.

———, 1997, *Indological Miscellanea*, 474 pp., Pune.

Dash, Vd. Bhagwan, 1975, *Embryology and Maternity in Āyurveda,* 147 pp., Diary Publ., Delhi

Ferguson, L., 1988, A Catalogue of the Alexander Thom Archive held in the National Monuments Record of Scotland, pp. 31-131, in: *Records in Stone*, ed. by C.L.N. Ruggles, 1988, xvii+519 pp. Cąmbridge Univ. Press.

Filippi, G.G., 1996, *Mr̥tyu. Concept of Death in Indian Traditions.* 258pp., D.K. Printworld, New Delhi.

Filliozat, J., 1955, L'apport de l'étude des religions de l'Inde à la science de l'homme, in: *NUMEN II*. Suppl. Leiden, pp. 108-19

———, 1991, *Religion, Philosophy, Yoga*, Collected articles, Motilal Banarasidass, Varanasi, 484 pp.

Bergaigne, A, 1878-83, *La religion védique d'après les hymnes du Rig-Veda,* vols. I-III.

Gadgill, M. and M.D. Subash Chandran, 1992, Sacred Groves, 183-87 in: *Indigenous Vision,* 304 pp., India International Centre and Sage Publ., New Delhi.

Ganapati, S.V., 1982, *Sāmaveda*, 491 pp., Motilal Banarsidass.

Ganapti, G.F., 1934, *The Struggle for Existence*, Williams and Williams, Baltimore, 163 pp.

———, 1935, Vérifications expèrimentales de la thèorie mathèmatique de la lutte pour la vie, in: *Actualitées scientifiques et industrielles*, 277, 61 pp.

Graves, R., 1960 (ed.), *The Greek Myths*, 2 Vols. Penguin Books.

Griffith, R.T.H., 1889, *The Hymns of the Rigveda*, 707 pp., 1986 edn. Motilal Banarsidass.

———, 1893, repr. 1991, *The Sāmaveda Saṁhitā*, 500 pp., Nag Publ., New Delhi.

———, 1899, repr. 1990, *Yajurveda Saṁhitā*, 620 pp., Nag Publ., New Delhi.

Hale, W.E, 1991, *Asura in Early Vedic Religion*, 226 pp., Motilal Banarsidass.

Hillebrandt, A., 1876, *Uber die Göttin Aditi*, Bresslau.

———, 1877, *Varuṇa and Mitra*, Bresslau.

———, 1891, *Vedische Mythologie I. Soma und verwandte Götter*. Bresslau, English transl. S.R. Sarma: Vedic Mythologie, 1980, v.1, 476 pp., 1981, v. 2, 488 pp., Motilal Banarsidass, Delhi.

Hutchinson, G.E., 1959, Il concetto moderno di nicchia ecologica, in: *Memorie Istituto Italiano di Idrobiologia*, 11.

———, 1961, The Paradox of the Plankton, *American Naturalist*, 95, 137-45.

Jain, S.K., 1985, *Medicinal Plants of India*, Book Trust of India, 180 pp.

Kashikar, C.G., 1990, *Identification of Soma*, Tilak Maharashtra Vidyapeeth Pune, 1-50.

Keith, A.B., 1920, repr. 1981, *R̥gveda Brāhmaṇas: the Aitareya and Kauṣītaki Brāhmaṇas of the R̥gveda*, 555 pp., Motilal Banarsidass.

Köhler, W., 1947, *Gestalt Psychology*, Liveright Publishing Corporation, 222 pp., New York.

Kumbhojkar, M.S. and V.D. Vartak, 1988, Ethnobotanical Studies on Wild Edible Grapes from Sacred Groves in Western Maharashtra, *J. Econ. Tax. Bot.* 12, 2, 257-63.

Lièvre, V. and J.Y. Loude, 1990, *Le Chamanisme des Kalash du Pakistan*, ed. CNRS, Paris, 558 pp.

Loude, J.Y. and V. Lièvre, 1984, *Solstice païen*, Presses de la Renaissance, Paris 361 pp.

———, 1987, Fêtes d'été chez les Kalash du Nord Pakistan, in: *L' éthnographie*, 100-01, pp., 191-220.

Ludwig, A., 1876-88, *Der R̥gveda*. 6 vols. Prag.

MacKie, E., 1988, Investigating the Prehistoric Solar Calendar, pp., 206-31, in: *Records in Stone*, ed. by C.L.N. Ruggles, 1988, xvii+519 pp., Cambridge Univ. Press.

Mandler, J.M., 1990, A new Perspective in Cognitive Development in Infancy, in: *American Scientist*, 78, 3, 236-43.

Marazzi, U., 1984, *Testi dello sciamanesimo siberiano e centro-asiatico*, ed. UTET-TEA, Torino, 610 pp.

Margalef, D.R., 1956, La teoria de la información en ecologia, in: *Memorias Real Academia de Ciencias y Artes*, Barcelona, 32; 373-449.

——, 1958a, Temporal succession and spatial heterogeneity in plankton, in: *Perspectives in Marine Biology*. A.A. Buzzati-Traverse (ed.) Univ. of California, Berkeley.

——, 1958b, *Information Theory in Ecology*, 2nd ed., W.B. Saunders Co. Philadelphia.

Müller, M., 1849-74, *R̥gveda Saṁhitā*, the *Sacred Hymns of the Brāhmaṇas, together with the Commentary of Sāyaṇācārya*. 6 vols. 2nd edn. London.

Müller, F.M. and H. Oldenberg, 1895, *Vedic Hymns*, No 32 and 46 of the Series: *Sacred Books of the East* ed. by F.M. Müller 1979 ed., repr. 1990 Atlantic Publ. and Distr. New Delhi, v.1, xv+476 pp; v.2, x+500 pp.

Nadkarni, K.M., 1976 (ed.), *Indian Materia Medica*, v.1, 1319 pp., v.2, 968 pp., Popular Prakshan Pvt. Ltd., Bombay.

Nath, J., 1996, *The Dasas, Dasyus and Raksases in the R̥gvedic Literature*, Sanskrit Pustak Bhandar, Calcutta, 124 pp.

Odum, E.P., 1971, *Fundamentals of Ecology*, 3rd edn., W.B. Saunders Co. Philadelphia, xiv+574 pp.

Parker, P., 1991, Temple of Imra, Temple of Mahandeo: a Kafir Sanctuary in Kalash Cosmogony. *Bulletin of the School of Oriental and African Studies*. Univ. London, 54, I, 75-103.

Pandey, K., 1982, *Marriage Mantras* (Sanskrit, Tamil, English). Ramayana Printing Works, Madras. First Publ. 1971.

Patil, D.R., 1946, repr. 1973, *Cultural History from the Vāyu Purāṇa*, 348 pp. Motilal Banarsidass, Varanasi.

Pettinato, G., 1992, *La saga di Gilgamesh*, 427pp. Rusconi, Milano.

Piaget, J., 1952, *The Origin of Intelligence in Children*, transl. M. Cook, International University Press.

Radin, P. 1941, *La Religion Primitive, sa nature et son origine*, Gallimard, Paris, 242 pp.

Ramakrishnan, P.S. 1992, Shifting Agriculture and Sustainable Development, xvii+424 pp., *Man and Biosphere Series*, v.10, UNESCO, Paris.

Renou, L., 1956, *Hymnes Spéculatifs du Veda*, 276 pp. UNESCO ser. *Connaissance de l'Orient*, Collection UNESCO d'Oeuvres Représentatives, Gallimard, Paris.

Robertson, G.S., 1887, *The Kafirs of the Hindukush*, Facsimile repr., by Sang e-Meel Publ., Lahore, 656 pp. 1 map.

Ruggles, C.L.N., 1988 (ed.), *Records in Stone*. Papers in Memory of Alexander Thom, xvii+519 pp., Cambridge University Press.

Saint-Exupéry, A., 1921, Le Pettit Prince.

Saraswati, S.S.S. and S. Vidyalankar, 1980, *Rigveda Saṁhitā*, Ten vols. Veda Pratishthan, New Delhi.

Sastry, T.S.K., 1985, *Vedānga Jyotiṣa of Lagadha; in its Ṛk and Yajus Recensions,* 74 pp., Indian National Science Academy, Delhi.

Schuré, E., 1899, *Les Grands Initiés*, ed., by Laterza, 1989, I Grandi Iniziati, 480 pp.

Sharma, B.N.K. 1978, *The Brahmasūtras and their Principal Commentaries*, 3 vols. Bharatiya Vidya Bhavan, Bombay.

Sivananda Swami, 1977, 2nd edn., *Brahma Sūtra*, 686 pp., Motilal Banarsidass.

Vannucci, M., 1989, *The Mangroves and Us.*, 203 pp., Indian Association for the Advancement of Science, New Delhi.

———, 1991, Sacred Groves or Holy Forests, No. 32, in: *Concepts of Space, Ancient and Modern*, ed. by Kapila Vatsyayan, Indira Gandhi National Centre for the Arts, 665 pp.

———, 1992, Tradition and Change, pp., 23-34, in: *Indigenous Vision*, 304 pp., ed. Geeti Sen, Sage Publ. Inc., India and India Int. Centre, New Delhi.

———, 1994 b, Conscious and Unconscious Time. A Biological Perspective, in; International Seminar on *Kāla* —. Time, organised by Kapila Vatsyayan for the Indira Gandhi National Centre for the Arts, New Delhi.

———, 1994 c, *Ecological Readings in the Veda*, 216 pp., D.K. Printworld, New Delhi.

———, 1995, Common Roots for Transfer of Culture, in: *Prakṛti*, vol.5. *Man in Nature*. K. Vatsyayan (ed.) pp., 225-44, New Delhi.

———, (under press). The Origin of the Cult of Demeter, in: *ABORI*, Pune.

Vatsyayan, K., 1983, *The Square and the Circle of the Indian Arts*, xi+159 pp., Roli Books International, New Delhi.

Vesci, U.M., 1985, *Heat and Sacrifice in the Vedas*: 335 pp., Motilal Banarsidass, Varanasi.

Volterra, V. 1926, Variazioni e fluttuazioni del numero di individui in speci animali conviventi, in: *Memorie Reale Accademia dei Lincel*; 6; 2; 181-87.

———, 1928, Variations and fluctuations of the number of individuals in animal species living together, in: *Journal du Conseil*, 3; 1-51.

Wanninayaka, P.B., 1982, *Āyurveda in Sri Lanka*, 88 pp., Ministry of Health Publications, Colombo.

Whitney, W.D., 1905, repr. 1984, *The Atharva-Veda-Saṁhitā*, 2 vols., 1046 pp., Motilal Banarsidass.

Index